Greeted with Smiles

AMERICAN MUSICSPHERES

Series Editor
Mark Slobin

GREETED WITH SMILES

Bukharian Jewish Music and Musicians in New York

Evan Rapport

OXFORD
UNIVERSITY PRESS

OXFORD
UNIVERSITY PRESS

Oxford University Press is a department of the University of Oxford.
It furthers the University's objective of excellence in research, scholarship,
and education by publishing worldwide.

Oxford   New York
Auckland   Cape Town   Dar es Salaam   Hong Kong   Karachi
Kuala Lumpur   Madrid   Melbourne   Mexico City   Nairobi
New Delhi   Shanghai   Taipei   Toronto

With offices in
Argentina   Austria   Brazil   Chile   Czech Republic   France   Greece
Guatemala   Hungary   Italy   Japan   Poland   Portugal   Singapore
South Korea   Switzerland   Thailand   Turkey   Ukraine   Vietnam

Oxford is a registered trademark of Oxford University Press
in the UK and certain other countries.

Published in the United States of America by
Oxford University Press
198 Madison Avenue, New York, NY 10016

© Oxford University Press 2014

Library of Congress Cataloging-in-Publication Data
Rapport, Evan.
Greeted with smiles : Bukharian Jewish music and musicians in
New York / Evan Rapport.
pages cm.—(American musicspheres)
Includes bibliographical references and index.
ISBN 978–0–19–022313–7 (hardback : alk. paper) 978–0–19–937903–3
(paperback : alk. paper)—ISBN 978–0–19–937906–4 (on-line component)—
ISBN 978–0–19–937905–7 (electronic text)—ISBN 978–0–19–937904–0
(on-line file)   1. Jews, Bukharan—Music—History and criticism.
2. Jews—New York (State)—New York—Music—History and
criticism.   3. Jewish musicians—New York (State)—New York.
4. Music—New York (State)—New York—History and criticism.   I. Title.
ML3776.R26 2014
780.89'92407471—dc23
2014006596

1 3 5 7 9 8 6 4 2
Printed in the United States of America
on acid-free paper

For Sarah, Alice, and Charlie

Dar dasti rafiqon guli navrastai noz
Mo ro begiriftand bo tabassum peshvoz

In the hands of friends, young beautiful flowers,
They greet us with smiles

—Ilyas Mallayev, "Yalalum," 1999

Contents

List of Figures

List of Transcribed Music Examples

List of Audio Music Examples

Audio examples included by permission of the artists. Selection 3.3 also included by permission of Theodore Levin and Shanachie Records. Selections 3.4, 4.3, 4.4, 4.6, 6.1, and 6.2 are previously unpublished field recordings by the author.

Selected Biographical Sketches

Roshel Aminov (b. 1951, Dushanbe, Tajikistan)

Roshel Aminov is an important teacher and a highly respected performer with a deep and thorough knowledge of Central Asian classical music. He learned his repertoire directly from his father Neryo Aminov, one of the most illustrious composers and maqom performers of the twentieth century. He primarily sings and plays the tanbūr and sato, and his brother, Imonuel, plays the doira. In 2002, Aminov began teaching under the banner of the Traditional School of Bukharian and Shashmakom Music, located on the sixth floor of the Queens Gymnasia, a Jewish day school sponsored by the Bukharian Jewish Congress. He also sings Jewish religious repertoire.

Tamara Katayeva (b. 1947, Samarqand, Uzbekistan)

The accomplished singer and dancer Tamara Katayeva was born into a family of famous artists. Her father, Pinkhas Kurayev, and her mother, Frida Mulloqandova, were members of the Bukharian Jewish Theater company in the 1930s and 1940s. Frida Mulloqandova, a ballet master, was the sister of Gavriel and Mikhoel Mulloqandov, both legendary maqom singers. After studying medicine, Tamara moved to Dushanbe in 1969, joining the ensemble "Gulshan," where she specialized in light-classical lyric songs. She relocated to Tashkent and continued to perform there until immigrating to New York in 1990. In New York she joined Ilyas Mallayev's Ensemble Maqom as a featured singer and dancer, and she also acts in the "Bukhara on the Hudson" ("Bukhara na Gudzone") theater company.

Ezro Malakov (b. 1938, Shahrisabz, Uzbekistan)

One of the Bukharian Jewish community's most celebrated singers, Malakov learned much of his repertoire from his mother, Yeshuo Borukhova, the daughter of Rabbi Ari Borukhov (1896–1940) and granddaughter of the Chief Rabbi of Shahrisabz, Mullo Obo Deroz (1844–1936). In 1976 Ezro Malakov moved to Tashkent, where he worked as a singer in the national radio and TV orchestras and recorded several albums. He came to Queens in 1992 and soon after began singing as a cantor at a major Bukharian synagogue, Congregation Beth Gavriel. He performs with the two highest profile Bukharian ensembles, Ensemble Shashmaqom and Ensemble Maqom. In 2007 he published the landmark *Musical Treasures of the Bukharian Jewish Community*, which contains notated transcriptions and audio recordings of over one hundred Bukharian religious melodies. One of Ezro Malakov's brothers, Menaḥem Malakov, is also an esteemed hazzan.

Ilyos Mallayev (b. 1936, Mary, Turkmenistan—d. 2010, New York)

Ilyos Mallayev was widely considered to be the greatest poet of his generation and one of the community's most knowledgable musicians. He grew up in Kattakurgan, Uzbekistan. He moved to Tashkent in 1951 and soon began working in professional groups, including the Uzbek Song and Dance Ensemble (1952–1960), the ensemble of the legendary dancer Tamara Khonum (1953–1956), the Folk and Variety (Estrada) Orchestras of Uzbekistan Radio (1956–1962), and the Symphonic Variety (Estrada) Orchestra of Uzbekistan Radio (1962–1992). He toured widely, spending three years in Moscow in the 1950s and visiting the United States in the early 1960s. He became known for his poetry, instrumental virtuosity, innovative compositions, and vaudeville entertainment style. He immigrated to New York in 1992 with his wife, the singer Muhabbat Shamayeva, and their children. In Queens, he led Ensemble Maqom, performing classical music, folk music, and original repertoire with Shamayeva, Tamara Katayeva, Ezro Malakov, Yosef Abramov, and Matat Barayev.

Roshel Rubinov (b. 1966, Shahrisabz, Uzbekistan)

Roshel Rubinov is a skilled poet, masterful singer and instrumentalist, and noteworthy composer; the depth and breadth of his talents have positioned him as one of the younger Bukharian Jewish musicians most prepared to carry the torch. From 1983 to 1987 he attended the Mirzo Tursunzoda Art Institute in Tajikistan, where he studied Central Asian classical music with Neryo Aminov, Barno Isḥoqova, Shoista Mullojonova,

Nison Shoulov, and Abduvali Abdurashidov. He immigrated to Queens in 1995. Rubinov writes Persian poetry in the classical forms and meters, having studied poetry with Abubakr Zuhuriddinov in Tajikistan and Ilyos Mallayev in New York. He is presently one of the busiest Bukharian Jewish professional musicians. The group in which he performs, Mazal Tov, often plays multiple celebrations per week.

Muhabbat Shamayeva (b. 1944, Bukhara, Uzbekistan)

Muhabbat Shamayeva is one of the true singing stars of Central Asia. In 1963, she joined Yunus Rajabi's Radio Uzbekistan Ensemble in Tashkent. She recorded hundreds of songs for the national archives and holds the highest national title awarded, "People's Artist of Uzbekistan." She married her fellow entertainer Ilyos Mallayev in 1965, and they immigrated together in 1992. She is one of the most popular Bukharian singers in New York, featured in Ensemble Maqom and on several recordings. Mallayev and Shamayeva's children, Raj, Nargis, and Violetta, are important figures on the contemporary Bukharian music scene.

Avrom Tolmasov (b. 1956, Samarqand, Uzbekistan)

Avrom Tolmasov is generally regarded as one of the greatest living Bukharian singers, the most recent outstanding talent of a renowned musical dynasty. He was raised in Samarqand, where he learned Central Asian classical music from his father, Gavriel Tolmasov, and his father's uncles, the legendary Mikhoel Tolmasov and Isroel Tolmasov. He is famous for his vocal range, virtuosic instrumental technique, gripping style, and versatile repertoire. In addition to being a renowned tanbūrist, he plays guitar, sitar, soz, and other instruments. He moved to Israel in 1988 and New York City in 2002. After a decade in New York, Tolmasov returned to Israel. Tolmasov's nephew, Roman Tolmasov, is also a very accomplished solo musician.

Acknowledgments

I would like to begin by thanking Stephen Blum, my dear advisor, mentor, and friend. He introduced me to the Bukharian Jewish community. He guided my research through the completion of my dissertation and has continued to be a crucial sounding board for me. It is no exaggeration to say that my studies and conversations with Professor Blum have fundamentally changed the way I think about and listen to music.

Thank you to Mark Slobin for supporting this book project from its inception. I could not have asked for a better guide through the process of writing my first monograph. It has been a true privilege to work with Mark, Suzanne Ryan, and the team at Oxford University Press in bringing this book to completion.

I will always be grateful for the generosity and kindness of my Bukharian friends. Ezro Malakov has been my primary consultant for over a decade now, and I am truly blessed that he took such a strong interest in my work. Ezro-aka's artistry, knowledge, and dedication to the livelihood of the Bukharian Jewish community in New York and throughout the world is astounding. He and his wife, the wonderful Bela Khaimova, hosted me on more occasions than I can count and always treated me like a member of the family. Roshel Rubinov, like Malakov, is a brilliant musician and extremely devoted to his fellow Bukharian Jews. During the dissertation research that laid the groundwork for this book, Rubinov taught me tanbūr week after week, patiently working with me and explaining the ins and outs of maqom and what it means to be a professional Bukharian Jewish musician. He freely gave of his time, demonstrating his unselfish spirit. I owe a special thanks to Roshel Aminov, who also taught me tanbūr during my dissertation research, and who spent many hours answering my questions and providing his useful perspectives. Thanks also to Tamara Katayeva, Ilyos Mallayev, Muhabbat Shamayeva, Avrom Tolmasov, and Roman Tolmasov for their wonderful music and for their time and candor in interviews. I would also like to express my appreciation to Lana Levitin,

Albert Malakov, Jacob Malakov, Khaiko Malakov, Yosef Munarov, Rafael Nektalov, and Ilya Yakubov.

Two fellowships helped make this book possible. My experience at Harvard University as a Harry Starr Fellow in Judaic Studies during the 2012–2013 academic year proved to be invaluable. Kay Kaufman Shelemay and the other Starr Fellows—Judah Cohen, Maureen Jackson, Daniel Jütte, Edwin Seroussi, Amy Wlodarski, and Stacy Wolf—helped me think through many complex issues. By a stroke of tremendous serendipity, I spent the year working only a few blocks from the home of my fellow scholar of Bukharian Jewish life, Alanna E. Cooper, and I am grateful for our many inspiring conversations and for her generous hospitality. Thanks to Jim and Liz Vezina and to Jerry Lim and Maia Lynch for hosting me during this period. A Dorot Post-Doctoral Fellowship at the NYU Department of Hebrew and Judaic Studies during the 2007–2008 academic year provided a stimulating atmosphere for me to reconsider my graduate research as a monograph project and set the stage for the next phase of my research. I would especially like to thank Hasia Diner for her guidance and insight.

I have been fortunate to receive a great deal of support and mentorship from many of my senior colleagues, including Walter Zev Feldman, Jane Gerber, Ellie Hisama, Angelika Jung, Mark Kligman, Theodore Levin, and Peter Manuel. A special thanks to Ivan Raykoff for providing criticisms and conversations during the writing of the manuscript. Thanks to Ethel Raim and Pete Rushefsky at the Center for Traditional Music and Dance for their generous sharing of the Center's Bukharian archival materials. I would also like to thank Alessandra Ciucci, Alexander Gelfand, Farzaneh Hemmasi, Galina Paliy, Will Prentice, and Furqat Pulatov. Thanks to the anonymous readers of my proposal and manuscript, who gave such thoughtful and constructive comments.

I gratefully acknowledge the work of my student assistants, generously supported by The New School: Derek Baron, Anthony Jillions, Sofia Savchenko, and Valerie Tregubenko. While pursuing this research at the CUNY Graduate Center as my dissertation, I received crucial support from a dissertation-year fellowship and the Baisley Powell Elebash Fund. Thanks to David Adler for editing an earlier version of the manuscript. Jerry Lim expertly helped me create the maps found in the book's introduction.

Words cannot express the gratitude due to my friends and family. I would like to especially thank my parents, Margery and Dennis Rapport, my in-laws, Liz and Jim Vezina, and my sister and brother-in-law, Wendy and Misha Grinberg, for commenting on earlier drafts and hosting me for writing retreats.

Above all, thanks to my wife, Sarah Vezina, and my children, Alice Coco and Charles Sidney. I love you.

Note on Transliteration and Translation

Bukharian Jews speak, write, and sing in at least four languages in addition to English (Tajik Persian or "Bukhori," Russian, Hebrew, and Uzbek), each with regional variations. For most of the twentieth century, their primary alphabet for each of these languages was Cyrillic, with the exception of Hebrew. Many also continued to learn how to read and write the Hebrew alphabet for texts in Persian, as Hebrew was historically used for all the Judeo-Persian languages. The Perso-Arabic script, the standard for Persian and Turkic languages in Central Asia before the twentieth century, is virtually unknown among Bukharian Jews today. In the United States, Bukharian Jews are increasingly using the Roman alphabet for all of these languages, a trend gaining hold globally with the rise of the Internet.

Bukharian Jews have an open and impartial approach to transliteration perhaps due to this dizzying linguistic and orthographic variety, much of which is the result of externally imposed policies. However, some standard transliteration practices are emerging. The basis of my transliteration system in this book is Edward Allworth's romanization system for Tajik Persian, as it produces spellings similar to those used by Bukharian Jews. The exceptions are the use of the half-ring (') for ъ, e for э, and ī for й. My transliteration system is provided as Table i.1.

For consistency I also transliterate from the Cyrillic spellings of Hebrew words used frequently in the general Bukharian Jewish environment described in the book (e.g., *shiro* and not *shira* or *shīrāh* for שירה, spelled широ in Cyrillic and nearly always "shiro" in Roman by Bukharian Jews). Common English forms are used if they appear as main entries in merriam-webster.com or *Merriam-Webster's Collegiate Dictionary,* 11th edition; thus, I use *Bukhara* and *Torah,* not *Bukhoro* or *Tūro,* unless the word appears in a song title ("Iroqi Bukhoro," "Vasfi Tūro"). Since Bukharian Jewish speakers often mix and match plural suffixes (the Hebrew word *nigun* might be pluralized as *nigunim, niguns,* or *nigunho*), I simply use -s

Table i.1. Transliteration table. Vowels usually scanned as short are marked by a superscript 1, those usually scanned as long are marked by a superscript 2. Some can be interpreted as short or long depending on the use.

Roman	Cyrillic
A a^1	A a
B b	Б б
Ch ch	Ч ч
D d	Д д
E e^2	Э э, E e
F f	Ф ф
G g	Г г
Gh gh	Ғ ғ
H h	Х х
Ḥ ḥ	for Hebrew ח
I i^1	И и
Ĭ ĭ^1	Й й
Ī ī^2	Й й
J j	Ч ч, ДЖ дж
K k	К к
Kh kh	Х х
L l	Л л
M m	М м
N n	Н н
O o^2	O o
P p	П п
Q q	Қ қ
R r	Р р
S s	С с
Sh sh	Ш ш
Shch shch	Щ щ
T t	Т т
Ts ts	Ц ц
Ū ū^2	Ӯ ӯ
U u^1	У у
V v	В в
Y y	Ы ы
Ye ye	E e (after a vowel)
YO yo	Ё ё
YU yu / IU iu	Ю ю
Z z	З з
Zh zh	Ж ж
ʻ	Ъ ъ
ʼ	Ь ь

or -es, indicated with a hyphen in the first appearance (*nigun*-s first and then just *niguns*). The ultimate aim of these many decisions is to provide reasonably consistent spellings that will be recognizable to Bukharian Jews themselves, as well as readers familiar with English-language scholarship on Bukharian Jews and Central Asia, while also not requiring too much compromise or a steep learning curve for those who are used to conventional romanizations from Perso-Arabic script or the Hebrew alphabet.

Vowels require special attention as their values are important for prosody. Scholars of Iranian Persian should be aware that *e* (*meravad*) and *o* (*maqom*) are the long vowels usually rendered as *ī* (*mīravad*) and *ā* (*maqām*) from Perso-Arabic, and *i* (*hofiz*) is the short vowel usually rendered as *e* (*hāfez*).

Unless otherwise specified, all quotes from speakers are transcriptions from English or my own translations from the speaker's native tongue, usually Tajik Persian. Italics indicate stress and square brackets are for points of clarification. Sometimes I bring special attention to a specific word that a speaker used by putting the original in parentheses or elaborating further in a footnote, but Bukharian speakers switch languages so often that it would be untenable to draw attention to it in every case. For example, in one interview, Ezro Malakov regularly alternated between calling the Book of Psalms "Zaburi Dovid" (Persian and Arabic, but pronouncing David's name according to Hebrew and not the Persian and Arabic Dāwūd), "Tehillim" (Hebrew), and "Psalmy Davida" (Russian), and his switching seemed to hold no special significance. Foreign words are italicized in their first appearance only, except for special emphasis or clarification (e.g., in quotations, lists, or new chapters).

Finally, although English-language scholars have tended to use the spelling *Bukharan*, I use *Bukharian* since this spelling is overwhelmingly preferred among Bukharian Jews themselves. I use *Bukharian* only in reference to Bukharian Jews; I do prefer *Bukharan* when referring to anything generally related to the city, province, or historical emirate of Bukhara (as in *Bukharan court*).

About the Companion Website

Greeted with Smiles

Introduction

It is October 7, 2007, at Beth Gavriel Synagogue on 108th Street in Queens, New York. Tonight is a celebration for *Simḥat Torah*, or in Bukharian parlance, the *Sefar Tūī* (Torah scroll celebration). The Torah is perched atop the centrally located *bimah* dressed as a bride, wrapped in beautiful scarves and covered in an embroidered *jomma* coat (Figure i.1).[1] The small synagogue is filled to capacity, with participants of all ages, men on one side and women on the other. Between the two groups, in front of the bimah, sits the Torah's *ḥoton* (groom) for the evening. He has paid handsomely for this honor. Waiters and waitresses roam the room, serving large portions of *samsa* dumplings, fish, and *plov*—the meat and rice dish required at any celebration. Vodka flows freely. A lively fundraising auction takes place, with music punctuating the completion of each sale: *"Du hazor dolar yak, du hazor dolar du* [two thousand dollars once, two thousand dollars twice], *muzyka* please!" (Figure i.2).

An ensemble featuring some of the Bukharian Jewish community's most celebrated musicians, including Ezro Malakov, Roshel Rubinov, and Avrom Tolmasov, entertains those in attendance.[2] The band, dressed in fashionable suits, play their electric guitars and synthesizers along with the old-fashioned *doira* frame drum through a heavily amplified sound system. They perform a variety of songs over the course of the evening, expressing the multifaceted character of being a Bukharian Jew in New York at the beginning of the twenty-first century. Joyous religious songs capture the spirit of the holiday and the delight of freely practicing Judaism. A persistent 6/8 dance rhythm accompanies upbeat party songs associated with Bukharian weddings and other life-cycle celebrations. And classic *maqom* melodies, joined with meaningful Persian lyrics written by poets spanning the generations, hark back to Central Asia and stir feelings of nostalgia among those gathered here in a city so far from where their lives began.

1

Figure i.1. Avrom Mirzokandov dances at a Simḥat Torah celebration at Beth Gavriel, 2007. The Torah is on the bimah wrapped in scarves and a jomma. Photo by the author.

Figure i.2. Mullo Avrom leads an auction at Beth Gavriel, accompanied by Ezro Malakov and Roshel Rubinov. Photo by the author.

Greeted with Smiles: Bukharian Jewish Music and Musicians in New York is a study of the musical life of this fascinating community, a quintessential American immigrant group at the turn of the twenty-first century. Bukharian Jews are part of the recent waves of immigrants from an unprecedented variety of countries, and a kind of Jewish immigrant that was previously mostly unknown on American shores. Their experiences, like those of their contemporaries, are unavoidably tied to the still-dominant paradigm of multiculturalism, promoting an acknowledgment of cultural differences and an acceptance of new groups' places in the American "mosaic." With intense energy and diverse creative responses to their new circumstances, Bukharian Jews are reconsidering their historic otherness and distinct traditions in terms of American ideas of ethnicity, revealing the many pressures and opportunities of multicultural New York. And in doing so, their musical activities in the public sphere are changing the city's cultural landscape and ideas of the American—and specifically Jewish American—experience.

* * *

Historical Background: Continuity in the Face of Rupture

Bukharian Jews began immigrating to New York City in significant numbers during the 1980s and 1990s as part of the extraordinary waves of Jewish migration from the Soviet Union accompanying the end of the regime. These Bukharian Jews—Persian- and Russian-speaking Jews from the area covered by present-day Tajikistan, Kazakhstan, Kyrgyzstan, Turkmenistan, and most of all Uzbekistan (home of the community's eponymous city of Bukhara)—settled primarily in and around the Forest Hills, Rego Park, and Kew Gardens neighborhoods in Queens, with immigration exploding around the dissolution of the Soviet Union in 1991.[3]

After a continuous presence in Central Asia since ancient times—conceivably dating back to the Babylonian Exile of the Jews in 586 BCE—the Jewish population left Bukhara, Samarqand, and other oasis cities en masse at the end of the twentieth century.[4] The United States is currently home to roughly half of the recent Bukharian Jewish emigrants, conservatively estimated at about 28,000 (Kaganovitch 2008).[5] Most of the other half emigrated to Israel, joining the substantial Bukharian community that first settled there in the late nineteenth century. It is also not uncommon for Bukharians to move to New York after having emigrated to Israel, or vice versa. There are some Bukharian Jewish immigrants in Europe, especially in Germany and Austria, and in other US cities such as Atlanta and Denver, and there remains a very small number of Bukharian Jews in Central Asia itself.

While their unprecedented "exodus" (Ochildiev 2005:170) established an ostensible schismatic break with the past, Bukharian Jews recognize a great deal of continuity between their lives in Central Asia and in New York. Bukharian Jews in New York perpetually draw on their past to understand and navigate their contemporary immigrant situation. They do not imagine an unbreachable gulf between "Old World" and "New World" or think of their former lives as something to be shed and discarded in the process of reinvention or assimilation. Rather, they consider their lives in Central Asia to be a precedent for the American multiculturalist context and are adapting their traditions as models and resources.

A few of these points connecting Bukharian life before and after mass migration are treated in greater detail in this Introduction. (1) Throughout their history, Bukharian Jews lived in multicultural cities (e.g., Bukhara, Tashkent, and New York) as a distinct minority group, where they both participated in the local environment and resisted assimilation, cultivating separate traditions specific to their community. (2) They successfully managed discrimination and changing political tides—from the threat of forced conversion and inequalities of the pre-Soviet era, to the oppressive and erratic policies of the Soviets—developing an ability to thrive in difficult situations that has served them well in New York. (3) Their mass migration at the end of the twentieth century has a precedent in that Bukharian Jews regularly migrated to, from, and within Central Asia before their current dispersion, and they consistently maintained a "classic" diasporic consciousness in which the Land of Israel serves as a spiritual home.[6] Music has played a key part in each of these points, as Bukharian Jews have consistently excelled in diverse musical repertoires that provided social mobility as well as multiple avenues of expression.

Minority Life in Multicultural Cities: Participation and Exchange while Resisting Assimilation

Bukharian Jews lived consistently as a very small minority in Central Asia—less than 1 percent of the population—and almost exclusively in the cities. The majority populations of these cities are Sunni Muslims, and depending on the location of the city, usually Uzbeks (Turkic-speaking) and Tajiks (Persian-speaking). Urban life in Central Asia anticipated multicultural New York in that Bukharian Jews primarily resided in neighborhoods, *mahalla*-s, in what now might be considered "ethnic enclaves" of diverse cities alongside members of other ethnoreligious minorities, such as Shi'a Muslims ("Ironi," "Forsi," or "Marvi," originally from Iran), Armenian Christians, and Indian Hindus.[7] By the end of the nineteenth century, "Bukhara [the emirate] was a vast multi-ethnic state.... Tajiks, certain Turkic and Arab entities, Hindus and Jews lived in settled communities" (Arapov 1993:15); the city itself also included populations of ethnic minorities such as Afghans, Russians, Caucasian peoples, other Turkic-speaking people (Kazakhs or Kyrgyz), and "Gypsies" (Sukhareva 1967:117–81; Naumkin 1993:59–91; Djumaev 2008:54).

Confined to Jewish quarters under Muslim rule, life in the private community environments of the mahallas both forced and enabled Bukharian

Jews to continue their distinctive traditions and resist assimiliation while they interacted with the diverse groups around them. Assimilation per se is an ongoing, serious concern for Bukharian Jews—they use the Russian *assimilatsiya*—but the particular conception of assimilation depends on their circumstances. Retrospectively understood as conversion (forced or otherwise) to Islam and then as abandoning the Jewish faith under pressure from Soviet atheistic policies, assimilation in New York is associated with fears surrounding the loss of an externally mandated, clearly defined, and separate Jewish identity, complicating the overall characterizations among Bukharian Jews of America's widespread freedoms as blessings.

Concepts such as assimilation and multiculturalism rely on a group identifying itself as such, along with notions of difference ("us" and "them"). It should be underscored that the Central Asian Jews' status as a distinct minority group, so central to their experiences in New York, predated and continued during the Soviet era. Under Muslim rule, Jews were considered a separate group and subject to particular rules and restrictions. After the Russians successfully wrested Central Asia from the khans who ruled feudal Bukhara, Kokand, and Khiva, eventually establishing the Uzbek and Tajik Soviet Socialist Republics in 1924 and 1929, the Soviet government officially constituted new Uzbek, Tajik, and other Central Asian ethnonational categories, drawing on some linguistic and regional affiliations but also ignoring and replacing existing senses of identity. "The romantic concept of nation as being the whole of persons united by a common mother-tongue was introduced into Central Asia where it met with several not clearly shaped indigenous concepts of nation (as being the whole of persons united by either religious belief, attribution to a professional group, citizenship or tribal links)" (Baldauf 1991:80). In the Soviet system, the Jewish nationality was considered wholly incompatible with the Uzbek and Tajik categories (an "Uzbek Jew" would be an impossibility), coinciding with the important point that, unlike Uzbeks and Tajiks, Jews already had a group identity. Due to the categorical separation of Jews and their neighbors in Central Asia, I refer to the dynamics between Bukharian Jews and Muslims and other non-Jews throughout the book as "intercultural." Meanwhile, Bukharian Jews consistently identified as part of broader global Jewry, so the complex relationships between Bukharian Jews and other Jewish communities are described throughout the book as "intracultural."

Despite categorical distinctions, Jews in Central Asia (like Jews all over the world) shared much of the culture and folkways of their neighbors, including language and literature, food, dress, customs, art, and music. For example, Persian is their mother tongue just as it is for Tajiks and the general population of Bukhara and Samarqand, as well as Afghanistan and Iran (the dialect Bukharian Jews speak is Judeo-Tajik, which Bukharian Jews refer to as Bukhori, Bukharian, or the Bukharian Jewish language, historically written with the Hebrew alphabet). Under Soviet rule, Bukharian Jews in the region, like their neighbors, became Russian speakers and Cyrillic readers as well.[8] Music was an intensely productive arena for interaction and collaboration between Jews and their neighbors, especially in the realm of the classical repertoire known as maqom, discussed in Chapter 3, and the sphere of popular entertainment, discussed in Chapter 5.

Indeed, the history of exchange between Muslims and Jews in Central Asia is remarkable. One older Bukharian man (Ilya Yakubov) told me that the Jews of pre-Soviet Kokand would use a corner of the Friday mosque for prayer following the Muslims—an unusual situation; even if an exaggeration, the fact that this man believed this attests to the closeness of Jews and Muslims in the region. And Bukharian Jews still maintain a high level of connection to their former homes. They continue to have strong business and personal contacts in Central Asia, and some, including Boris Kandov (president of the Congress of the Bukharian Jews of the USA and Canada), are known to be supportive of the current governments, including Islom Karimov's in Uzbekistan and Emomalī Rahmon's in Tajikistan.[9] As discussed in Chapter 6, Bukharian Jews regularly organize *ziyorat* (pilgrimage) tours to Central Asia to visit Jewish cemeteries, synagogues, and other important sites, and they send funds to their home cities to ensure the upkeep of these locations. Bukharian musicians such as Roshel Rubinov sometimes travel to Central Asia to record. In 2000, Ilyos Mallayev's Ensemble Maqom performed in Tashkent, Bukhara, and Samarqand in concerts organized by the Uzbek Consulate.

Managing Discrimination and Adapting to Changing Political Tides

Bukharian Jews' vigorous participation in general Central Asian society is notable considering the difficulties they faced. Their ability to adapt was frequently limited and contained by those in power. Under the Muslim khanates, Bukharian Jews were subject to the various policies (enforced with varying degrees of severity) that applied to most Jews in Muslim lands under the Pact of Umar: they were restricted from wearing certain clothes, prohibited from riding on horseback, prohibited from building new synagogues, confined to living in Jewish Quarters, and forced to pay disproportionately large taxes (Amitin-Shapiro 1931:10–12; Hourani 1991:47; T. Levin 1996:91–92; Cooper 2012:20). And although the Russians ended the emir's discriminatory policies and introduced medicinal and scientific technologies, Soviet policies could be equally, if not more, brutal. The Soviet Union's official policy of enforced atheism was especially difficult for the religious Bukharian Jewish community. Tolerance of Jewish religious practice ebbed and flowed tremendously, with especially dark periods during Stalin's purges in the 1930s, the "Black Years" of 1948–1953, and the end of Khrushchev's reign (1957–1964) (Pinkus 2007; Ro'i 2008:58).[10] To persevere and participate in society despite these challenges required developing serious adaptation strategies, such as keeping various repertoires and styles out of the public sphere, strategies they have applied to their lives as immigrants.

Considering that Jews had lived in Central Asia for centuries through all kinds of unfavorable circumstances, the en masse emigration of Bukharian Jews might be difficult to comprehend. Although life during the Soviet Union was difficult and restrictive, Bukharian Jews had weathered equally severe storms through the generations, and they had relatively positive relationships with their neighbors. However, like Jews in the western part of the USSR, Bukharian Jews were attracted to the religious freedoms and economic opportunities of the United States, Israel, and Europe (Cooper 2011). For Jews in Central Asia, the climate seemed foreboding at the end of the Soviet Union, as growing neonationalistic movements in the Central Asian countries created fear among the Jewish populations. Tajikistan had fallen immediately into a state of civil war. Some Jews describe being fearful that the Central Asian republics would go the way of Iran and become Islamic states (Ezro Malakov and Alisher Alimatov, personal communication), the revolution of 1979 still fresh in their minds (even though the opposite ended up happening, with the former Soviet leaders remaining in charge and suppressing Islamist movements; see Whitlock 2002).

Incongruously—but with unfortunate frequency—the successes that Jews had despite the formidable obstacles of nationwide anti-Semitism and suppressive policies were used against them as evidence of their secret connections to the Soviet authorities and international powers (Human Rights Watch 1995; Rotar 2005). In Uzbekistan, the country with the most Bukharian Jews, President Islom Karimov's ruthless crackdown on militant Islamist groups such as Hizb ut-Tahrir fueled backlash against Jews. While many Jews maintained positive and productive relationships with their Muslim neighbors, others began to experience anti-Semitic graffiti, slurs, insults, and threats (see Kenvin 2010:99–126 et passim for recollections and documentation of arson, vandalism, and other acts of violence against Jews). "Uzbekification" also made other non-Uzbek people uncomfortable, and the Russians, Germans, and other "foreigners" who once populated ethnically diverse cities such as Tashkent started to leave Uzbekistan in significant numbers. The fall of the Soviet Union also led a significant number of Muslim Central Asians to resettle in New York. Some Bukharian Jews have aided and welcomed their migration, while in other cases the renewed situation of Central Asian Jews and Muslims as neighbors in New York has led to resurfaced tensions.

Migration and Diasporic Consciousness

Although Jews lived in Central Asia for so long, migration was a regular adaptation strategy and an important part of their history. Complicating the picture, while Bukharian Jews were extremely rooted in Central Asia, they also maintained a diasporic consciousness that deemed Central Asia part of the *golut* (exile), after which would be redemption and return to Zion, the Land of Israel. Bukharian Jews were consistently aware of and in contact with other Jewish communities (discussed in Chapter 4), in contrast to their frequent representation as lost and isolated. Bukharian

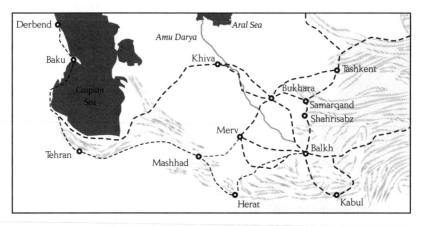

Figure i.3. Map of selected Central Asian trade routes in the sixteenth and seventeenth centuries. Map by the author with Jerry Lim (with information from Bregel 2003:69).

Jews were some of the earliest Zionist immigrants to Palestine, establishing the Bukharan Quarter in Jerusalem at the end of the nineteenth century (Cooper 2000:144–60). Migration to and from Palestine/Israel continued throughout the twentieth century. By 1914, about 1,500 Bukharian Jews lived in Israel, another wave of immigration at the beginning of the 1930s brought 4,000 more, in the 1970s another 10,000, and at the beginning of the 1980s, another 7,000—"by the late 1980s some 29,600 Bukharan Jews were living in Israel," reaching an estimate of about 65,000 after the fall of the USSR (Kaganovitch 2008:111).

Jews in Central Asia also migrated within the region over the course of their history. A branch of Persian Jewry, along with Jews in Iran and Afghanistan, Bukharian Jews traveled to and from cities such as Bukhara, Mashhad, and Herat to escape political tumult or discrimination, or to pursue economic opportunities. As merchants, they moved around the Silk Road and Muslim world for centuries; written evidence from Central Asia and the Cairo Geniza "attests to the mobility of Iranian Jews, especially between the 9th and 11th centuries CE" (Moreen 2010:398; "Iranian" includes Central Asia in this statement). Jewish merchants in the nineteenth century were known to travel to Europe, India, and China (Cooper 2012:73–75). Figure i.3 shows just a few of the many trade routes linking Central Asian cities, including many with Jewish populations, in the sixteenth and seventeenth centuries. These intercity connections are especially important when considering Jewish geographies, which may only roughly intersect with national borders.

Hardships also spurred migration. Some Jews in Central Asia came after fleeing persecution in Iran: oppression under the Safavids resulted in substantial migration from Iran to Central Asia (Calmard 2003:812; Sahim 2003:368–69; Netzer 2007), and the large-scale forced conversions of the Jews in Mashhad in 1839 (the so-called Allahdād) also brought refugees to

Figure i.4. Map of current Central Asian national borders, with superimposed borders of khanates of Bukhara and Khiva during the Russian protectorate period at the beginning of the twentieth century. The gray area surrounding the Aral Sea indicates the water's edge during the Russian protectorates. Map by the author with Jerry Lim (with information from Bregel 2003:91).

Central Asia. Before the Soviet era, many Bukharian Jews left the Bukharan emirate for cities such as Samarqand that had already been absorbed into Russian Turkestan, where the Russians had extended greater freedoms and opportunities (see Figure i.4).[11] Stalin's terrors in 1930s and 1940s sent many Jews in the other direction, to Afghanistan, Iran, and India (Kaganovitch 2007; Koplik 2008).[12] Thus, the migration to New York, Israel, and Europe at the end of the twentieth century can be seen as part of a continuum rather than a totally unprecedented break.

The Contemporary Bukharian Diaspora and Multicultural New York

The history of migration and the almost complete dissolution of the community in Central Asia has culminated in a vast and complex diaspora, mapping closely onto the conditions of globalization as defined by Robin Cohen in terms of a world economy, international migration, the development of global cities, cosmopolitanism, and a deterritorialization of social identity (R. Cohen 1997:157). Bukharian Jews maintain transnational governing bodies, such as the World Bukharian Congress, as well as international economic networks driven by wealthy members of the community such as the diamond magnate Lev Leviev, who supports many Bukharian institutions.[13] Bukharian networks overlap with other international trade systems and other Jewish diasporas, with particularly intricate dynamics between Bukharian Jews and Ashkenazic Jews—the dominant Jewish group worldwide—and the Sephardic Jews that trace their origins to the expulsions from the Iberian peninsula in 1492 and 1497.[14] Sephardim, although a minority of global Jewry often positioned at the margins with respect to Ashkenazim, constitute a hegemon of sorts in relation to Bukharian Jews, who are at the margins of the margins. Bukharian musicians, already of great importance to the community and deeply cosmopolitan, have shaped and strengthened the Bukharian diaspora, traveling and performing throughout the world, and writing poems and songs that speak to their current condition of dispersion.

Although I consider the global diasporic issues in this book, particularly with respect to the Jewish religious repertoire (Chapter 4), my study deals primarily with the American multicultural context in which Bukharian Jews in New York specifically live. Even members of this exceedingly diasporic and international community must deal with the day-to-day conditions of immigrant life and their local environment. Bukharian Jews in New York may be strongly connected to Tel Aviv, Vienna, and Samarqand, but even with the Internet, air travel, satellite TV, and Skype, they still must adapt to life in the United States, with its specific social mores, ideas of religion, and categories of ethnicity and race. The musical life of Bukharian Jews in New York, with its distinct approaches to the classical, religious, and popular repertoires, is directly related to the particular qualities of multicultural New York at the end of the twentieth and beginning of the twenty-first century.

Bukharian Jews in New York arrived during a moment of mainstream and widespread multiculturalist ideology and, along with massive numbers of immigrants of unprecedented diversity, were part of a shift that redefined New York's identity as a cosmopolitan city of immigrants and ethnic enclaves. In Queens, the "meltingest pot" (Mehta 2003) borough with the most foreign-born residents and where most Bukharian Jews reside, an astounding 138 languages were reported as spoken in the 2000 census, with Bukhori existing side-by-side with endangered languages such as Vlashki and Mamuju (Roberts 2010). As shown in Figure i.5, the central Queens neighborhoods in which most Bukharian Jews currently live are representative of the heavy immigration transforming the borough in general: according to 2000 census data, 1,028,339 Queens residents were foreign-born, accounting for 46.1 percent of the borough's population.[15] This trend continued through the 2000s; by 2011, the percentage had risen to 47.8 (New York City 2013:51).[16] Bukharian Jews in New York have new neighbors—African Americans, Latin Americans— and newly kindled relationships with old neighbors—Iranians, Afghans, East Asians. The landscape of Jewish New York, dominated by Jews of Ashkenazic descent for one hundred years, changed drastically with the arrival of Bukharian Jews and others from the former Soviet Union, such as Georgian Jews and the "Mountain" Jews from Dagestan. Jewish institutions adopted multiculturalism from a Jewish perspective, giving Bukharian Jews opportunities to connect with powerful Jewish organizations and individuals. Bukharian Jews' encounters with New York's religious freedom, multicultural atmosphere, and influential Jewish networks

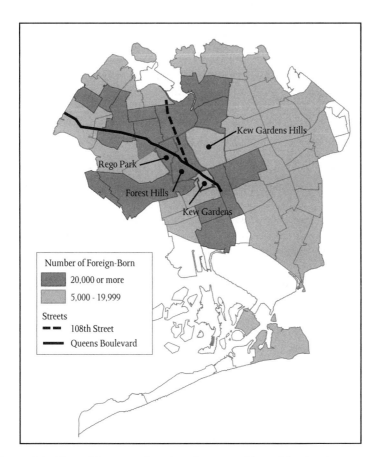

Figure i.5. Map of Queens, showing demographics of foreign-born residents. Map by the author with Jerry Lim (with data from New York City 2004).

resulted in an extremely favorable view of immigration, best expressed in Ilyos Mallayev's popular song "Yalalum": "in the hands of friends, young beautiful flowers / they greet us with smiles" upon coming from Asia to America.[17] Yet Bukharian Jews have also had to newly define themselves as a discrete ethnic group; manage tensions with non-Jews, other Jewish communities, and within their own community; and face the significant losses and gains that always accompany large-scale migrations.

Bukharian Jewish Repertoires and Roles: Navigating Change by Adapting Traditions

Most Bukharian Jews participate wholeheartedly in American society at large despite their often marginal status, just as they did in Central Asia. Although articles in mainstream media outlets such as the *New York Times* and the *New Yorker* frequently limn the community as isolated, mono-lithic, and insular, Bukharian Jews are a diverse group that has overcome significant linguistic and cultural barriers to become an essential part of the city's life.[18] Professional musicians, with their experience managing diverse situations and negotiating relationships with Bukharian Jews' "others," are perhaps the most active agents engaging the Bukharian Jews' contemporary immigrant situation, directing and responding to the community at large as they adapt to life in the United States.

The study focuses primarily on the generation of immigrant musicians in middle to upper age (in their forties to seventies), who spent their formative years in Central Asia and directly experienced upheaval and pivotal change in relocating to the United States. Based on an extensive period of research of over twelve years with these particular musicians as well as supplemental interviews and countless conversations with many non-musicians or amateur musicians, students, younger and older people, spouses and relatives—including some quoted throughout this book, such as the community activist Aron Aronov and Ezro Malakov's nephew Jacob Malakov—I found that professional musicians were extremely invested in the status and identity of the community and that others looked to them as leaders in situating the community in New York.

Bukharian Jews self-consciously use music to define and transform their circumstances, every aspect of Bukharian Jewish life finding some form of expression in melodies, poems, and rhythms. Bukharian Jews brought with them three major overlapping but distinct musical repertoires from Central Asia, which they continue to develop in relation to their changing environment. One repertoire is maqom or heavy (*vazmin*) music, the music most explicitly linked to the American multicultural context as the Bukharian Jewish "ethnic music." Another repertoire is Jewish religious music, which has become an intense area for growth and change as Bukharian Jews revisit and revive their own distinct traditions while negotiating an extremely different landscape of Jewish connections and practices. A third repertoire is party or light (*sabuk*) music, which reflects Bukharian Jewish Americans' self-image as cosmopolitans, but which is also in tension with the pressures of multiculturalism.

Maqom, or Central Asian classical music, is a symbol of old Central Asia as well as the "world music" representation of Bukharian achievement in the most explicitly multicultural settings. Maqom—a broad category that includes the specific repertoire known as *Shashmaqom* ("six modes") associated with the Bukharan court—is a product of fruitful interactions between Jews and Muslims, the intercultural relationship that defined Bukharian Jewry in Central Asia. In New York, maqom continues to be the primary repertoire in which Bukharian Jews explore their relationships with non-Jews and the majority culture. Befitting its role as a symbol and a heritage music, maqom has developed into a small repertoire of representative selections from a wide variety of regions and styles. Contemporary maqom captures the historical memory of Central Asian life, reminiscent of feudal, pre-Soviet times, although its current state owes much to Soviet ideology. However, maqom is not only a look backward. Highly concerned with perpetuating Bukharian traditions, poets and composers both young and old continue to set new poems to the old tunes and to update the classics for today's ears.

Religious repertoire has become a crucible for Bukharian Jewish life in New York, a communal expression of the most pervasive quality of Bukharian life—the practice of the Jewish religion—as well as a manifestation of the complex intracultural relationships between Bukharian Jews and other Jewish communities. Religious repertoire is a male-dominated sphere of performance, although women participate in mixed contexts as listeners. Religious repertoire captures the particular ways in which Bukharian Jews navigate two coexisting yet competing currents, both related to multiculturalist ideology: toward assimilating to more general manifestations of Jewish culture, and toward retaining or creating a unique Bukharian Jewish identity. Contradicting the conventional wisdom that religious music is static when compared with secular music, religious repertoire is the site of the most rapid change in America, with Bukharian Jews exploring religious life in unprecedented ways after the repressive environment of the Soviet Union. Religious music is essential for a constant stream of life-cycle events and the Jewish calendar—weddings, funerals, holidays, sacred meals—and as such is contemporary and alive, yet religious repertoire also carries the significance, weight, and associations of history and heritage that Bukharian Jews ascribe to maqom. Unique Bukharian traditions, including the singing of Hebrew and Persian hymns set to maqom melodies, are being revived, maintained, and even created, sitting side-by-side with new songs and styles culled from other Jewish communities.

Party music, or "light" music, captures Bukharian cosmopolitanism—a defining quality of Bukharian identity internally, but one that is rarely presented outside the community. In party music, Bukharian Jews demonstrate their own version of multiculturalism, as they define their own "others" through an ever-growing amalgam of languages and styles. Party music expresses the Bukharian Jewish professional musicians' ability to thrive in wide-ranging situations, and the community's self-conception as a group that, unlike other groups, appreciates music other than its "own." Yet the internal quality of the party repertoire illuminates one of the major limitations of multiculturalism—despite a rhetorical embrace of diversity, multiculturalist institutions influence how communities present themselves in terms of singular, bounded, ethnically marked styles. The music played for weddings, bar mitzvah celebrations, and other parties is called "light" in contrast to the "heavy" maqom repertoire; without the obligations that accompany maqom, party music helps Bukharian Americans celebrate immigrant life with great flexibility. But although associated with newness and change, party repertoire has a historical basis, as Bukharian musicians thrived as popular entertainers in Central Asia. Perhaps unexpectedly, the role of party musician and the aesthetics of the light repertoire have remained two of the more consistent aspects of

Bukharian Jewish life through the transition of mass migration to the United States.

The professional musician is at the center of Bukharian Jewish musical life, performing these repertoires for the community in appropriate situations and guiding Bukharian Jews through their immigrant experiences. "Professional" (Bukharian Jews use the English word, a loanword in Russian) does not necessarily indicate that the musician makes his or her sole living from music—some do, some do not.[19] Rather, it indicates a high level of ability, achievement, and community recognition of the musician's artistry. Roshel Rubinov compared a professional musician's repertoire to ammunition in a gun: the gun must always be loaded to be effective, and a performer must always be prepared to play just as a soldier must always be ready to use his weapon. Tamara Katayeva explained that for each event, "you need to be prepared. If I'm singing for Navruz [Persian New Year], I have to prepare something special for Navruz. If it's a Mother's Day party, I have to sing about mothers. For Shabbat, about Shabbat. You must always be prepared." In New York, Bukharian Jewish musicians have adjusted and expanded their repertoires and styles to address the community's rapidly changing needs and desires, many of which stem from newfound religious freedoms. Musicians are well suited to leading the Bukharian community through processes of adaptation and adjustment, having developed adaptation strategies in Central Asia while navigating interactions outside the community.

The professional master classical singer known as *hofiz* is extremely important to the Bukharian community.[20] At least since the end of the nineteenth century, Bukharian Jews populated the ranks of maqom singers, providing a great source of pride and leadership. Great hofizes of the past such as Levi Bobokhonov, Gavriel Mulloqandov, and Mikhoel Tolmasov are known and respected as heroes among Bukharian Jews. During the Soviet era women joined the formerly restricted ranks of maqom singers and had momentous achievements. In the United States, the role of hofiz is crucial as Bukharian Jews make their mark on the mainstream "world music" landscape, and contemporary hofizes such as Avrom Tolmasov are inheritors of this Bukharian legacy. Hofizes also keep the globally dispersed Bukharian diaspora connected, as they travel and perform for Bukharian communities worldwide.

Equally important is the religious singer known as *ḥazzan*. The ḥazzan is responsible for crucial sections of worship, carrying the congregation's words to God. In Bukharian congregations the ḥazzan is always male, and the role is dependent on community recognition rather than ordination by a cantorial school. A Bukharian ḥazzan may lead most of the service, or he may sing at decisive moments that require an expert vocal display. Under the Soviet regime, the Jewish religion was officially suppressed and went "underground," and while individuals from rabbinical or cantorial families learned the religious repertoire at home they rarely performed it publicly. This situation has completely changed with the religious freedom of the United States, and the role of the ḥazzan has once again become a prominent public one. The classical singers Ezro Malakov and Ochil Ibragimov also work as ḥazzans in the United States.

The party repertoire is dominated by the pop singer, inheriting the role of the *estrada* (or "show") entertainer from the Soviet Union. Pop singers such as Yuhan Benjamin and Nargis Mallayeva perform at weddings, nightclubs, and community events. Much Bukharian light music is rooted in the traditional wedding repertoires, especially the music of the female wedding entertainer called *sozanda*. Pop singers also mix and match musical styles from around the world, incorporating the most recent international hits into their diverse repertoire in order to get people dancing. A self-sustaining piece of Bukharian musical life, many singers and instrumentalists with classical training perform light repertoire to satisfy their primary source of income, the wedding.

These are vocalist roles, and the singer has a special part to play in the Bukharian community. But Bukharian Jews have also thrived as composers and filled the ranks of instrumentalists for all three repertoires. During the Soviet era, Bukharian Jews became prominent teachers at conservatories and performers with government orchestras and theater companies, and they contributed essential new compositions to the classical repertoire. And although not a focus of this book, Bukharian Jews also became noted performers of European classical music, as violin virtuosi, opera singers, or even as players of adaptations for traditional Central Asian instruments. Yakhiel Sabzanov composed a well-known opera, *Bozgasht* (Return), and Suleïmon (Solomon) Yudakov wrote the melody for the Tajik national anthem (see Reikher 2009–2010 for more examples).

Rather than stick to only one repertoire or practice, Bukharian Jews have by and large diversified as professional minority musicians who are adept at performing in a variety of situations. The great maqom singer Shoista Mullojonova performed *Eugene Onegin, Carmen,* and *The Tsar's Bride* (Benyaminov 1992:92). Ari Bobokhonov inherited the entirety of his family's maqom repertoire and also mastered European classics on the *rubob*. The Mulloqandov family provides a good example of the various roles Bukharian Jews have mastered, continually adapting to the changing times: "People's Artist of the Uzbek SSR" Gavriel Mulloqandov was a singer, composer, and famous maqomist, while his son Roshel became an opera singer; Gavriel's brother, Mikhoel, was also a "People's Artist," *tanbūr* player, singer, and theater performer; Gavriel's sister, Frida Mulloqandova, was a singer and performer in a touring theater, and her daughter, Tamara Katayeva, went on to become an accomplished singer and dancer in Central Asia and, after immigrating in 1990, the United States.

Bukharian professional musicians quickly adapted to the opportunities and challenges presented by their new home in New York. They perform at Carnegie Hall and Lincoln Center as part of multicultural programs, bringing their exotic music, dance, and costumes to audiences interested in "world music." At libraries and community centers, Bukharian musicians take part in programs designed to educate their neighbors about

Jewish life in a Muslim society that is located in a part of the world many Americans know nothing about. Meanwhile, Bukharian professional musicians continue to develop and perform their distinct religious repertoires and cosmopolitan party music at local celebrations such as weddings, bar mitzvah parties, and circumcision rites. Masters of Bukharian Jewish song lead prayers in synagogue, providing an aesthetic and moving worship experience, and they preside at memorials, helping people grieve and remember the deceased.

Bukharian Jewish professional musicians are able to traverse unfamiliar and quickly changing terrain with an uncommon versatility born from constantly shifting social and political circumstances in Central Asia. By applying their deep-seated skills to the New York multicultural environment and then developing them further, Bukharian Jewish professional musicians are quintessential examples of contemporary ethnic minority and immigrant musicians, as well as consummate representatives of a globally important figure, the Jewish professional musician operating both in and out of majority contexts. Ezro Malakov, Roshel Rubinov, Ilyos Mallayev, Muhabbat Shamayeva, and others seem able to adjust their repertoires and performance styles to any situation. Ezro Malakov will transform a library into a roomful of dancers, preside over Congregation Beth Gavriel's Saturday morning services, and sing classical melodies on the stage of Lincoln Center; in Uzbekistan, he will also bestow Muslim blessings on his old friends and neighbors. At a library in Brooklyn attended mostly by older Russian Jewish residents, Muhabbat Shamayeva sang Yiddish songs to complement the unfamiliar Central Asian songs in her performance. Roshel Rubinov can perform masterful interpretations of Central Asian classical music as well as Elvis Presley and Ricky Martin songs. In each case, these professionals reach their audience despite major challenges (for example, many of the older musicians do not speak English), and the variety of styles and songs at their disposal is a source of constant surprise.

Along with their ability to move from situation to situation, Bukharian Jewish musicians are highly concerned with defining and maintaining their distinct heritage. The community's need to both change and keep its traditions distinct is a balancing act long familiar to Jews and other immigrants and minority groups, but Bukharian Jews are distinguished by the intensity of their activities. Primed by their various experiences as a distinct ethnic group in Central Asia through the Soviet period, Bukharian Jews have capitalized on New York's well-established character as a patchwork of ethnic communities and the city's embracing of multiculturalism. Ezro Malakov found the initiative to spearhead an effort to record hundreds of Bukharian Jewish hymns, including many newly commissioned works, resulting in the monumental publication *Musical Treasures of the Bukharian Jewish Community*; immediately following this project, he proceeded to produce recordings of new musical settings for all 150 Psalms.[21] Ilyos Mallayev and Roshel Rubinov compose and sing poems written in the centuries-old Persian meters and forms, demonstrating an unusual commitment to keeping these genres vibrant. Roshel Aminov established a school dedicated to the teaching of the classical Shashmaqom repertoire. Bukharian Jews have drawn on multiculturalist ideas to develop a unique Bukharian Jewish ethnicity, with professional musicians leading the way.

From the Musician's Point of View: Lived Practices, Not Abstractions

It is difficult to spend more than a few hours in Queens without hearing the praises of Avrom Tolmasov, Shoista Mullojonova, Ilyos Mallayev, or Ezro Malakov, and nearly every celebration is accompanied by almost constant, supremely amplified music. Frequent encounters with these prominent professional musicians led me to focus my research on their stories and activities immediately upon beginning my research activities. One unexpected benefit of the "subject-centered musical ethnography" (Rice 2003) that I pursued was a freedom to circumvent the rabbit hole of a nationalist musical ideal—one music associated with one people and one language—that continues to trouble Jewish music research, despite being intrinsically unsuited to the historical conditions of Jewish life.[22]

Focusing on the diverse and sometimes messy or paradoxical activities of these musicians, rather than starting from a predetermined abstraction of "Jewish music," provided a path for understanding the multiethnic, multifaceted, and multilingual realities of Jewish people in diaspora (Slobin 1986a). All of the various products and activities of the community are what collectively constitute Bukharian Jewish American music and culture, a bundle of responses to the new questions and concerns Bukharian Jews have perceived after migrating en masse to a new environment governed by multicultural ideology. As Stephen Blum notes, drawing on Robert Musil, "such concepts as 'race and culture, people and nation' should be understood as 'questions, and not answers; not substrata of phenomena, but complicated phenomena in themselves; not sociological elements, but results; in other words, products and not producers' (Musil 1978:1366, tr. 1990:162). The 'products' are put to use by actors, who offer competing answers—best interpreted, in turn, as new questions" (Blum 1994:277). I have done my best to illustrate and interpret some of the competing answers of Bukharian Jewish musicians to the questions of multiculturalism rather than rendering a judgment on multiculturalism per se or offering an absolute definition of Bukharian Jewry and its borders.

In accordance with my treatment of Jewish music, multiculturalism, and identity, the three repertoires delineated in this book are "products put to use by actors," not permanent categories or "producers" themselves. My empirical definitions of repertoires conflict in some cases with conventional understandings, especially in the case of the theoretical ideal typically associated with maqom. Musicians are often uninvolved or unconcerned with discussions of musical structures and theory, and even the most interested and knowledgable musicians typically have practice-based understandings of their music that differ from the understandings of theorists. As the Persian prince Kai Kā'ūs (11th c.) advised musicians one thousand years ago, "Do not always play the royal melodies, citing the rules of music (*shart-i mutribī*).... While you are applying the rules of music people will become drunk and leave. So see what each person likes most and deduce what they want" (Kaykāvūs 1994:192 [translation mine]; see also Djumaev 1992:148–49). The Bukharian Jewish professional musicians described in this book, in part due to their liminal minority status (since theoretical ideals became associated with "nations" that excluded Jews from their categorical boundaries), understand maqom and other repertoires above all as resources for performance, apart from their interest in abstract ideals or their level of theoretical knowledge.

My own experiences as a professional musician (I have a background as a professional saxophonist), my eagerness to study Central Asian classical music performance, and my availability to assist on recording projects further focused my study on the activities of professional musicians. Due to my background and my interests, almost all of my research was specifically related to the connections between repertoire and the musical life of professionals. I studied the tanbūr (long-necked lute) with two instructors, Roshel Aminov and Roshel Rubinov. My lessons with Aminov were formal, one-on-one rote instruction as part of his music school. My lessons with Rubinov were free (a rarity in this world, and for this he deserves my unending gratitude), at his house, also in one-on-one rote instruction, but open-ended and filled with lots of informal conversation that heavily shaped my ideas about Bukharian Jewish musical life. My initial experiences with Ezro Malakov were in assisting him with the preparation of his book and CD set, *Musical Treasures of the Bukharian Jewish Community*, as I recorded him and his fellow musicians on my MiniDisc and checked over transcriptions.

While my background and identity created fast relationships with some musicians and quickly directed my research, these factors also limited my work. For example, my identity as an Ashkenazic Jewish man granted me access to male gatherings and helped create a close, almost familial relationship with some musicians (especially Ezro Malakov), but on the other hand, although I interviewed and became well acquainted with several women musicians (especially Tamara Katayeva), I did not participate in or witness any women-only events. I also chose to abide by the community's standards of Jewish law when conducting research, which meant that I never took notes or used electronic devices on the Sabbath. Other choices similarly characterized my research. For example, I decided to learn and conduct my research primarily in Persian, enabling me to speak with older members of the community, read and understand poetry, and have the intimate discussions that communication in a mother tongue seems to foster. However, my inability to understand spoken Russian obscured aspects of

Bukharian life, such as some public speeches (the Russian-language research in this book was conducted with the help of translators).

Jewish music scholars have frequently written on the issues of being both an insider and an outsider (Summit 2000:5–9; Koskoff 2001:xii–xvi; Slobin [1989] 2002:xiv–xvi, 1993:3–5; J. M. Cohen 2009:16–18; Cooper 2012:3–8 et passim), but the mixture of access and obstacles connected to identity is only one factor to consider due to the extremely multilingual and multisited situation of Bukharian Jews. The scholarship on Bukharian Jews is much like Rumi's fable from the *Masnavi* of the elephant in the dark, each person feeling a different part of the animal and offering a description—an accurate representation of that person's interaction with the subject, but a partial illustration of the whole. Most scholars have conducted their research in one or two languages, whereas many Bukharian Jews are competent or fluent in at least three. Surprisingly, with the exception of Mark Slobin's essay on Bukharian music in Israel (1982b), this book is the first English-language publication on Bukharian Jewish music based on ethnographic research conducted primarily in Persian, the Bukharian mother tongue.[23] Regarding fieldwork locations, it would be impossible to cover every site of the Bukharian diaspora, which spans the entire globe—and some of these geopolitical entities, such as the Soviet Union, do not even exist anymore. I conducted research in Central Asia and Israel in addition to New York but only for very short periods of time, yet even scholars conducting broad multisited fieldwork on the community, such as Cooper (Central Asia, Israel, and New York) and Levin (Central Asia and New York) can describe only a small piece of the Bukharian experience. But with these factors in mind, a body of work is emerging that explores this fascinating community from a variety of angles. I hope *Greeted with Smiles*, despite its limitations, makes a contribution to this literature and represents the community responsibly.

* * *

I think of the book as a performance of classical Central Asian music, with each chapter capturing my sense of a particular genre or rhythm. The Introduction is an opening instrumental *tasnif* to attune the ears and create an amenable atmosphere for performance, laying the groundwork for discussing the central question of the book: how does Bukharian Jewish musical life in New York shed light on the circumstances, governed by multiculturalism, facing new American immigrants? Chapter 1, "Performing Bukharian Jewish History," is a *sarakhbor*, the opening vocal statement that announces the mode. In a slow *zarbi qadim* ("ancient rhythm"), this chapter discusses how the New York community understands their historical circumstances as setting the stage for their current activities, based on an interpretation of Ilyos Mallayev's play *Levicha Hofiz* about Levi Bobokhonov, singer for the last two emirs of Bukhara. Chapter 2, "Adapting Bukharian Jewish Musical Life to Multicultural New York," is a series of *tarona*-s (songs) introducing the particular ideas of American multiculturalism engaged by Bukharian Jews as they transform and adjust the music brought from Central Asia to shape and construct Bukharian Jewish American ethnicity.

Chapters 3, 4, and 5 are in-depth discussions of three repertoires expressing different aspects of Bukharian American life: Maqom (classical or "heavy" music), Jewish religious repertoire, and party music ("light" music). Each chapter contains an explanation of the repertoire—particularly necessary to clarify what musical practices are under discussion, since the definitions I outline sometimes conflict with the conventionally accepted point of view. Following each definition are several subsections that shine light on various ways in which changes to the music relate to the multicultural environment in New York. I imagine these three chapters as a short suite of signpost pieces based on a specific rhythm. Chapter 3, "Maqom: Bukharian Jewish Classical Music," is in the *talqin* rhythm, a difficult "limping" pattern that ebbs and flows. Like maqom in general, talqin is heavy, played by professionals and appreciated by connoisseurs. Chapter 4, "Religious Repertoire: 'Like Mushrooms after the Rain'" is in the *nasr* rhythm, serious but welcoming and versatile. Chapter 5, "Party Music: Expressing Cosmopolitanism," is in the *ufor* rhythm, the upbeat 6/8 dance meter that dominates weddings and other celebrations, and which typically ends maqom performances, leaving audience members on a high note.

Chapter 6, "Ziyorat," is a lyric song to close the performance. A reflexive and reflective chapter, I take an experience accompanying Ezro Malakov and thirty other Bukharian Jewish Americans on a pilgrimage to Central Asia as an opportunity to think about the project as a whole. This experience also allowed me to revisit the local realities of Bukharian Jewish musical life in New York in terms of the global Bukharian diaspora.

1

Performing Bukharian Jewish History

Ilyos Mallayev's Play *Levicha Hofiz*

Remembering Old Bukhara

For three days in 1999, the Bukharian Jewish émigré community transformed the Queens Theater in the Park into old Bukhara when a large cast of the major singers, dancers, and poets in New York performed Ilyos Mallayev's play, *Levicha Hofiz* ("Levicha the Singer"). The play is loosely based on the life of Levi Bobokhonov (1874–1926, nicknamed "Levicha"), last court singer to the Bukharan emir.[1] After two years of preparation under the direction of Boris Katayev, contemporary stars such as Avrom Tolmasov, Roshel Rubinov, Muhabbat Shamayeva, and Ezro Malakov inhabited the roles of their musical ancestors, in a defining moment for Bukharian Jews in New York (Figure 1.1).

Levicha Hofiz provides a unique window onto Bukharian Jewish history. The play, written by and performed for Bukharian Jews, is not a story of battles and treaties or an attempt at an objective historical account, but an untold story of Central Asia from the point of view of a marginalized religious minority. In this way, the play is a traditional piece of Jewish storytelling, drawing creatively on historical events and personages to demonstrate continuity with persistent Jewish themes and narratives, especially the constantly shifting relationships between Jews and their others, and the need to resist assimilation while participating in majority society. Most significantly, *Levicha Hofiz* illuminates Bukharian Jewish history from the perspective of contemporary Bukharian New Yorkers, showing how the past is interpreted as a model and inspiration for the present and future. As shown in the play, Bukharian Jews see a direct connection between their lives in Central Asia and New York, with the conditions of multicultural Bukhara setting the stage for their contemporary activities.

Figure 1.1. From the *Misvo-Sa`udo* (Circumcision Celebration) in *Levicha Hofiz*, 1999. From left to right: Ezro Malakov (as Yusufi Gurg), Roshel Rubinov (Levi Bobokhonov), David Barayev (Mūrdekhai Tanburi), Vyacheslav Katayev (Il'evu Hofiz), Isak Katayev (Ota Jalol Nasirov). Photographer unknown.

The play opens in 1902 when Levi is a precocious virtuoso approaching thirty.[2] The great Shashmaqom master Ota Jalol hears Levi playing in the mahalla of Bukhara and takes him on as a student. For the crime of teaching Shashmaqom to a Jew, Ota Jalol is summoned along with Levi to the palace of Emir Olim Khon.[3] In a turn of events, after an inspired performance the emir enlists Levi as his personal singer. Levi's new position means that his voice is the emir's property and as such he is prohibited from singing among the general populace. According to the rulings of the emir's ministers, Levi is also obliged to convert to Islam (although he never does).[4] Through narration we learn that time passes, the emir has gone to study in St. Petersburg and returned, and although Levi has continued as the palace singer, the emir's ministers are increasingly ill-disposed toward him.[5] Another story arc involves the Jewish female court entertainer (sozanda) Shishakhon, who desires Levi. Manipulating the influence of the emir's mother, Shishakhon arranges to be given to Levi as a gift—a second wife. Levi cannot accept this "gift" as it goes against Jewish law.[6] Further disobeying the emir's commands, Levi also independently records for a scout from the Riga-based recording label "Pishushchiĭ Amur" and continues to sing privately among common people.[7] The ministers and Shishakhon plot against Levi, using Levi's repeated "disobedience" as evidence. In a final stroke, the chief minister alters a praise poem that Levi has written for the emir into an insult. The emir throws Levi in prison. To convince the emir to free Levi, Ota Jalol leverages his close relationship with Olim Khon's late father, Abdulahad Khon. Levi flees Bukhara for Samarqand, where he devotes himself to passing on the maqom tradition to his students.[8] Aged beyond his years, Levi dies at fifty-three.[9]

In *Levicha Hofiz*, Mallayev suggests striking parallels and continuities between life in early twentieth-century Bukhara, the Soviet era, and New York. One of the most significant themes is that "otherness" is an essential condition for Bukharian Jews. The Bukharian Jews must constantly define themselves in relation to the majority culture—in the case of the play, the Muslim population and the policies of the ruling elites. Musicians, actively involved in interactions with "others," navigate the multicultural scene, serving as representatives of the community.

Ilyos Mallayev represents early twentieth-century Bukhara as a diverse hub of music and literature. This urban mix serves as a precedent for life in cosmopolitan Soviet Central Asian cities such as Tashkent as well as multicultural New York. Levi Bobokhonov and the other Jews in the play are actively involved with the city's culture, with music a particularly important site of collaboration and exchange. Jewish and Muslim men and women are represented as friends and musical collaborators, sharing a heritage of Shashmaqom urban art music and refined Persian poetry; the play opens with an interfaith gathering of Levi and Yusefi Gurg, both Jews, enjoying a Shashmaqom session with the great Muslim maqom master Domullo Halim Ibadov and other noted maqomists of the day.

But Mallayev's play also shows the separateness of the Jewish community and the difficulties for a religious minority within this multicultural environment. Being Jewish in Bukhara means being not-Muslim: resisting pressures of conversion and assimilation that come with professional life beyond the walls of the mahalla. While Central Asian Jews and the Muslim majority population privately associate as equals, their public encounters are restricted by hierarchies, laws, and social mores. As members of a religious minority, Bukharian Jews must constantly balance their private community lives with their public professional lives. This includes the relationships between Jews and Muslims, men and women, and Central Asians and Russians. *Levicha Hofiz* brings into focus the point that Bukharian Jews themselves see a continuous and consistent need to read the shifting terrain of these relationships, from their pre-Soviet history up to the present.

Assimilation lurks as a continuous pressure for Levi. Assimilation of course has different meanings in different situations, and at the end of the Bukharan emirate assimilation primarily meant the threat of forced conversion. The last emirs of Bukhara, the Manghits, introduced forced conversion in the mid-eighteenth century (Sukhareva 1966:173–78; Mukhtarov 2003:58; Zand et al. 2007:259) creating small communities of *anusim* called *chala*-s, meaning "neither one nor the other": they were not considered full-fledged members of the Muslim *'ummah*, and as outward converts to Islam could not be fully accepted as Jews either.[10] In cities with Jewish neighborhoods, such as Bukhara, chalas lived near but apart from the Jews. Forced conversion was a problem for Jews throughout the Muslim world, and it had already become a serious issue for Iranian Jews under the Safavids (Moreen 1987, 1990; some Jews in Central Asia and Afghanistan were originally Jews from Safavid Iran who fled these persecutions). However, anusim typically only superficially converted to Islam, continuing to practice Judaism in secret. Given enough time, anusim often found themselves in a position to return to Judaism, either under a new ruler or by migrating to a new environment. But in the emirate returning to Judaism was a form of apostasy and punishable by death, so even when the opportunity arose, the situation was dangerous and fraught—the tide could quickly turn back again.[11]

In the first scene in *Levicha Hofiz* at the court, the emir, the chief judge (*Qozikalon*), chief minister (*Qushbegi*), and chief religious advisor (*Sheikh-ul-Islom*) portray Ota Jalol's teaching of maqom to Levi and Levi's presence at the palace as against Islamic law, and they demand that Levi convert to Islam as a condition of his being the emir's personal singer. Indeed, the emir's enlisting of Levi's services is represented in the play as a tragedy, not a triumph. In this way, Levi faces a common dilemma for prominent Jewish professionals working in majority situations outside the confines of a Jewish enclave. Prominent European Jews faced comparable obstacles as their profiles grew and positions went higher; Gustav Mahler, for example, had to convert to Roman Catholicism before he could accept the job of Kapellmeister of the Vienna Philharmonic. The first Jewish "palace singer" known in Bukhara, Borukh Babayev, known as Kalkhok (1845–1891, Kalkhot in some accounts), who played at Muzaffar's court (Djumaev 2004:93), seems to have converted to Islam (become chala) as a condition of his role as the emir's singer, but moved to Samarqand soon after its annexation by Russia in order to return to Judaism (Rybakov 2013).[12]

A major part of Levi's story for contemporary Bukharian Jews is that Levi remains Jewish despite the pressures exerted by the emir's ministers. But conversion is a constant threat throughout the play, and Levi's resistance is circumscribed and completely dependent on his extraordinary voice and talent. Levi does not deny his Judaism or apologize for it, and he handles mockery at the court with poise, but he is also unable to actively advocate for himself and must depend on Ota Jalol, as a Muslim, to argue on his behalf. Levi never vocally refuses to convert to Islam; he simply avoids it, leaving it to the ministers to press the issue. Similarly, he pleads with the emir not to give Shishakhon to him as a gift, citing the Jewish religion, but the matter ultimately goes unresolved like the conversion. Mallayev's play captures a minority perspective in that Levi's life is a process of continual problem solving and quotidian heroism, and in some cases, to be good human being—authentic to himself and his community—he must be a "bad" servant. His passive resistance is ultimately as much of a threat to the emir's power as active opposition, and he is punished for his actions, or inactions, just the same. And of course, migration is always looming as a possibility, and Levi finally leaves Bukhara for Samarqand.

Music provides a solution to the challenges faced by the Jewish community. Levi and the other Jews in the play thrive in multiple situations through a mastery of various repertoires, styles, and techniques. Classical maqom is a forum for Jewish-Muslim exchange and the repertoire that raises Levi to the high status of court singer and then, through his students and his recordings, his claim to immortality. Levi is a master of various maqom performance styles, ranging from formal presentations for the emir to the informal salon atmosphere of private gatherings. (In a scene cut from the play's performance, Levi also participates in an *ashulai kalon* contest—a genre associated with the Ferghana valley—when Berkinboï Hofiz, the court singer for the khan of Kokand, visits.) The courtly dances of the sozanda entertainers in the service of the emir's mother serve as the equivalent of maqom for Jewish women, granting them fame and access to elite circles, and establishing another one of the spaces for interactions between Jews and Muslims. Although it is not represented in the play, sozandas helped guide sections of rituals such as circumcision ceremonies for both Muslims and Jews (Djumaev 2008:60–63).

The Jews are also dedicated to their own music and culture, represented in the play with a *misvo-sa'udo* (circumcision celebration) where Levi and the other Jewish men sing the hymn "Yigdal." The maintenance of a Jewish repertoire, apart from the shared artistic repertoires in which Jews generally participate, remains a key strategy for Bukharian Jews to keep traditional private life and distinct traditions intact. The play also features playful *mutribi* verses (*mutrib* is a word for "musician," implying a light style) sung to frame drum accompaniment by a comic figure, Kari Yahudo. Mikhali Karkigi, Shishakhon, and the other sozandas demonstrate mastery of private *mushoira* poetic contests of humor, praise, and innuendo, a stark contrast to the formal presentational dances performed for the emir and his retinue.[13] Mallayev highlights the versatility of Levi and the other professional musicians in the play, drawing a direct line from the past to Bukharian Jews' present-day strategy of maintaining, adjusting, and adapting different repertoires for a range of appropriate situations.

Of the many professional and musical situations in the play, Levi Bobokhonov's dilemma concerning his Gramophone Company recordings deserves special consideration for its contemporary resonance. In Mallayev's play, Levi is a proto–"world music" artist, and his decision to make recordings against the emir's wishes demonstrate Levi's awareness of the world beyond Bukhara. At the beginning of the twentieth century, record labels such as the Gramophone Company were extending their international reach to record and disseminate minority and ethnic musics. Bukhara and the other Central Asian court cities were sites on a musical Silk Road, with the company's representatives coming to record the legendary singers for their exchange value—a situation with strong contemporary echoes, as labels record and market "world music" singers such as Yulduz Usmanova and Munojot Yŭlchiyeva from these same cities and traditions (Various Artists 2005). According to Will Prentice (unpublished liner notes), Levi and Hoji Abdulaziz Rasulov were the major prizes for the Gramophone Company, and Levi was paid a large sum for his recordings: an exclusive contract of 3,000 rubles for three years, although he ended up recording for only a few days (for comparison, the representative who negotiated the contract, Fred Tyler, earned 6,000 rubles per year). Figure 1.2, a label from one of Levi's seminal recordings, mirrors the multicultural "world music" atmosphere portrayed by Mallayev. Note the multiple alphabets: Cyrillic, Perso-Arabic, and Roman. The script along the bottom indicates an important element in the record's appeal; both the Cyrillic and the Perso-Arabic transliteration proclaim Levi Bobokhonov as "the noble Bukharan emir's soloist" (the Persian reads "solist' impuratūri a'zami amiri bukharsqi levi bobu khonuf," using the Russian "solist" instead of "hofiz," and "bukharski" instead of "bukhari"). Notably, the record featured Levi's image. His records were the only Central Asian 78s to feature a likeness, in another indication of his star power (Jung 2010:12).

Mallayev's portrayal of pre-Soviet Bukhara in *Levicha Hofiz* demonstrates the usefulness of ideas of the Central Asian past to the American present. Mallayev and other Bukharian Jews look to a figure like Levi Bobokhonov, portrayed as skillfully managing difficult situations and

Figure 1.2. Amour Gramophone 14-12844/5, Levi Bobokhonov, "Sabo/ Avji Sabo." From private collection of Roshel Rubinov. Reproduced with permission.

unwilling to abandon his integrity and values, as a model for managing immigrant life in New York. Levi and the various musical styles and repertoires at his disposal provide avenues for thriving within the multicultural atmosphere of old Bukhara, and for managing and exploring the intercultural pressures and meaningful exchanges between Bukharian Jews and their others. Furthermore, couched within Mallayev's play are messages regarding Soviet Central Asia, providing a connecting thread from the beginning to the end of the twentieth century.

Vestiges of Soviet Central Asia in *Levicha Hofiz*

Although a representation of pre-Soviet Bukhara and performed in post-Soviet New York, *Levicha Hofiz* expresses aspects of Soviet times and the circumstances Bukharian Jews faced for most of the twentieth century while they continued to balance participation in majority society with resistance to assimilation. The play is based on a piece of historical fiction by Yoqub Hayimov written in 1982, and as a product of the Soviet era, the story contains many artifacts of Soviet ideology and the restrictions under which artists were forced to work.

The representations of the emir and his court clearly reflect Soviet ideology and artistic restrictions, in which feudal society and religious governments had to be shown as cruel and corrupt. In conversations with several of my interviewees, including Ochil Ibragimov, I was told that Levi was not thrown in prison, and that Olim Khon was a great patron of the arts and a friend to Levi.[14] Living in exile in Kabul following his overthrow, Olim Khon continued his patronage of Jewish musicians, arranging for the release of the Eliezerof brothers from prison; the Eliezerofs, musicians who fled from Samarqand to Afghanistan in 1935, performed for the emir for nearly two years before immigrating to Palestine (Slobin 1982b:229–30). Bukharian Jews are keen to put Olim Khon in a favorable light. In an interview regarding *Levicha Hofiz* the poet Mikhoel Zavul, who played the emir, said, "We should not forget that Olim Khon was a highly educated man, speaking Russian and French. One of his wives was a French woman.... At the end of the play he did release Levicha from captivity" ("Mudzhiza" n.d.).[15] At a striking moment during the play's performance, after all of the play's dialogue has taken place in Persian, the representative from Amour Gramophone gains an audience with the emir and speaks Russian to him, saying, "we probably need an interpreter?" The emir replies, "We do not need a translator. I studied at the Military Academy in St. Petersburg. I do not know the Russian language?" The audience spontaneously clapped for this line, in appreciation for the emir as well as the representation of Central Asians as multilingual and worldly.

Another interpretation of *Levicha Hofiz* is that the emir and his court serve as a proxy for the Soviet system. Conversion to Islam, for example, could be seen as analogous to the show of atheism required of Jews participating in high Soviet stations. Artists often disguised critiques of the

Soviet Union for fear of censorship and repressive measures. One of the major themes of the play is the stark contrast between public life, circumscribed by government policies, and private situations, in which everyday people ignore or disregard those policies in order to maintain their spiritual and community life. Contrasts between the public and private spheres are crucial to remember when discussing Bukharian Jewish life during the Soviet Union, when religious, linguistic, and other aspects of traditional life continued in private despite policies intended to end them.

In the play Levi is also overly concerned with playing "for the people" or "for the folk" in Soviet-inspired terms. Ota Jalol's "one condition" for taking Levi on as a student is that he continue to play for the people. This aspect of the play is strongest at the circumcision celebration scene, a party for Mullo Yaqov, a poor man who only invited poor guests. "In our *millat* (ethnic group) we care for the poor" says Bobojoni Mazori, a thief with a heart of gold and a music lover. The adversary in the scene is Aboi Chatoq, a buffoon of a rich man who tries to get Levi arrested, still in a rage over Levi's earlier refusal to play for his son's wedding. The representation of Aboi Chatoq as a corrupt traitor and the poor as completely noble is probably overdone and a relic of Soviet conventions.

Ilyos Mallayev clearly related to Levi Bobokhonov's story, and his representation of Levi's times reflects his view of the issues he and his contemporaries faced in their own careers as they flourished in general society. Much like the characters in *Levicha Hofiz*, Bukharian musicians in Soviet Central Asia adapted to governmental policies, outwardly adjusting while privately maintaining their traditions. For example, although the Soviets pushed monolinguistic relationships between newly created "nationalities" of Uzbek and Tajik and those respective tongues—many urban Central Asians had typically been competent in both languages—Bukharian Jews often increased their exceptional multilingual skills, keeping their mother tongue while thriving as singers in Persian, Uzbek, and Russian (and in some cases Hebrew, privately). Similarly, Jewish musicians *added* Russian and European music to their repertoires rather than *replace* Central Asian music with European.

On one hand, Mallayev, Muhabbat Shamayeva, and others successfully adapted to the pressures of Soviet Central Asia, with great achievements as professional musicians during the twentieth century. Bukharian singers, instrumentalists, dancers, and actors prospered, building upon the successes of Levi Bobokhonov and others in the feudal courts to reach new heights. Levi's students Gavriel Mulloqandov (1900–1972) and Mikhoel Tolmasov (1887–1969) both received the Soviet national "People's Artist" honorific, in 1936 and 1937, and Shoista Mullojonova, Berta Davidova, and many others followed (see Figure 1.3). The Soviet authorities allowed and encouraged women to participate in the world of classical maqom, which had previously been restricted to men, and Jewish women became some of the most famous and prominent classical singers of the era.[16] The sozanda tradition continued as well, with Tūhfakhon

Figure 1.3. Grave of Berta Davidova (1922–2007), People's Artist of Uzbekistan (*Narodnaya Artistka Uzbekistana*). Jewish cemetery in Tashkent. Photo by the author.

(Yafo Pinkhasova) achieving legendary status as the most important sozanda of the twentieth century.[17]

Several of my Bukharian interviewees, including Ilyos Mallayev and Muhabbat Shamayeva, spoke specifically about the period under Sharof Rashidov from 1959 to 1983 as being particularly favorable for Bukharian Jewish performers, and Bukharians still adore the music of the large Soviet maqom orchestras of the time (see also T. Levin 1996: 268–69; Dugger 1997).[18] Ezro Malakov and Isak Katayev were featured performers in the national maqom orchestras, Katayev's sixtieth birthday in 1986 even commemorated with a large outdoor music concert at the Senate building in Tashkent's Revolution Square (now Independence Square [*Mustakillik Maĭdoni*]). During Soviet times, Ari Bobokhonov (Levi's grandson), Neryo Aminov, Barno Isḥoqova, and other Bukharian Jews also filled the ranks of instructors at the national music conservatories in Uzbekistan and Tajikistan. In the maqom contexts of orchestras and conservatories, productive collaboration between Muslims and Jews took place to an unprecedented degree.

On the other hand, Jewish ethnicity often limited careers and presented difficulties in Central Asia. Ilyos Mallayev was discouraged from his more personal pursuits, and his Jewish identity curtailed the extent to which his poetry was performed (T. Levin 1996:267). After Rashidov's death in 1983, Mallayev and Shamayeva faced greater obstacles and restrictions. On a similar note, the "People's Artist" award had irony attached to it, in that as members of a separate "nation" in the Soviet taxonomy, Jewish recipients were not considered part of the Uzbek or Tajik "people" whose art they expressed. However, it should be underscored that these restrictions and limitations came from "the system, not the [common] people," in Ochil Ibragimov's words.

Bukharian Jews faced threats of assimilation during the Soviet era, but of a new sort from those faced under the emirs. Some "Russified" Bukharian Jews in Tashkent, for example, did lose fluency in Bukhori, speaking Russian as their mother tongue. And although at first, in the late nineteenth century, the Russians extended greater religious and civic freedoms to Jews in Central Asia, the Soviets officially repressed Judaism and everyday practice became very difficult for many Bukharian Jews. Levi Bobokhonov's dilemma continued to resonate: for many Jews to achieve successes in public life, they had to suppress, deny, or hide their religious beliefs.

The representation of Levi maintaining a separate private and community life in the face of governmental restrictions and discrimination echoes life in Soviet times, especially resonant with respect to Jewish religious practice. Continuing the double existence of Bukharian Jews, religious practice moved underground, with celebrations and religious rites often held in the home instead of the synagogue. For example, while Ezro Malakov and his brothers were growing up, they studied Judaism at home in secret with tutors hired by their father Asher. (Much depended on the particular person, town, and community, and of course, the governmental administration in power at the time.) However, as Ro'i indicates, "Whatever the reason (or reasons), the Bukharan Jews did not forego the ways of their religion. Nor, apparently, did they feel the same compulsion to do so as did most of Soviet Jewry. At no stage did the Bukharan Jews associate with, or accept, the call of the Soviet regime and its ideology to modernise and secularise at the expense of their traditions and ethnic and cultural identity" (Ro'i 2008:74). Some Bukharians think that their comparatively tolerant situation had to do with the fact that Islam was similarly suppressed by the Soviets, and Central Asian Muslims and Jews shared a desire to maintain their religious lifelines. The explosion of Jewish religious music and practice in New York should thus be seen not as a newfound interest but more like a dam breaking, after many years of an intense building of desire to openly and freely practice Judaism.

Levicha Hofiz and New York

The post-Soviet era is embodied in *Levicha Hofiz* in the play's very existence and its performance at an important theater in New York. Even the most tolerant Soviet period pales in comparison to the freedom and support Mallayev found in the United States for his personal passions. As he explained to me, "I found acceptance for my work in America.... There [in Uzbekistan] I couldn't create these books [of poetry], or discs, or this play about Levicha. All of these things I did here [in the United States]." The play is an open celebration of Jewish identity and Jewish history, and the role of the Jewish hofiz, that could not have been mounted in Soviet Central Asia. Before the play's premiere, the actors spoke on this particular significance of the performance. For Ezro Malakov (who played Levi's senior contemporary Yusufi Gurg), the play was a crucial reminder that religious Jews can follow Levi Bobokhonov's example without fear, in an unprecedented historical moment for Bukharian Jews.

Levicha Hofiz served as a public platform for Mallayev and the Bukharian community to take advantage of their post-Soviet situation. In the United States, many Bukharian Jews have found themselves at liberty for the first time to publicly position themselves as they wish in relation to their former neighbors. They have actively asserted to Uzbeks and Tajiks their role in maqom's history and the centrality of maqom to Bukharian Jewish life, as well as the arbitrary character of Soviet-drawn national boundaries. *Levicha Hofiz* was itself a repudiation of Levi's circumscribed speech in front of the emir and his ministers. Importantly, Uzbeks and Tajiks favorably received the play. Rashid Alimov, the representative of the Republic of Tajikistan to the United Nations, attended *Levicha Hofiz* and declared the play a "miracle" (*mu'jiza*) (Nektalov 1999). Z. Khojimetov, the consul general of Uzbekistan in New York, hoped the play could be staged in Samarqand, Bukhara, and Tashkent ("Mudzhiza" n.d.).

Levicha Hofiz was also an opportunity for the Bukharian Jewish musicians to demonstrate their astounding versatility. Their ability to master multiple styles, and even styles of different ethnic groups, is a point of pride for the contemporary community. Not only did the play feature performance styles ranging from heavy to light, but the musicians also inhabited the roles of their Muslim neighbors. Ilyos Mallayev's cameo appearance in the play is as the *muazzin* who performs the Muslim call to prayer. The Bukharian musicians inhabited the Muslim characters drawing on the closeness of Jewish and Muslim life in Central Asia, where Muslim greetings and mannerisms were a normal part of everyday interactions.

But above all, *Levicha Hofiz* was an attempt to take stock and define the Bukharian Jewish community in New York, as one major response to encounters with American multiculturalism and a newly perceived pressure to think about Bukharian Jewish ethnicity, identity, and history in clear and concrete terms. Through *Levicha Hofiz*, the community portrayed a pivotal historical reference point—the transition from the Bukharan emirate to Russian rule—and constructed a persona embodying the hopes and concerns of the community as a whole. In the years following *Levicha Hofiz*, Levi Bobokhonov's symbolic importance has only grown. The second annual "Shashmaqom Forever" concert, held at the Queens Theater in the Park on 10 August 2013, was dedicated to him. In an interview with Roshel Rubinov regarding the concert, Rafael Nektalov marveled at how the image of Levi Bobokhonov "suddenly, in a new country" began to "attract like a magnet" (Nektalov 2013).

The fact that Ilyos Mallayev, Boris Katayev, and the large cast galvanized Bukharian Jewish Americans around a story of a musician is significant: musicians have consistently served as representatives of the community both internally and externally, and maqom—Levi's main repertoire—has been the repertoire of choice for Bukharian Jews in the public arena. Levi's actions and those of his community are used as a model for the present in many ways. As in Central Asia, Bukharian Jews in New York live in a mahalla, Forest Hills, where they continue their community existence. And musicians remain emissaries, interacting to a significant degree with Bukharian Jews' "others," representing and defining the community.

Internally, *Levicha Hofiz* demonstrated the centrality of tradition to the Bukharian Jewish community and their living connection to Central Asian music. Lineage, tradition, and the importance of maqom from generation to generation is powerfully expressed as two young contemporary masters "play," in both senses of the word, the role of Levi: Roshel Rubinov as the younger Levi, and Avrom Tolmasov as the older Levi. Tolmasov is a direct musical descendant of Levi, his uncles Mikhoel and Isroel Tolmasov being two of Bobokhonov's most renowned students, portrayed learning from Levi at the end of the play among other great maqomists Gavriel and Mikhoel Mulloqandov and Hoji Abdulaziz Rasulov. (Before dying Levi says, "I pass my voice to Mikhoel Tolmas, my tanbūr to Mikhoel Mulloqand.") Gavriel and Mikhoel Mulloqandov's niece Tamara Katayeva, one of the few contemporary singers with some knowledge of the sozanda repertoire, played Shishakhon. Mūrdekhai Tanburi's grandson, Osher Barayev, played Bobojoni Mazori. Maqom, traditional dance, and classical poetry are living practices for the Bukharian Jewish community in Queens, the echoes of Levi's century-old recordings heard in Roshel Rubinov's performances at restaurants and community parties, not just the staged historical spectacle of *Levicha Hofiz*.

The two different Levis represent generational issues facing the community and a serious concern about the passing on of tradition. The young Levi develops his art while learning from masters and adapts according to the challenges of his environment. The older Levi is reflective; now a master himself, he devotes himself to transmitting his knowledge. The contemporary analog is palpable, as the older Levi is living in Samarqand in exile, forced to leave Bukhara due to circumstances beyond his control. Ilyos Mallayev and the older generation of musicians in New York, similarly distant from their homes, naturally worry about the future of Bukharian Jewish music and tradition with the community uprooted from Central Asia. And the figure of Levi Bobokhonov continues to represent the generational issues surrounding tradition. With Mallayev's death and Rubinov's aging into more of a senior role in the community, Rubinov in particular has become increasingly devoted to embodying Levi's legacy. At the 2013 Shashmaqom Forever concert, Bobokhonov's 1911 recordings played over the house speakers. Rubinov then sang along with Levi for "Ufori Mūghulchai Segoh" and then eventually performed the song himself, making the lineage abundantly clear.

To many viewers in the Bukharian community, the broader message of *Levicha Hofiz* is the need to resist assimilation while adapting, no matter what the circumstances and encounters with others may be. *Levicha Hofiz* is especially poignant in the wake of mass migration to multicultural New York, where Bukharian Jews feel the pressure of various kinds of assimilation as well as the desire to maintain their distinctiveness. They express the fear of losing their traditions in connection with freedom and migration, although the nature of that loss is contested and often ambiguous. To one reviewer, the theme of assimilation and conversion "gives the conflict a religious-national color, which adds drama and makes it extremely topical and emotional." And regarding Levi's conscience and commitment to community principles: "How important it is in our ultra-modern reality, when everything seems to be permissible and accessible, before our eyes the family is crumbling, to remember these timeless values!" ("Mudzhiza" n.d.).

In the light of the dizzying complexity of the contemporary Bukharian diaspora, intensely multilingual and multicultural, and straddling nations and transnational economic networks, Mallayev's play is a reminder that such conditions may not exactly correspond to the core beliefs of everyday people. In fact, globalization, diaspora, and concomitant increased encounters with new "others" often intensify and reinforce boundaries, traditions, and a community's sense of unity. Bukharian Jews in New York consider themselves both modern cosmopolitan New Yorkers and members of a community deeply committed to their traditions and history. As shown in *Levicha Hofiz*, contemporary Bukharian Jews see their past as part of a continuum, as they aim to maintain their distinct heritage while adapting to changing circumstances. In New York around the turn of the twenty-first century, that specifically meant defining a distinct Bukharian Jewish ethnic identity with its attendant musical practices, which could exist alongside other ethnicities in a multicultural environment.

2

Adapting Bukharian Jewish Musical Life to
Multicultural New York

When Michael Bloomberg says that New York is a melting pot,
I tell Michael Bloomberg, "please, don't say to my people that it is
a melting pot, because we want to integrate into the American
society, but at the same time we want to preserve our Bukharian
Jewish identity." So why don't we call it, like New York is a mosaic,
consisting of so many colors, and we are some of those colors.
—Aron Aronov, director of the Bukharian
Jewish Museum (Rosehope 2011)

The arrival of Bukharian Jews in New York during the 1980s and
1990s coincided with a mainstreaming of multiculturalism, and multiculturalist policies and ideas have continued through the beginning of
the twenty-first century. Multiculturalist ideology resonates with the skills
and strategies that Bukharian Jews developed in Central Asia as members
of a multilingual religious minority, with professional musicians especially well positioned to navigate New York's scene. Bukharian Jews have
explicitly drawn on multiculturalist ideas as a way to adapt to the American
environment while avoiding assimilation to a general American identity,
or to a broadly defined Jewish American identity. However, in a multiculturalist paradigm, those who identify as belonging to a group are compelled to define themselves in terms of a bounded singular identity
represented by distinct cultural aspects—and this pressure to define group
characteristics can be construed as another kind of assimilation.
Bukharian Jews must also reckon with multiculturalism as a legacy of
decades of cultural work, much of it conducted by earlier Jewish
Americans, in ways that are significantly affecting contemporary
Bukharian musical life. Broadly speaking, Bukharian Jews' musical

choices reflect the impact of multiculturalist ideas on the opportunities and challenges faced by recent immigrants, the ways in which new arrivals must deal with the legacies of their predecessors, and the need for new New Yorkers to define themselves in relation to a patchwork of other "ethnic groups" similarly negotiating their group identity through cultural products.

As Aron Aronov demonstrated in this chapter's epigraph, Bukharian Jews read and actively engaged the terrain of American multiculturalism, largely rejecting a "melting pot" assimilationist or hybridization model in favor of a pluralistic "mosaic."[1] The "glorious mosaic" or "salad bowl" metaphor characterized multiculturalism in the 1980s and 1990s and up to the present day, symbolizing a worldview in which groups of different backgrounds live together, interacting with and learning from each other while maintaining their own distinct traditions (King 2000:34). Multiculturalism as "the politics of recognition" (Taylor 1992) remains especially strong in New York, a city deeply rooted in, and proud of, its history as a center of immigration and its ethnic enclaves. Bukharian Jews embraced mosaic multiculturalism as a way to adapt to the New York environment without compromising their identity and values. They retrospectively interpreted their Central Asian experiences as a distinct "nationality," reevaluating their historical "otherness" in terms of the American multicultural context.

Music is a primary arena for Bukharian Jews to negotiate multiculturalism. Multiculturalism is essentially constituted in terms of *cultural* products, and music, as it is for many communities, is in many ways the most flexible, adaptable, and performative cultural sphere in Bukharian life. Futhermore, music has consistently been the main area in which Bukharian Jews have successfully participated in intercultural situations. Bukharian Jewish musical life in New York especially reflects "mosaic" multiculturalist ideology in that Bukharians are choosing, by and large, to adapt and adjust their existing repertoires to their contemporary situation and present them alongside singular representations of music from other cultures rather than participating in mainstream forms or "reinventing" their music.

To thrive in a multicultural environment, groups must still in a way assimilate. On the broadest level, American immigrants must often newly consider the very nature of their group identity, and what cultural activities they can claim as distinct or even unique in order to represent themselves. At the First Congress of the Bukharian Jewish Community of the United States and Canada (2–3 May 1999), Lev Kandinov succinctly captured this shift in self-conception, remarking, "For about fifty-five of my sixty-seven years of life I never thought about who I am. Only now can I recognize myself as a civilized Bukharian Jew" (A. Yakubov 2005:70). "Bukharian" only becomes a meaningful modifier in relation to encounters with Jews who identify differently; these encounters became commonplace and unavoidable with immigration to New York, and took on a particular quality in the city's multicultural environment. Kandinov's comment not only points to the smoothing over of differences between Jews from various Central Asian towns and backgrounds to a general "Bukharian" category, but also the foregrounding of "Bukharian Jew" as a label in the American context that should be recognized.

The American multicultural context and the culture-contact encounters accompanying migration have brought the multiple senses of identity that Bukharian Jews had in Central Asia to the fore, especially their ideas of Jewishness. No longer able to take for granted their particular notions of Jewish identity and practice, Bukharian Jews must reconcile a new sense of otherness with respect to a Jewish American identity that has been dominated for a century by Ashkenazic Jews of European descent, as Ashkenazic and Bukharian Jews have many significant differences in their customs and histories. Bukharian Jews also found that Jewishness in the United States is not categorically opposed to "American" the way that "Jew" was excluded from the definition of "Uzbek" or "Tajik" in Soviet Central Asia, giving Bukharian Jews an opportunity to define a "Bukharian Jewish American" identity for themselves.

In forming their Bukharian Jewish American identity, Bukharian Jews have had to resolve an ontological difference between their long-held essentialist sense of Jewish identity and the American attitude that Judaism, despite carrying a heavy legacy of racial otherness, is ostensibly a matter of choice, affiliation, and a personal or private belief system. Bukharian Jews generally hold an externally (due to Soviet nationalities policies) and internally attributed sense of Jewishness as something biologically determined, a race or nationality, and an incontrovertible essential fact. For Bukharian Jews, the American idea that Judaism is a matter of affiliation rather than biology, a matter of choice divorced from externally determined definitions, and generally Ashkenazic, has raised questions about the passing on of their tradition and culture. Having come to the United States for religious freedom, they now fear losing their distinct history and traditions. In response to these questions, Bukharian Jews are actively defining who they are and self-consciously making their "ethnicity" a priority.

From Melting Pot to Mosaic Ideologies among Jewish Americans

The choices and activities of Bukharian Jews in New York are made in relation to the specific models, paradigms, and narratives of multiculturalism that earlier Jewish Americans produced or embraced. The tangled but overall shift in emphasis from melting pot to mosaic (or sometimes "salad bowl") is particularly salient for Jewish Americans. Aronov's rhetoric in this chapter's epigraph echoes that of contemporary advocates of multiculturalism, especially within a Jewish American context. For example, regarding his decision to support a Bukharian Jewish history class at Queens College in 2009, director of Jewish Studies Mark Rosenblum said, "The college is not a melting pot. It's a salad bowl where students retain their cultures, while respecting others" (Kadinsky 2010). However, as evidenced by the repeated references to the melting pot ideal (even to negate it) by Aronov, Rosenblum, and Mayor Bloomberg, the mosaic or salad bowl never fully replaced the melting pot, which remains a forceful concept in the American, and specifically Jewish American, imagination.

Bukharian immigrants encountered a distinct conception of Jewish identity and a tension between melting pot and mosaic ideals that is a legacy of active cultural work by earlier Jewish Americans following the major waves of immigration from Eastern Europe (Frank 1997; Gilman 2006, especially chapter 3). These European Jewish immigrants and their descendants, through cultural representations, heavily invested in the idea of the American melting pot, which they hoped or imagined would allow them to transcend their historic racial otherness and leave behind the "Old World."[2] The melting pot was initially cast in racial terms, as in the concept's namesake play *The Melting-Pot*, in which Jews are merely one of the "races of Europe melting and reforming" in America, "God's crucible" (Zangwill [1909] 1919; Sollors 1986:66–101; Gilman 2006:73–84).[3] (Demonstrating the persistent sense of Jewish "otherness" in a cross-cultural perspective, Jewishness is primarily defined in *The Melting-Pot* as "not Christian" in relation to the majority culture, just as Jewishness is "not Muslim" in *Levicha Hofiz*.) George Gershwin, for example, used melting pot ideas and aspirations to create an American music based in America's diversity; he called *Rhapsody in Blue* a "musical kaleidoscope of America—of our vast melting pot, of our incomparable national pep, our blues, our metropolitan madness" (quoted in Pollack 2006:297), and in the process transcended and defused the racial and ethnic world of Jewish vaudeville.[4]

Meanwhile many American Jews vigorously advanced an anti-racial vision of Judaism. American attitudes about Jewish identity were heavily shaped by the Jewish Enlightenment and eventually Reform Judaism, a European and American movement that promoted an ethical, rather than national or ethnic, basis for Judaism (Satlow 2006:32–36, 250–66). Reform Judaism was seen as a bridge between "modern, rational science and certain core principles of Judaism, such as the resurrection of the dead" (Diner 2004:120), and helped establish a playing field in which Judaism, or even aspects of Jewish practice generally held to be essential and fundamental, such as keeping the dietary laws of *kashrut*, could be considered matters of personal choice.

And although there were significant tensions between Jewish racial identity and white identity in the United States up through the end of World War II, in the postwar era American Jews seriously gravitated toward the stance that Judaism was a religion, culture, or way of life, but not a "race."[5] The concept of ethnicity in particular had already emerged in the prewar period as "not only a model for pluralism, but a defense against the racialization of the Jews" (Prell 2011:102). After World War II the racial component of Jewish belonging and otherness effectively became the property of anti-Semites, attributable to the horrifying consequences of racial theory and racist thought that became reality in the Holocaust (Gilman 2006:183; Rosman 2007:23). But even with the wholesale rejection of Jewish identity as a "race," senses of Jewish belonging and otherness—Jewish "peoplehood"—remained a major concern for Jews.

The full-fledged emergence of ethnic identity politics and multiculturalism in the 1960s and 1970s provided an attractive solution to the dilemmas of assimilation and race for many American Jews (see, e.g., Galchinsky 1994:362, in which he critiques the trend). African American, Latin American, Native American, and Asian American scholars and activists heavily shaped multiculturalist thought and academic programs (Gutierrez 1994) as members of groups that were excluded or marginalized in the assimilationist and melting pot ideologies that privileged whiteness and European ancestry (the original "cultural pluralism" model was also Eurocentric [King 2000:27–32], but even so it set the stage for multiculturalism). The Smithsonian Folklife Festival began in 1967, providing a highly visible stage for cultural presentations by a wide variety of ethnic groups. A culmination of multiculturalist trends such as Takaki's history *A Different Mirror* asserts that "indeed, the study of diversity is essential for understanding *how* and *why* America became what Walt Whitman called a 'teeming nation of nations'" (Takaki [1993] 2008:6), covering several groups "that illustrate and illuminate the landscape of our society's diversity—African Americans, Asian Americans, Irish Americans, Jewish Americans, Mexican Americans, Muslim Americans, and Native Americans" (Takaki [1993] 2008:6). Ethnicity became a primary organizing category to describe group affiliation in multicultural societies, seen as an all-embracing term of self-identification and choice that avoids or encompasses the "heavily charged" term of race (Sollors 1986:39).[6] Nevertheless, ethnicity and race remain intertwined in American society, which is still racially organized, and "ethnic"—originally from the Greek translation of the Hebrew *gōy* ("nation," gentile, non-Jew)—has carried with it a sense of otherness, difference, low economic status, "or, in America, as not fully American" (Sollors 1986:25).

For American Jews, the concepts of ethnicity and multiculturalism seemed to provide avenues for retaining difference and distinctiveness without fully paying the "price of assimilation" required to fully integrate into American society (Goldstein 2006:209–39). Multiculturalism also enabled the reclaiming of words that had been negatively associated with Jews: the "marginal man," typified by the Jew, for example, "arises in a bi-cultural or *multi-cultural* situation" (Stonequist 1935:1, emphasis mine; see also Gilman 2006:62–63). The associations of "ethnic" with otherness and the lower class, "diaspora" with the unwanted condition of Jewish exile (Rosman 2007:38), and "cosmopolitan" with Stalin's codeword for "Jew" in his purges—and now floated as the next step past multiculturalism (King 2000:275–76; Appiah 2006b)—can all be said to have undergone similar transformations from negative to positive associations for Jews.

Multiculturalism had made significant inroads into the cultural institutions and the educational system of the New York to which Bukharian Jews immigrated in the 1980s and 1990s. Schools such as Forest Hills High School, attended by many Bukharian Jews in Queens, hold a yearly "world expo," where "every nation, every nationality, Indian, Korean, Chinese, Israeli, Russian, has their own club or group and gives a performance" (Yosef Munarov, personal communication); the high levels of immigration and overwhelming national diversity represented in Queens make this kind of multiculturalist event a salient opportunity for learning and exchange among new neighbors. Organizations such as the Ethnic Folk Arts Center and World Music Institute sponsored multicultural performances, and the National Endowment for the Arts began sponsoring the National Heritage Fellowship, "honoring American folk artists for their contributions to our national cultural mosaic" in 1982 (the accomplished Bukharian singer Fatima Kuinova received the honor in 1992 and is to date the only Bukharian to win this award). Ethnomusicology classes, programs, and faculty were central concerns in the discussions surrounding multiculturalism and multicultural education during the 1990s in the United States (Wong 2006). Jewish American culture of the 1970s and 1980s also became increasingly multicultural and pluralistic, from the "revival" and reethnicization of the klezmer repertoire by such groups as Kapelye, the Klezmer Conservatory Band, Brave Old World, and Andy Statman and Zev Feldman (Kirshenblatt-Gimblett 2002), to the burgeoning interest shown by Jewish American scholars in little-known Jewish communities, including Bukharian Jews.

Yet while the mosaic vision of multiculturalism and the "politics of recognition" establishes a platform for exploring, defining, and asserting group identity, multiculturalist initiatives also suppress internal diversity, exerting pressure for people to determine a group identity and to draw boundaries around it. The notion of world Jewry as a "mosaic" itself, composed of many Jewish groups and Judaisms, is essentially in tension with the pressure to clearly define one Jewish identity with an accompanying historical narrative and set of cultural practices. Bukharian Jews are continuously walking this line in the United States, as the category of "Jewish American" is thorny for Bukharian Jews: they are Jewish Americans, but they have very different stories from the Ellis Island and Lower East Side Jewish American narrative described in *A Different Mirror*. Similarly, they are "Asian Americans" as well, but they share even less identification with the imagined "Asian America" (Zheng 2010:13).

In the 2000s, cultural figures and scholars began seriously critiquing and moving away from multiculturalism to promote the increased recognition of diversity within groups and individuals. With the 2000 Census, for the first time in history Americans were able to choose more than one race. President Barack Obama self-identifies as African American, while his diverse genealogy "reflects a nation's diversity" (Kantor 2009). In *Yellow Face* (2008), David Henry Hwang reflected on his experiences as an Asian American playwright, his relationship to his ethnicity, and the issues of ethnic categorization; as he stated in an interview about the play, "your ethnic identity does not explain who you are, if anything, it's one piece in a complicated picture of who we are, but it's not the answer, the way it maybe felt more in the '70s and '80s."[7]

But although "anti-essentialist understandings of social boundaries and cultural forms have gained widespread acceptance, [and] the terms 'ethnic group' and 'culture' have come under scrutiny ... most [Bukharian Jews] continue to speak about themselves (and are spoken about by others) as though they belong to a discrete, definable ethnic group with a clearly identifiable culture" (Cooper 2008:188). Despite multiculturalism's many shortcomings, the generation of Bukharian immigrants who arrived at the end of the twentieth century self-consciously took up its ideas, which resonated with their self-conceptions and the path they imagined for their

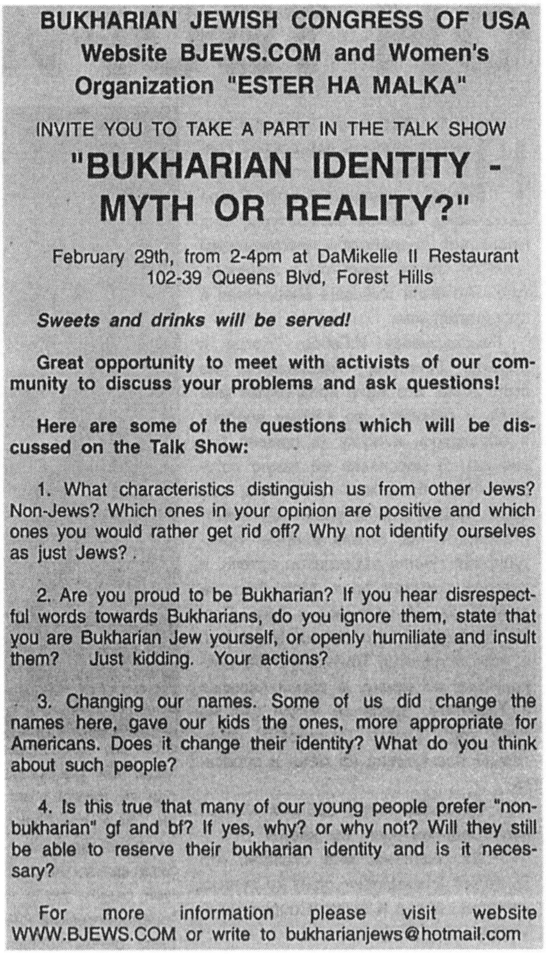

> **BUKHARIAN JEWISH CONGRESS OF USA**
> **Website BJEWS.COM and Women's**
> **Organization "ESTER HA MALKA"**
>
> INVITE YOU TO TAKE A PART IN THE TALK SHOW
>
> ## "BUKHARIAN IDENTITY - MYTH OR REALITY?"
>
> February 29th, from 2-4pm at DaMikelle II Restaurant
> 102-39 Queens Blvd, Forest Hills
>
> *Sweets and drinks will be served!*
>
> **Great opportunity to meet with activists of our community to discuss your problems and ask questions!**
>
> **Here are some of the questions which will be discussed on the Talk Show:**
>
> 1. What characteristics distinguish us from other Jews? Non-Jews? Which ones in your opinion are positive and which ones you would rather get rid off? Why not identify ourselves as just Jews?
>
> 2. Are you proud to be Bukharian? If you hear disrespectful words towards Bukharians, do you ignore them, state that you are Bukharian Jew yourself, or openly humiliate and insult them? Just kidding. Your actions?
>
> 3. Changing our names. Some of us did change the names here, gave our kids the ones, more appropriate for Americans. Does it change their identity? What do you think about such people?
>
> 4. Is this true that many of our young people prefer "non-bukharian" gf and bf? If yes, why? or why not? Will they still be able to reserve their bukharian identity and is it necessary?
>
> For more information please visit website WWW.BJEWS.COM or write to bukharianjews@hotmail.com

Figure 2.1. "Bukharian Identity—Myth or Reality?" Advertisement in *Bukharian Times* weekly, 2004. Reproduced with permission.

community. Mosaic multiculturalism continues to dominate Bukharian Jewish attitudes toward their place in American society, as well as their relationship to other Jewish communities. Multiculturalism's paradoxical embrace of diversity and insistence on group conformity resulted in significant tensions between familiar Jewish American narratives and Bukharian Jewish experiences, inspiring some of the most intense debates over, and creative responses to, questions of Bukharian Jewish ethnicity and identity (Figure 2.1).

Jewish Multiculturalism and Bukharian Jews

Intracultural exchanges between communities have consistently defined the Jewish diaspora. In recent generations, interest in the variety of the Jewish experience has escalated with each wave of immigration from around the world to Palestine/Israel and the United States, and with the advent and spread of recording technology. Already in the early part of the twentieth century, the biographies and repertoires of many musicians point to an excitement throughout the diaspora accompanying increased access to world Jewish repertoires. Examples include Bracha Zephira, the noted singer of Yemenite descent who grew up among multiple immigrant communities in Jerusalem before Israel's founding, and who interpreted songs from "the Sephardi, Persian, and Bukharan communities," among others, in a European art-song style (Hirshberg 1990); Isaac Algazi, the ḥazzan from Izmir who lived in Istanbul, Paris, and Montevideo, and whose multifaceted corpus of recordings included a 1909 recording of two back-to-back versions of "Hayom Harat Olam," one in an unmeasured performance in the Turkish *makam segah* and the other one *alla Franka* ("French," or Western style) (Seroussi 1989; Ottens and Rubin 2002); and A. Z. Idelsohn's *Hebräisch-Orientalischer Melodienschatz*, which presented melodies from a number of Jewish communities brought together in Palestine (Bohlman 2002a:48–59).

Contemporary Jewish intracultural exchanges are usually couched within the language of multiculturalism. The Center for Jewish History in New York "represents in institutional terms this dialectic between unity and diversity—the multicultural Jewish nation.... [T]he constant discussion of this diversity and difference, is a particularly American (Jewish) obsession" (Aviv and Shneer 2005:145). The music at New York's B'nai Jeshurun synagogue expresses the contemporary spirit of Jewish multiculturalism; the version of "Lekhah Dodi" on their CD is a medley of "traditional European, attributed to L. Lewandowski, traditional Turkish and Bulgarian, traditional Hassidic," gathering intensity and rhythmic excitement with each melody (Coleman 1999). With the rise of the Internet, the sharing of Jewish repertoire has reached dizzying heights. For example, the "Piyut Archive" site www.piyut.org.il, supported by the Avi Chai Foundation and other sponsors, catalogs texts and recordings of piyyut performances from thirty-two "Jewish Ethnic Traditions"; the site has over forty recordings of "Yedid Nefesh" alone. In addition to the general "world music" landscape, Bukharian Jews have emerged as a significant group in this specifically Jewish multicultural environment.

Jews interpret multiculturalism as a contemporary version of the preexisting models for understanding and accepting Jewish cultural difference throughout the diaspora. For Jews, the American multiculturalist ideal of multiple ethnic groups that together constituted America, e pluribus unum, resembles the biblical conglomeration of tribes that constituted the Israelites. The singular Jewish people as a confederacy of discrete ethnic groups is what Alanna Cooper identifies as the "*Edah* Paradigm" (Cooper 2012:120–23) in contrast to the "Center-Periphery Paradigm" (Cooper 2012:31–32) that aims to locate a central Jewish religious authority.[8] The Hebrew word *minhag* also provides a useful precedent for multiculturalism, referring to the myriad legal interpretations, customs, and cultural expressions developed by communities with specific histories in diverse places among various neighbors. For Bukharian Jews, the idea of multiculturalism also dovetailed with the pluralist conception of the Soviet Union as a collection of diverse mutually exclusive nationalities, each with its distinct cultural qualities.

To the Bukharian American wedding singer Yuhan Benjamin, the multiple communities of the Jewish people are a plov, a Bukharian equivalent to the salad bowl. In this emblematic Bukharian dish, meat, spices, rice, and vegetables come together to make one food but still retain their unique and individual tastes. Just as Jewish Americans in general embraced multiculturalism as a mode of participating in American society without losing their heritage, Bukharian Jews understood multiculturalism as a way to participate as a distinct and self-contained group of Jewish Americans. The middle-aged and older generation of immigrants feared losing their "Bukharianness" as a by-product of their freedom and saw the existing Jewish American culture as heavily assimilated, a cautionary tale. Roshel Rubinov was uneasy about "too much freedom" in the United States, which would result in Bukharian Jews choosing not to observe religious laws or intermarry ("intermarriage" is itself, of course, a cultural construction depending on ideas of otherness [Sollors 1986:71–75]). Even many younger Bukharian Jews voice a striking resistance to many mainstream Jewish American ways, and express concern over looming assimilation however ambiguously and vaguely defined. Multiculturalism provided a way in which Bukharian Jews could adapt their existing identity from Central Asia to an American paradigm and still engage the global unity of the Jewish people.

Yet the appeal of multiculturalism should not lead us to overlook the continued importance of the Jewish "Center-Periphery Paradigm." For Bukharian Jews, the tribal, multiculturalist conception of the Jewish people and the idea of a cohesive Jewish identity and narrative coexist, and in much the same manner that they put musical repertoires to various uses, these paradigms serve different purposes in Bukharian Jewish life. The idea of a singularity linking all Jewish people—described by Roshel

Aminov as unified through "one God, one prayer, one Hebrew language" (personal communication)—sustained Bukharian Jews as a religious minority, and they are deeply attached to the idea of Jewishness as an essential inborn otherness that can be traced back to Ancient Israel, even biologically determined, which separates Jews and their neighbors. Whereas contemporary scholars of Jewish identity might locate such an attitude—a "given nature of Jewish Peoplehood" (Cooper 2012:25–28)—in the past (Aviv and Shneer 2005), it still holds real resonance for many Jews, even those such as Bukharian Jews who exist on the periphery. As Satlow notes, "The practice of defining Judaism normatively and essentially has had a remarkable staying power" (Satlow 2006:3).

Bukharian Jews' Soviet experience as a discrete "nation" or millat incompatible with the nationalities of the republics in which they lived reinforced their essentialist conception of Jewishness.[9] After the 1930s, Bukharian Jews were classified along with all other Jews in the Soviet Union as "Jew," a nationality designation throughout the entire USSR marked on one's passport regardless of the republic in which one lived.[10] The Jewish nation was considered to be mutually exclusive of the Uzbek (Sunni Muslim, Turkic) nation and the Tajik (Sunni Muslim, Persian) nation, "Uzbek" and "Tajik" being new concepts as ethnic nationalities (see Hirsch 2005:165–86; Adams 2010:35; Cooper 1998, 2012:19–20). Unlike Uzbeks and Tajiks, linked to the new nations of Uzbekistan and Tajikistan, Jews were a "dispersed nationality without a home republic" (Katz 1975:355) and according to Stalin's definition only a "nation on paper," not a fully fledged nation with a common territory, language, and economic life (Katz 1975:380; Altschuler 2007:542). Bukharian Jews in New York continue to distinguish themselves from "Uzbeks," "Uzbek people" (khalqi Ūzbekī), "Tajiks," and "Tajik people" (khalqi Tojikī) when remembering life in Central Asia; a Jew from Uzbekistan would never naturally refer to himself or herself as an "Uzbek." Rather than hide their nationality, as did many Jews in the western part of the Soviet Union, Bukharian Jews were uncommonly proud of their "passport" nationality. In the United States, Bukharian Jews have retained the Soviet conception of "Jew" as a nationality or ethnic categorization, fundamentally apart from other nationalities.

Their deep-seated commitment to both a singular Jewish peoplehood and their community's distinct culture compel Bukharian Jews to constantly consider their place in global Jewry—to identify their senses of intracultural belonging and otherness. Despite the lofty aims and rhetoric of multiculturalism, Jewish or otherwise, serious tensions and hierarchies exist between groups. In the atmosphere of intensive exchange that characterizes the contemporary Jewish diaspora, Jews of every background are involved in learning each other's ways. Bukharian Jews today view the learning of Sephardic and Ashkenazic melodies as a broadening and deepening experience in the same manner that Ashkenazic and Sephardic Jews might learn Bukharian or Yemenite melodies to include in their own worship experiences. However, the small number of Bukharian Jews and the forces of immigration raise the very real concern that younger Bukharian Jews will only learn Ashkenazic or Sephardic ways and lose their distinctive melodies. Furthermore, in the economics of multiculturalism and globalization, Bukharian Jews' unique culture is a valuable resource that they need to protect.

Bukharian Jews' position with respect to other Jews is directly related to their long history in Central Asia and deep ties to the culture of their non-Jewish neighbors. This is the norm rather than the exception; however, the unfamiliarity of the Central Asian environment among non-Bukharians, especially Jews of Ashkenazic descent, has marked them as an other. Representations of Bukharian Jews by Ashkenazic Jews are typically marked by aspersions about the Bukharian Jewish "character" based on the close relationship between Bukharians and their non-Jewish neighbors. A. Z. Idelsohn's early study of Bukharian Jewish song (1922), for example, described Bukharian Jews as "naive," "cunning," "short-tempered," and "idle," and imagined, "In their faces, their physique and in their mental disposition, there are features of the Altai and Tartar character, imposing a suspicion that much non-Jewish and even non-Semitic blood flows in their veins" (1922:15; this was probably not meant as a compliment).[11] Bukharian Jews are well aware of these representations. Rafael Nektalov called Idelsohn's writing about Bukharian Jews "racist" (using the English word).

Although Idelsohn's work is dated, such stereotypes are persistent. In decades marked by the the Israeli-Palestinian conflict, the Iranian Revolution, and the September 11 (2001) terrorist attacks on the United States, Bukharian culture's strong affinities with its Muslim environment in particular can have a negative connotation for other Jews or automatically seem un- or anti-Jewish. A young Bukharian woman who attends Touro College in Manhattan said that she felt that the other students (i.e., Jews, but not Bukharians) "don't even really think we're Jewish, because we come from a Muslim country." Alla Lupyan-Grafman, Janet Malcolm's Ashkenazi acquaintance from Minsk, "cited some of the more extravagantly stereotypic characterizations [held by Western Soviet Jews toward Bukharians]: the Bukharans were alien and not altogether civilized—savage, tribal people, capable of violence, even of murder. They were Jews but not proper Jews, more like Muslims than like Jews" (Malcolm 2011:31). Such associations are ironic considering how strongly Bukharian Jewish identity has been located in self-perceived differences from the Muslim majority among whom they lived in Central Asia.

Tensions, stereotypes, and misunderstandings go both ways. Just as Ashkenazic Jews characterize Bukharian Jews as too Muslim, many Bukharian Jews find Ashkenazic Jews too Christian. As noted, many have explained to me that American Jews heavily succumbed to assimilation, quickly trading in their precious culture and values in order to gain higher social status. Bukharian Jews also considered the neighboring Ashkenazic community in Central Asia which emerged during the Soviet era to be assimilated—Bukharian Jews, since they kept their practices and identity were "real Jews" while Ashkenazic Jews were not (Cooper 2012:168; on the Ashkenazic community in Central Asia, see Z. Levin 2008b). Bukharian Jews usually view forms of Jewry widespread among Ashkenazic Jews in New York, such as Reform and Conservative Judaism, with skepticism, bemusement, or even disdain.

Embracing Jewish multiculturalism, diversity, and cultural pluralism provides a natural tool for legitimizing Bukharian Jewish life in intracultural encounters. Bukharian Jews have spearheaded multiculturalist initiatives dedicated to promoting Bukharian distinctiveness. Aron Aronov established a Bukharian Jewish museum, housed with artifacts and pictures from Central Asia, and Bukharian Jewish youth are regularly brought to the museum to learn about their heritage. Imonuel Rybakov began teaching a class on Bukharian Jewish history at Queens College in the fall of 2009, mostly populated by young Bukharian students, who are required to do family tree and oral history projects. At an end of the semester party, one student improvised a speech:

It's hard, but it's also Bukharian culture and Bukharian history. Plus, so much of our community has taken this class.... And I just want to tell you and whoever created this class with you that it's truly a great course, and I wish you could actually teach more often to our community, future generations, because I have a feeling with our generation, pretty much everyone sitting here, our children will lose the Bukharian culture. And it's happening. Assimilation, as you said, is happening increasingly fast, it's drastic, it's skyrocketing. And one thing I don't want to lose is my culture, my values, the way I was raised, because I'm nice to people. If someone comes to my house, I don't tell them, you know, "here's a cup of water," you know, I put out sunflower seeds, the whole bit. And I think that's what I believe is a good thing to pass on to my children, a good thing to pass on to future generations, because I believe that the Bukharian culture, itself, we're like a fist. We're strong. We need everyone. If you lose a finger then you're not a whole. Like kicking out one of the legs of a tripod. If you don't have a tripod, you don't have anything pretty much. And that's why I believe that teaching this class is pure essential, very essential for our Bukharian culture.[12]

At the same time, assimilation to broader Jewish American identities, largely Ashkenazic and Orthodox in nature, is attractive to many Bukharian Jews, especially the ways in which the search for a singular Jewish identity intersects with Judaism as a way of life and belief system. Jewish religion presides over Bukharian Jewish behavior and interpersonal relationships, including music-making practices, and Bukharian Jews in general are highly concerned with the correct ways of practicing the religion, from dietary restrictions to gender roles. Although they recognize the unique aspects of their culture, Bukharian Jews typically see Judaism as a God-given inheritance that demands proper understanding and dedication. Ashkenazic Jews, as the dominant Jewish group in New York for over a century, have the strongest authority with respect to matters of Jewish religious law, and Bukharian Jews are often inclined to follow Ashkenazic opinion in cases of discrepancy. Discussed in Chapter 4, musically these questions concern such topics as the participation of women, as religious authorities have increasingly followed Orthodox, ultra-Orthodox, and Hasidic rabbis on particular interpretations of Jewish law. These authorities do not allow women to sing in front of men, or strongly discourage such practices, and have curtailed such traditions as female mourners (also today linked to Bukharian Jews' Muslim milieu). Bukharian Jews have heated debates among themselves and with non-Bukharian Jews over the legitimacy of those aspects of their minhag.

Ethnic Music in Multicultural New York

In constructing a distinct Bukharian Jewish American ethnic identity in accordance with multiculturalism, Bukharian Jews have adjusted the musical repertoires that they brought to New York to fit their new environment. The three main repertoires—maqom, religious, and party—are key resources, intimately connected to the multiple Bukharian meanings of "us" and "them," as "the concept of repertory entails a fundamental sense of 'otherness,' of difference.... Thus, 'my/our' repertory implies an awareness of 'his/her/their/your' repertory" (Bent and Blum 2001:197). Maqom, a "national" music in the Soviet Union, has been adapted to represent Bukharian Jewish "ethnicity" in multicultural—both "American" and "Jewish"—mosaics. Internally, Bukharian Jews adopted the methods and language of multiculturalism to preserve their distinct religious repertoire and retain a meaningful sense of otherness and essential Jewish difference. Bukharian Jews also adapted their own vision of multiculturalism to their party repertoire, an already cosmopolitan mix of music of different cultures, nations, or ethnic groups. Maintaining these three repertoires with different performance contexts is itself a multicultural and pluralist approach, a "plov" musical corpus with different ingredients each representing part of the Bukharian Jewish identity.

The particular activities surrounding these three Bukharian Jewish repertoires speak to the similarities of Bukharian Jews to other recent immigrant communities in New York. Like other immigrant communities, Bukharian Jews are faced with new ideas of "us" and "them," and are balancing their constantly shifting environment with an anchored sense of identity by maintaining diverse repertoires for multiple performance contexts.[13] New relationships and new categories for understanding identity are worked out in the repertoires and performances of ethnic heritage ensembles, wedding bands, and religious singers. The process of adapting immigrant identity and culture to American multiculturalism requires a balancing of internal differences to present a unified front, a defined ethnicity. And as we will especially see with new uses of the maqom and religious repertoires, in a multicultural environment, marginalization and exoticization becomes an asset with exchange value, a cultural property and a national resource.

Bukharian Jews, like other contemporaneous immigrants to multicultural New York, present their ethnicity on mainstream stages with folkloric ensembles combining local styles and genres. The Bukharian Jewish ensembles Shashmaqom and Maqom, or the Chinese American ensembles Music from China and Melody of Dragon, are among those who have found success in mainstream situations with a presentational repertoire that combines and collapses distinctions between classical, light-classical, and various regional folk musics.[14] The maqom repertoire is the centerpiece for these Bukharian ethnic heritage ensembles, which package an authentic folk culture that general audiences can appreciate as exotic while the immigrant community celebrates its appearance on high-profile American stages. Bukharian Jews in New York are newly able to claim maqom as their own, their number of accomplished musicians far exceeding those among the Uzbek and Tajik immigrant population.

The ethnic folkloric ensemble is an excellent professional niche for immigrant musicians, based on the significant number of musicians who, before immigrating, had careers primarily as Western classical, pop, or jazz musicians. Israel Mallayev and Osher Barayev, for example, are Bukharian Jews who taught and performed Western classical music in Central Asia but perform in ethnic heritage maqom or folk ensembles in New York.[15] Immigrant musicians are typically faced with a new awareness of their own culture, and perhaps the fragility of traditional musics, and at the same time, they encounter fierce competition in the classical, pop, and jazz spheres. These conditions set the stage for some enterprising musicians to adjust their repertoires and rethink their careers to highlight their "ethnic" music. Questions of professional opportunity, of course, should not be treated cynically. They are of the utmost importance to immigrants, who are above all striving to carve out a way of life in an unfamiliar environment, often tackling massive obstacles such as language barriers.

Bukharian Jewish religious repertoire serves a specific need as an internal heritage music, defining the group's ethnicity in relation to the global Jewish community. But tellingly, religious repertoire rarely surfaces on mainstream multiculturalist stages, and usually does not even appear in Jewish-specific multiculturalist contexts. Religious repertoire is participatory and protean, unlike the clearly bounded presentational repertoire of maqom and its light-classical and folkloric cousins. Also, religious repertoire is absorbing a huge amount of influence from other Jewish communities as Bukharian Jews are engaging more Jewish religious repertoires than ever before.

While New York's multicultural environment has helped spur the growth of heritage ensembles that unite immigrant communities for external and internal audiences, concerts and events solely for the community often capture a much wider aesthetic range, with presentational "ethnic" repertoires representing only a small portion of the concert. The tendency among performers and presenting institutions to minimize internal diversity is especially apparent in the lack of representation on mainstream stages of the Bukharian party repertoire. Party music operates as a self-representation of Bukharian Jews' own multicultural and cosmopolitan aesthetics, their own idiosyncratic take on diversity and cultural pluralism. Marc Augé has claimed that "respect for differences, the idea of the right to be different, the notion of a 'multicultural' society—all these, while generating noble-sounding expressions—may actually furnish an alibi to a ghetto ideology, an ideology of exclusion" (Augé [1994] 1998:99); this idea has been borne out to a degree in Bukharian Jewish musical life. While mainstream, externally directed events presenting Indian American, Chinese American, and other communities feature acoustic ensembles, regionally marked costumes, and other elements designed to convey an aura of authenticity, internal events use canned recorded accompaniments and styles unheard during performances for general audiences, such as contemporary pop songs. Immigrant weddings may feature American pop or global dance music, with only the most judicious use of classical or folk music, often heavily amplified and rhythmically updated. The blisteringly loud Russian, Israeli, or Spanish songs heard at a Bukharian wedding would be out of place at a World Music Institute concert and the audience's desire for unique and "authentic" folk culture, as would the diverse repertoire sung at an anniversary concert for the Chinatown-based Univoice Chorus, which sang "Mozart's Coronation Mass in C Major ... spirituals, a Hebrew folk melody, a Filipino folksong, and several Chinese art songs and folk melodies" (Zheng 2010:185).

The next three chapters detail some of the major adjustments and changes Bukharian Jewish professional musicians made to the maqom, religious, and cosmopolitan party repertoires as they have adapted to life in multicultural New York and helped to define a distinct Bukharian Jewish American identity. Bukharian Jews have become active contributors to an American "cultural democracy" with their distinct Central Asian music and dance, as well as their food, clothing, and literature. With multiculturalism as the dominant ideology in New York, Bukharian Jews and their contemporaries have found ways to retain their culture and utilize it as a niche in a globalized society.

3

Maqom

Bukharian Jewish Classical Music

Bukharian Jews in New York strongly associate their culture, heritage, and community with maqom, Central Asian classical music.[1] Maqom is the foremost music of presentation of the Bukharian community, a highly symbolic repertoire—"we are Bukharian Jews, and this is our music"—for both internal community events and public concerts geared to non-Bukharian audiences. More than any other repertoire, maqom represents the Bukharian community on multicultural stages in New York (Figure 3.1).

The deep connection between Bukharian Jews and the maqom repertoire is based in their disproportionate representation as important performers, teachers, and composers of Central Asian classical music. For Bukharian Jews, the repertoire and its most famous Jewish exponents are inseparable. Maqom has historically been an important repertoire of the most visible professional musicians, so the role of the hofiz (master singer) is as symbolic as the repertoire itself, a distillation of the persistent challenges faced and rewards reaped by Bukharian star musicians.

Bukharian Jewish musicians historically put the maqom repertoire to a plethora of uses, and they have continued this approach by adapting the music to American multicultural performance contexts. Sometimes this means presenting maqom as a distinctly Bukharian Jewish repertoire. At other times, it means highlighting the repertoire's multiethnic heritage as a product of fruitful interactions between Jews and Muslims. As minority musicians in Central Asia, Bukharian Jews were used to navigating complex ethnic and national politics, and they approached maqom with a freedom that accompanied their outsiderness. The United States presents an opportunity for Bukharian hofizes to draw on these familiar strategies while asserting a sense of ownership in situations where they find

Figure 3.1. An ensemble performing maqom at a community event in Queens honoring the scholar and journalist Isḥoq Mavashev (hanging portrait). Back row (l. to r.): Osher Barayev (doira), Yosef Abramov (tor), Ezro Malakov (voc.), Abukhai Aminov (voc.), Rustam Khojimamedov (voc.). Front row (l. to r.): Matat Barayev (doira), David Davidov (tor), Ochil Ibragimov (tor), Muhabbat Shamayeva (voc.), Shoista Mullojonova (voc.). Standing to right: Ilyos Mallayev (tor). Photo by the author.

themselves with some wind at their backs, such as on the stage of the 92nd Street Y in Manhattan or other prominent Jewish institutions.

As Bukharian American ethnic heritage music, maqom is not only directed outward to non-Bukharian audiences but also directed inward at weddings and community celebrations and on locally produced CDs. For Bukharian Jewish Americans internally, maqom has been a crucial source for maintaining historical continuity and navigating the changes accompanying migration, and as such, the repertoire is a vital source of inspiration for contemporary expressions. Yet as life in Central Asia recedes in the community's collective memory, maqom faces challenges of dwindling audiences and rarefied performance contexts. Audiences for maqom are increasingly found among non-Bukharian world music aficionados or Jewish listeners newly interested in discovering exotic diasporic communities. At Bukharian events where most celebrants are young and raised in New York, such as weddings and bar mitzvah parties, maqom is usually performed as two or three selections near the end of the party, for the benefit of older Bukharians born in Central Asia or maqom connoisseurs. Members of the Bukharian Jewish community and non-Bukharian maqom audiences demand different aesthetic performances from Bukharian professional musicians, further complicating working musicians' need to balance what they want to perform with what they think people want to hear.

Defining the Maqom Repertoire

Maqom in Central Asia refers to melodic types or modes as well as the ordered repertoire or compound form that has come to characterize the major maqom repertoires of the region, the *Shashmaqom* ("six modes," associated with Bukhara), *Chormaqom* ("four modes," associated with Kokand and the Ferghana-Tashkent region), the *Altı-yarım makom* ("six-and-a-half modes," associated with Khiva), and the Uyghur *On ikki muqam* ("twelve modes," associated with Kashgar and the Xinjiang region of China) (Levin and Sultanova 2001:911). Previous studies of Central Asian maqom repertoires have focused on the formal structure and integrity of the maqoms as suites or cycles, especially the Shashmaqom (Karamatov and Radjabov 1981; T. Levin 1984; Jung 1989; As'adi 2000; and Levin and Sultanova 2001), and the repertoires' roles in twentieth-century nationalization and canonization efforts (T. Levin 1984, 1996; Djumaev 1993; During 1993; Harris 2008; Light 2008). However, these approaches have limitations for understanding maqom from a specifically Bukharian Jewish perspective. While the formal structure of the suites and nationalization are important factors in the Bukharian Jewish understanding of maqom, as minority professional musicians on the margins of Central Asian ethnic categories, and as holders of an international Jewish identity that existed apart from and in tension with Central Asian nationalities, Bukharian Jews have primarily approached maqom as a performance style and a resource with multiple uses, including social mobility, adaptation, and collaboration. In this section of the chapter, I elaborate several key factors that contribute to a Bukharian Jewish musician's definition of maqom: form and genre, spiritual associations, transmission, instrumentation, and compositional modes.

Form and Genre

Among Bukharian Jews, maqom generally means "classical music," with the same layperson's associations that phrase has in English except that most of the melodies are of unknown authorship. Bukharian Jews often interchange the general term *maqom* with *Shashmaqom* ("six modes"), which strictly speaking refers only to the set of six large-scale ordered repertoires or compound forms developed at the court of Bukhara, coalescing in the nineteenth century.[2] Together, these six named modes (*Buzruk, Rost, Navo, Dugoh, Segoh,* and *Iroq*) contain over 250 individual pieces. The Shashmaqom is not the only Central Asian court repertoire, but it is the repertoire associated with Bukharian Jews; of the other Central Asian maqoms, I have heard Bukharian Jews play melodies from only the Chormaqom. Bukharian Jews are some of the most prominent performers of the Shashmaqom, and they are heavily responsible for sustaining and transmitting the music during the Soviet era.

The six named ordered repertoires of the Shashmaqom are generally described as large-scale suites or cycles. After a short instrumental section called *mushkilot* ("difficulties"), the works proceed to smaller vocal suites that proceed generally from slow expository compositions (including the opening vocal pieces, called *sarakhbor*-s, which outline the mode) to upbeat dance numbers (including those in the 6/8 rhythmic genre called *ufor*). Each composition in the repertoire has a place in the larger scheme. A full performance of a long suite such as Buzruk would take several hours and cover more than thirty individual compositions.

The twentieth-century Soviet musicologists and musicians who notated, recorded, canonized, and promoted the repertoires as national musics, such as Yunus Rajabi in Uzbekistan, highlighted the completeness of the large-scale suites or cycles. However, in practice, maqomists (both Jewish and Muslim) rarely perform Shashmaqom repertoire in suites unless they are performing in an academic setting or another performance situation influenced by scholars or theorists.[3] Compare Rachel Harris studying the Uyghur Twelve Muqam in Ürümchi, who originally expected to hear "neatly arranged by mode and structurally consistent" suites based on the "public discourse": "I realized that, while introductions to the Twelve Muqam typically state that each suite takes two hours to play through, I had never, either in folk contexts or in professional stage performance, heard a full performance of a complete *muqam*" (Harris 2008:72).

Instead, Shashmaqom musicians prefer to draw from a small pool of particular pieces from the repertoire and perform them as stand-alone compositions, and for this reason, I refer to the maqoms as ordered repertoires rather than "suites." Musicians usually call these pieces *ohang*-s (melodies, tunes), supporting their conception of the pieces as autonomous; they also use terms that imply a melody's place in the larger repertoire, such as the Persian word *porcha* ("piece," especially of denominations of property), *shuʿba* ("branch," referring to grouped sections of the Shashmaqom), *qism* ("division," "portion"), or the Russian loanword *fragment*, but less frequently. As Ilyos Mallayev explained, "to play maqom correctly you must play it in the exact order, but for concerts, it is possible to play 'fragments,' and to perform it in other ways" (personal communication). Frequently, maqomists will connect and present three or so individual well-known melodies in their proper order to make medleys within shuʿba-s of a specific mode, skipping over transitional or obscure material. For example, Roshel Rubinov will often perform Talqini Bayot, Nasri Bayot, and Ufori Bayot as a short suite or medley. The method of performing shorter suites of recognized melodies and virtuoso sections, in the proper order and limited to a specific shuʿba, seems remarkably consistent. According to the matrix numbers, Levi Bobokhonov's Gramophone recordings followed this practice (e.g., Mūghulchai Buzruk + its *avj* (virtuoso culmination), Talqin[cha]i Mūghulchai Buzruk, Qashqarchai Mūghulchai Buzruk) (Prentice unpublished liner notes).

In self-named "maqom" ensembles, Bukharian Jews regularly present other repertoires and styles alongside selections from the Shashmaqom. They will include some melodies from the Chormaqom as well as *khalqī* ("folk") songs, which are pieces of a quality similar to those in the named modes and also of uncertain authorship, but which do not belong to any of the ordered repertoires.[4] Chormaqom melodies are always played as individual ohangs by Bukharian Jews. Other heavy genres include *ashulai kalon* ("great song" in Persian, also *katta ashula* in Uzbek) and *yakkakhonī* ("individual singing"), both of which are used by Bukharian Jewish hofizes as platforms to demonstrate vocal virtuosity. Ashulai kalon is a genre from the Ferghana valley, perhaps originating in the Sufi *zikr* (T. Levin 1996:297), in which two or more singers perform classical poems a cappella or accompanied by a tremolo drone, alternating in rising tessituras in a competition of sorts and culminating with the singers finishing together. A crucial component of ashulai kalon is the singer's use of a small dinner plate, held against the side of the mouth, to modulate the sound. In yakkakhonī singers trade poetic verses of four-line folk poems (*chorband*-s) until the singer who knows more lines than anyone else is left alone at the end of the session. Ezro Malakov explained that yakkakhonī is properly a women's genre, and Nurjanov (1980:126–27) similarly describes yakkakhonī as the solo song, without doira, following the *soqinoma* in the female sozanda repertoire (see also Reikher 2005–2006:75).[5]

Bukharian Jewish maqom ensembles emphasize "lyric songs" (*surudi lyrik*) above all. These are light-classical works by known composers called *bastakor*-s (Persian) or *kompozitor*-s (Russian), who started contributing to the classical repertoire in the late nineteenth century. These songs echo the style of Shashmaqom melodies and often employ classical poetry. This genre surged during the Soviet era. Bukharian Jews especially thrived as composers and oftentimes found excellent Bukharian Jewish interpreters. Gavriel Mulloqandov, for example, wrote "Qurbon Olam," a song which he performed himself, and which was also famously sung by both Ezro Malakov and Isak Katayev. Another example is Shoista Mullojonova's celebrated version of Yakhiel Sabzanov's "Ba Dilbar." Today, Bukharian Jewish ensembles in New York also feature recent compositions by Ilyos Mallayev, Roshel Rubinov, and Avrom Tolmasov.

Bukharian Jews also perform some light repertoires in maqom performance contexts and formal presentations, such as wedding songs ("Shastu Shastu Chor" and "Yor Yor") and the repertoire of the female wedding entertainer called sozanda. Although not maqom per se, these wedding repertoires appeared as "folklore" (the loanword *folklor* used in Russian, not *khalqī*) during the Soviet era, and almost every staged, classically oriented performance has some overlaps with the folklore repertoire as both classical and folkloric music constituted part of the larger sphere of "people's" music. The role of folkloric wedding music and the sozanda has significantly diminished in the everyday participational musical life of Bukharian Jews, moving it further into the realm of presentation. Despite reverence and love for the most famous sozanda of Soviet times, Tŭhfakhon (Yafo Pinkhasova), who immigrated to the United States in 1995 (she died in 2010), no Bukharian Jewish woman in New York has fully continued the sozanda tradition. Today some of the most important situations for the sozanda repertoire are folkloric staged performances mounted by scholars and presenters working to rekindle interest in this crucial role and repertoire. Walter Zev Feldman, for example, presented a night of sozanda performance at the 92nd Street Y as part of his "Music and Dance of the Jewish Wedding" series in 2004 (Feldman 2004). Some performers, such as the lyric song specialist Tamara Katayeva, have learned a little of the sozanda repertoire for such concerts.

Spiritual Associations and Signals of Tradition

Maqom implies music of a spiritual, serious, and traditional quality. Several terms overlap with maqom in this sense, including *vazmin/ vaznin* ("serious," "heavy"), *klasik* ("classical"), *an'ana* ("traditional"), *mushkil* ("difficult"), and *toza* ("clean," "pure"). In the words of Avrom Tolmasov, "[maqom] is like symphonic music, it's like jazz … it's very serious" (personal communication). Maqom is music for the spirit, with healing properties, as Roshel Aminov explained: "Maqom, Shashmaqom, everything in it is extremely beautiful. When I listen to it, it fills my soul (*neshomoi man*).[6] … Shashmaqom is like a drug. It gives one a long life. It is artistic (*san'atī*) … which gives a person a very long life. Why? This person becomes without sadness or worry" (personal communication).

The poems sung for maqom are spiritually uplifting and ethical texts by the classical Persian and Turkic poets, such as Hafez, Sa'di, and Fuzuli. Bukharian Jews also use maqom for Hebrew texts, as explained in the next chapter. Russian is not a suitable language for maqom. Bukharians view the poems and the Persian language as inherently able to teach good morals and values. Roshel Aminov published an edition of Persian poems (Aminov 2011), transliterated into Roman characters so that young Bukharian Jews who might not read Cyrillic can "learn the good [beautiful, right, honest] way" (*rohi nek*).

In accordance with maqom's serious, formal, and traditional qualities, maqom performers typically wear traditional clothing such as the formal ceremonial coat called *jomma* (Bukharian Jews' jomma-s are usually adorned with menorahs and Stars of David) and the embroidered skullcap called *kalapūshi zarin, zardūzī* ("gold-embroidered") or *qalpoq* (see Figure 3.2).

As a symbol of Bukharian Jewish tradition, maqom is a vital component of community celebrations. Maqom is associated with weddings (*tūī-s*) and other parties for life-cycle events, birthday or anniversary celebrations in

Figure 3.2. Ensemble Maqom dressed in *jommas* and *zarduzīs*. From left to right: Matat Barayev (doira), Yosef Abramov (soz), Tamara Katayeva (voc.), Muhabbat Shamayeva (voc.), Ezro Malakov (voc.), Ilyos Mallayev (tor). Photo by the author.

honor of important people, and events celebrating the community's accomplishments, where it is naturally balanced with lighter repertoires. During the Soviet era, even as maqom was becoming officially canonized and nationalized, it remained an essential part of tūīs, and it is still heard at weddings today. As Avrom Tolmasov says, "a tūī without 'Qurbon Olam' is not a tūī."[7] However, at today's parties, maqom is generally relegated to only a few selections, typically near the end of the event.

Transmission

Maqom is strongly associated with the master–student (*ustoz–shogird*) method, the face-to-face lineal transmission of melodies, rhythms, and poems. The bond between ustoz and shogird is deep, nearly sacred, and representative of the general importance of tradition in Bukharian life.[8] Bukharian Jews also prize blood lineage and the continuation of musical tradition within families. For example, Roshel Aminov's website proclaims: "His father instilled in him a respect for this ancient musical art of the East.... Thus he learned in the traditional way through oral transmission rather than through formal lessons.... These compositions were handed down from teacher (ustoz) to pupil (shogird) as is the tradition throughout Central and South Asia" (Amin and Amin 2004).

   Sound recordings created a form of transmission that did not require personal one-on-one relationships, although the ustoz-shogird relationship remains valorized in principle. Ochil Ibragimov mentioned that with recordings, one no longer needs an ustoz as in the old days, that it is enough to learn repertoire and develop one's style with the many recordings that were produced after the beginning of the twentieth century. Ilyos Mallayev learned the art of maqom from recordings rather than in a master-student situation. Roshel Rubinov described Avrom Tolmasov and

Rasul Qori Mamadaliev, whose recordings Rubinov greatly admires, as his *ustozoni ghoibona*, or "absent" masters.[9] As he told me:

> And I listened all the time to Avrom Tolmasov. He's my teacher. He didn't teach me ... face to face. All the time I listened to his tapes ... and the great singer Rasul Qori Mamadaliyev. I listened, listened, listened to his recordings, and now I play exactly like him. I loved the way Rasul Qori Mamadaliyev played tanbūr. He's a very good tanbūrist, a virtuoso.... He is my teacher, Rasul Qori—absent teacher (*ustozi ghoibona*). I never saw him, he never saw me.... I only listened to his music, how he's singing, and learned from him.

Although most maqomists consider the ustoz-shogird form of transmission ideal for maqom, the repertoire is also taught in groups. The system of teaching maqom in national conservatories flourished during the Soviet era, and Soviet-style conservatory music education continues to play an important role in contemporary maqom transmission. Even contemporary pedagogical contexts that highlight ustoz-shogird methods, such as the Tajik Academy of Maqom, utilize group methods within conservatory contexts. Roshel Aminov's Traditional School of Bukharian and Shashmaqom Music, discussed in this chapter, is an attempt to establish an educational institution for maqom among Bukharian Jews in New York.

Instrumentation: The Maqom Ensemble

Instrumentation is a key element of maqom. Maqom requires at least one melodic instrument, ideally a long-necked lute, and a rhythmic instrument, which is always the doira (frame drum with jingles). The long-necked lutes tanbūr and *sato*[10] have the strongest associations with the history and tradition of the Shashmaqom, not the least because they are considered to be very difficult to play; maqom is supposed to be mushkil, or difficult. Indeed, the tanbūr rarely appears in other contexts, and when used elsewhere is primarily intended to signal the world of traditional maqom or old Central Asia.[11] Today, *tor* (double-chested long-necked lute), violin or *ghijak* (spike fiddle), clarinet, and keyboard (such as a Roland G-600), depending on the situation, can be used without any loss in seriousness. Keyboard and clarinet are considered modern, and accordingly, players of these instruments often dress in suits or sport jackets (this applies only to men; women do not, in my experience, play instruments in performance ensembles). As shown in Figure 3.3, contemporary ensembles often mix old and new looks.

The smallest ensemble for maqom is a singer playing a tanbūr and accompanied by a doira. This format is linked in the contemporary imagination with pre-Soviet maqom performance, exemplified by the 78 RPM recordings made by Levi Bobokhonov and his brother Yu'ov in 1911 (Audio Example 3.1◑).[12] Levi accompanies himself on the tanbūr; his voice and the tanbūr execute the same melodic lines but in different ways,

Figure 3.3. An ensemble performing maqom at an internal community celebration. Osher Barayev (doira), Boris Kuknariyev (accordion), Shlomo (Stas) Kalontar (Roland G-600), Roshel Rubinov (sato). Photo by the author.

resulting in a heterophonic texture, and the tanbūr also sets up the voice during breaks. In contrast to the styles of today's masters such as Roshel Rubinov and Avrom Tolmasov, Levi rarely plays the tanbūr *as* he sings, and his tanbūr playing, although filled with subtlety, is not particularly virtuosic. Levi mostly uses the tanbūr rhythmically, attacking strong beats in coordination with his brother, and to set up or respond to his extraordinary vocal displays. The difference in tanbūr styles is linked to an increased interest in instrumental technique that developed during the Soviet era. The old performance style of maqom is also characterized by an informal, salon atmosphere, in which players encourage each other with interjections and exclamations, as opposed to a formal staged presentation; in the background on some of the recordings, Yu'ov occasionally can be heard calling out "ey, Levijon!"

On the other end of the spectrum from the tanbūr-and-doira duo is the large Soviet maqom orchestra format, the most famous example being the Uzbek State Radio maqom ensemble, started in 1927 and led by Yunus Rajabi (T. Levin 1996:47–50). These maqom orchestras featured combinations of regional instruments constructed in different sizes in emulation of the Western symphony orchestra. Instead of spare heterophony supporting one vocalist, maqom orchestras offered rich textures supporting choirs. The emphasis on collective singing sought to capture Soviet ideologies (Ochil Ibragimov, personal communication), although simultaneous singing can be heard on the 1909 recording of the celebrated Mullo Tuichi Hofiz included on *Before the Revolution* (Prentice 2002).

In another change reflecting Soviet ideology, women were allowed to participate for the first time in the "heavy" traditions. The sound of women's voices in the mixed-gender choruses of the large Soviet ensembles is perhaps the most immediate difference between Soviet and pre-Soviet recordings. Jewish women notably filled the ranks of maqom singers, largely free of the mores that restricted Muslim women from heavy public participation in music. Yet in New York, Bukharian religious authorities have increasingly adopted international "ultra-Orthodox" Jewish attitudes, with striking ramifications for female participation in the maqom sphere. Women are discouraged, for example, from singing at events with significant numbers of men in attendance (Tamara Katayeva, personal communication). Although women do still perform in many concerts for Bukharian and non-Bukharian audiences alike, no women appeared in a concert at Carnegie Hall in 2011 in honor of Turgun Alimatov, featuring Bukharian Jews and Uzbek musicians from Central Asia (including Alimatov's sons), or in the 2013 Shashmaqom Forever concert at the Queens Theater in the Park.

The Central Asian large maqom ensemble can be seen as a particular response to European aesthetics and to the parallel responses that took shape in surrounding Asian and North African countries. The twentieth century saw similar processes of ensemble growth with the development of the modern Chinese orchestra (Tsui 2001:227) and the Egyptian *firqa* in the 1930s (Castelo-Branco 2001:557). However, the large maqom ensemble also seems to be an earlier phenomenon. At the court, both large and small ensembles performed maqom: "In [nineteenth-century] Bukhara, each *makom* was performed by two *ṭanbūrs*, a *sato* or *ghidjak*, an Afghan five-string lute or *rubāb*, and three *doiras*. *Makom* suites might be performed as instrumental music or include vocal sections. The smallest ensemble consisted of a singer accompanied by a *ṭanbūr* and *doira*" (T. Levin et al. 2001:186). Conversely, the small format has been continuous to the present day. Maqom was performed by both small and large ensembles throughout the Soviet period.

Jewish performers thrived in the large ensembles, especially as vocalists. In Uzbekistan, Isak Katayev, Berta Davidova, Barno Ishoqova, and Ezro Malakov, and in Tajikistan, Shoista Mullojonova, Fatima Kuinova, and Neryo Aminov were featured singers of maqom backed by large ensembles. Audio Example 3.2◐ is Ezro Malakov's recording of "Mūghulchai Dugoh" with the Uzbek Radio and TV Orchestra. As seen in Figures 3.4 and 3.5, the Yunus Rajabi museum in Uzbekistan commemorates the accomplishments of some of these performers. Jean During (2005:153) describes professional musicians' participation in national orchestras as part of a "double game," in which "belonging to an orchestra gives them status and assures them of a minimum income," but these practical reasons must be considered along with the most important reason articulated among musicians: enjoyment. Although the stiffer orchestral aesthetic does not seem to be

Figure 3.4. Portrait of Ezro Malakov on the wall of the Yunus Rajabi museum in Tashkent. Photo by the author.

generally enjoyed by most contemporary scholars of Central Asian music, musicians often enjoy "submitt[ing] to the discipline demanded of the members of a national orchestra" (During 2005:153) as much as they enjoy playing in small ensembles.

In fact, the large orchestral maqom format remains a beloved aesthetic for Bukharian Jews, especially those older people who remember the performances of the 1960s and 1970s in the USSR. They consider that period a golden age for maqom in terms of recordings, performances, and the connoisseurship of listeners. As During observed, "Musicians do not give the impression of having been crushed by directives that went against their convictions and interests. The remarkable artistic level and the wealth of musical activity which could be found during the 1960s and continuing over the next 30 years are evidence of this. The best artists were recorded, produced records, performed on the radio, were well paid and given privileges" (During 2005:148). On a group pilgrimage to Uzbekistan in October 2010, cassettes of Soviet-era orchestral recordings featuring Neryo Aminov and Ezro Malakov played constantly on the tour bus, at meals, and during relaxation periods. In the United States, recordings in this style by Isak Katayev, Neryo Aminov, Shoista Mullojonova, and others have been reissued on CD, testifying to their continued appeal (Katayev n.d.; Mullojonova 2004; Aminov 2005). Ezro Malakov referred to the large

Figure 3.5. Display case in the Yunus Rajabi museum. Isak Katayev is in the lower left of the photograph at top. At the bottom left is an LP of Berta Davidova. Photo by the author.

ensembles as "modern," and held the instrumentalists of those ensembles in the highest esteem. Maqom ensembles in New York tend to have six or seven performers at most, but Malakov explained that the lack of large ensembles in the United States is not due to an aesthetic preference for smaller groups but because there is no institutional support for the orchestral format nor enough instrumentalists in New York to populate such a large group. Bukharian Jews' nostalgic appreciation for the ensembles of Soviet Central Asia serves as a reminder that maqom in New York, although it often sounds very different from the maqom of the Soviet era, is a stylistic continuation of familiar processes and not indicative of a self-conscious break with the past.

Compositional Modes

The core instrumentation of voice, tanbūr, and doira corresponds to clearly demarcated hierarchical categories of text, melody, and rhythm. The text (voice) is the most important element, the melody (tanbūr or other melodic instrument) supports the poetry, and the rhythm (doira) provides a foundation. The performers' status normally reflects their musical role, with singers having the highest status, followed by melodic instrumentalists (stringed instruments foremost), and finally, players of the frame drum. Although classical music and poetry are completely intertwined in Bukharian thought, singing (*khondan*, also "to read," or "to recite"), done by a hofiz, is considered a separate activity from playing music (*navokhtan*) on an instrument, done by a *muzykachi*. These three roles also match different levels of variation in performance. Vocalists ornament melodies and improvise cadential passages on vocables at the ends of poetic lines, instrumentalists decorate the melodic lines more subtly and explore variations in between vocal passages, and drummers usually keep the rhythmic pattern unchanged in the background, only rarely displaying flashy technique.

The combination of text, melody, and rhythm into compositions is primarily a process of "fitting together," "adapting," or "adjusting" preexisting components.[13] Completely new compositions in the usual Western classical sense—new texts, melodies, and rhythms—are unusual in the maqom sphere. Music-making remains rooted in tradition by keeping preexisting elements intact. This is a crucial point for understanding Bukharian Jewish music as well as Bukharian Jewish life in the United States. Bukharian Jews can be seen as primarily "adapting" and "adjusting" traditional modes of life rather than "reinventing" themselves.

Composition typically includes novel settings (Bukharian Jews use the verb *mondan*, "to set") of poems to melodies, with either the poem or the melody preexisting, or both. For an example of coordinating preexisting items from both the poetic and melodic repertoire, Ezro Malakov sings a standard poem attributed to Mirobid Saïido Nasafi (died between 1707 and 1711, Bečka 1968:509), to "Iroqi Bukhoro" (from Maqom Buzruk), ashulai kalon, "Navruzi Ajam," and other melodies.[14] For examples of one new element and one preexisting element, "Qurbon Olam" is Gavriel Mulloqandov's setting of a poem by Fuzuli to a novel melody, and "Sūhbati Dono" is a new poem of Ilyos Mallayev's to "Talqini Uzzol" from Maqom Buzruk (Audio Example 3.3🔊).[15]

The compositional mode of coordinating and setting depends on adherence to form. Classical poetry (*she'r*) must conform to poetic genres and metrical formulas, which suggest certain kinds of musical treatment. Poetic forms (*shakl*-s) include *ghazal, mukhammas, rubo'i, tarje'band, soqinoma, musaddas,* and *masnavi.* The most common form for musical settings, the ghazal, is composed of a series of couplets. The rhyme scheme is AABACADA, and so on, with the most important rhyming syllable or syllables occurring just before the end of the line.[16]

The mukhammas, a five-line poem rhyming AAAAA, BBBBA, CCCCA, and so on, is a genre commonly employed by a poet who wishes to base a new composition on a previously written work, either to demonstrate familiarity with poets of the past or to honor the work of his or her contemporaries.[17] Mallayev, for example, has written mukhammases on ghazals by the classic poets Mashrab, Maknuna, Jomi, and Hiloli, as well as his fellow Bukharian poet Mikhoel Zavul. Zavul, in turn, has written mukhammases on Mallayev's ghazals.

When the mukhammas is used for this purpose, the final two lines of every stanza are one couplet (AA, BA, CA, etc.) of the existing ghazal, and the first three lines are newly composed on the rhyme of the fourth line. The following mukhammas by Roshel Rubinov on Mallayev's ghazal "Sūhbati Dono" (Discourse of Wise People), with the rhyming syllables italicized, illustrates the way a new poem is built on top of a preexisting poem.[18]

Line and Author	*Rhyme scheme*
[Rubinov]	
Mardi dono oqilu bemislu beham*to* buvad,	A
Bovafoiu ham tavono sarbari dun*'yo* buvad.	A
Bah chi khush ast ahli dono doimo yak*jo* buvad,	A
[Mallayev]	
Har kujo dono buvad mehru vafo on *jo* buvad,	A
Lazzati bazmu tarab az sūhbati do*no* buvad.	A
[Rubinov]	
Kori nek karda ba olam khalqi khud kun sar*fa*roz,	B
Nekiro karda ba ob parto, vale az on *ma*noz.	B
Doimo pesh az ibodat kardanu vaqti *na*moz,	B
[Mallayev]	
Khoki poi ahli donoro ba chashmon sur*ma* soz,	B
Har kujo nodon buvad koni balo on jo buvad.	A

Translation:
[Rubinov]
A wise, smart person is incomparable and without equal,
The world is supported with faithfulness and also strength.
Smart people are always in one place with that which is good,
[Mallayev]
Everywhere wise people are, friendship and loyalty are there,
The pleasure of festivity and joy comes from discourse of wise people.
[Rubinov]
Doing good things makes your friends happy,
Do good things but don't boast about it.
Always be ready for worship and prayer time,
[Mallayev]
Dust from the feet of wise people is surma [collyrium] for the eyes,
Everywhere ignorant people are, it is a source of trouble.

Another crucial aspect of composition is the coordination of poetic meters—the rhythms that emerge from the long and short syllables of the words alone—and the underlying rhythmic cycle. In addition to conforming to specific forms, every classical poem adheres to a poetic meter (*vazn*) based on a quantitative system (*'arūz*) originally developed by Arabic poets and codified by al-Khalil in the eighth century. Poets writing in Hebrew, Persian, and Turkic languages adopted and adapted the 'arūz system in different ways.[19] A hofiz must have a proper understanding of ʿaruz: "poetry and music are attached to each other, and knowledge of ʿarūz meter is essential for every musician and composer" (Rubinov 2002:7).[20] Bukharian singers pay close attention to short and long durations of syllables when setting poetry to music: the norm is for short syllables to be given short musical durations, and long syllables longer durations. Long syllables are also generally placed on strong beats, and short syllables on weak beats.

Rhythmic cycles (*zarb*-s or *usul*) played on the frame drum provide the frameworks to which poetic texts and melodies are coordinated.[21] Like poetic meters, rhythmic cycles are composed of combinations of two contrasting elements: the low center stroke "bum" and the high rim stroke "bak." Many zarbs recur in the Shashmaqom repertoire, such as *sarakhbor, talqin, nasr, ufor,* and *mūghulcha,* shown in Example 3.1.[22] Every zarb has distinct associations and functions. For example, sarakhbor is stately, formal, and considered to be very old (it is also called *zarbi qadim,* or "old rhythm"). In contrast, ufor is a brisk, energetic 6/8 suitable for dance. Rhythmic cycles are conventionally paired with specific poetic meters (Karamatov and Radjabov 1981:111–12). For example, talqin rhythms are commonly joined with poems in the meter of *ramali musammani mahzuf*: four repetitions of the ramal foot (– ‿ – –) with the last foot apocopated to three syllables (– ‿ –).

Together, these musical principles, signals of tradition, spiritual associations, and transmission methods create a flexible definition of maqom that overlaps, but can also conflict, with the large-scale suite or ordered repertoire qualities of maqom. Tension between the multiple meanings and uses of maqom dates back to the Soviet period, when the Uzbek and Tajik government representatives introduced the categories of classical and folk music, and enlisted the large-scale repertoires as representatives of

Example 3.1. Five zarbs.

national musics. The tensions that characterize maqom are particularly poignant for Bukharian Jews, who contributed heavily to nationalist projects and were simultaneously excluded from the discourse due to the essentialist quality of the nationalist categories. In New York, the legacy of their Soviet minority status has manifested in a freedom and newfound desire to engage national questions.

Canonical Shashmaqom Editions and National Questions

In New York, Bukharian Jews present maqom as their ethnic heritage music. This is a natural extension of maqom's use as a national and classical music in the Soviet Union, concepts introduced to Central Asia by Viktor Aleksandrovich Uspenskiĭ with respect to the "Classical Music of the Uzbeks" in 1927 (Djumaev 2005). The Shashmaqom became associated with the Uzbek and Tajik nations, represented in canonical notations and presented by national ensembles. The Jewish relationship to the "national questions" surrounding the Shashmaqom is deep and complex, since Jews were closely involved with the work of nationalizing the repertoire, but from a national or ethnic standpoint, Bukharian Jews as a group were excluded from the discourse of ownership. The language of multiculturalism presents Bukharian Jews with a new set of questions and reasons for revisiting their relationship as a nation or ethnic group to the Shashmaqom, and they have various responses to these questions, sometimes claiming ownership (or co-ownership) of the repertoire and sometimes sidestepping the issue of ownership altogether by simply highlighting the contributions of Jewish musicians.

Music played a key role in establishing the discrete divisions of nations or peoples introduced by the Soviets, such as Uzbek, Tajik, Turkmen, and Kazakh. Thinking about musical repertoire in terms of national divisions was a significant shift from the late nineteenth and early twentieth centuries, in which repertoires were associated with regions, urban and rural distinctions, religious divisions, and classes. The new nationalities were matched with musical repertoires rooted in a singular folk, and religious connections were suppressed. The specific repertoire of the Shashmaqom serves as a quintessential example, with Soviet officials attempting to transform it from a polyglot urban repertoire with spiritual associations and a particular manifestation in the Bukharan court into symbols representing the Uzbek and Tajik nations (T. Levin 1984:80, 1996:46–47; Djumaev 1993:47–49, 2005; During 1994:127, 1998:108–10).[23]

Jews participated in these nationalization efforts but did not (and could not) claim ownership of the repertoire. Officially such claims were unsustainable and illogical, against the Soviet conception of nationality that treated Jews exceptionally. Throughout the entire Soviet Union, the Jewish people were considered to be a separate national group, overlapping with strong senses of Jewish otherness already pervasive both within and without the Jewish community. "Uzbek" and "Jew" were mutually exclusive national categories, not terms of citizenship or of religious faith (Cooper 2000:344). Unlike Uzbeks and Tajiks, Jews were considered rootless, without a distinct national culture, a direct extension of Richard Wagner's position that "Jews had no national culture of their own and were therefore condemned to be cultural strangers and imitative performers in European music, rather than original, creative artists" (Loeffler 2010:102; see also Slobin 1986b:254; Gilman 2008; Móricz 2008:4–7).

Officially sanctioned published notations were the most concrete manifestations of Soviet policies on the maqom repertoires. In 1924 the "publication of the Bukharan Shashmaqom, initiated by Abdurauf Fitrat [the prominent Uzbek *jadid* revolutionary] ... symbolized the legitimatization of the Bukharan Shashmaqom as an inseparable part of Uzbek national musical culture" (Djumaev 2005:175). Nationality was tied to language in the editions. In order to "prepare the way for a new Uzbek version" (During 2005:147), Viktor Uspenskiĭ's early notations of the Shashmaqom sponsored by Fitrat were published without the Persian poems Ota Jalol sang for Uspenskiĭ (Djumaev 1993). Following a suppression of the Shashmaqom during Stalin's rule, the Shashmaqom repertoire was revived and published with Turkic-language texts as the "people's music" of Uzbekistan in Yunus Rajabi's *Uzbek khalq muzikasi* or *Uzbekskaya narodnaya muzyka* (Rajabi 1959), and with Persian-language texts in Viktor Belyayev's Tajik edition of the Shashmaqom, introduced as "classical music of the Tajik people" (*muzikai klassikiĭ khalqi Tojik*) (Belyayev 1950:9).[24]

Bukharian Jews loomed large as informants for the Shashmaqom editions. Levi Bobokhonov was an informant for Uspenskiĭ's early notations.[25] Rajabi almost completely relied on Bukharian Jews, who had transmitted and maintained the repertoire under the very difficult conditions of Stalin's repression.[26] Rajabi's primary informant was Borukh Zirkiyev, but Mikhoel Mulloqandov, Mikhoel Tolmasov, and Yakub Davidov (the master instrumentalist and instrument maker David Davidov's father) also contributed (Rajabi 1959). Additionally, Zirkiyev was involved in Rajabi's Shashmaqom ensemble and the group's canonical recordings of the repertoire (Ochildiev et al. 2007:311).

During the Soviet era, Jewish musicians did received some recognition for their role in the maqom tradition. The portraits included in the Rajabi/Akbarov edition are Ota Jalol Nasirov, Ota Ghiyos Abdughani, Levi Bobokhonov, Mikhail Tolmasov, and Borukh Zirkiyev: three Jews and two Muslims. Yet by and large Jews were excluded or marginalized from the nationalist discourse. As Levin, who studied in Tashkent during the Soviet era, related, "During my year of study with Professor Karomatov at the Tashkent Conservatory in 1977–1978, he never mentioned Bukharan Jews in connection with the Shash maqâm or any other musical repertory. Other people discussed that connection in whispers" (T. Levin 1996:92).[27] As Uzbeks and Tajiks have sought to reintroduce Islam as an explicit creative element in their music following the demise of the Soviet Union,

Bukharian Jews remain on the sidelines in this culture battle.[28] As Laura Adams wrote, "One of the most important answers to the question of 'who are we?' in Uzbek national identity is 'we are Muslims'" (Adams 2010:61). However, their exclusion also gave Bukharian Jews license to approach maqom without the burdens of Soviet nationalist legacies, and they have been able to draw on this outsider attitude in their post-Soviet global diaspora.

Bukharian Jews hold conflicted thoughts about their relationship to the Shashmaqom as a nationality or ethnic group. If pressed about questions of ownership, Bukharian Jews may argue that Jews populated Central Asia before Muslims (i.e., before the Arab conquests), and some with whom I have spoken have used this as evidence that maqom is Jewish music, and not Muslim. When people point to the Jewish quality of maqom, they tend to focus on the accomplishments of individual musicians rather than the "music itself": the Jewish identity of the Bobokhonovs, Tolmasovs, Mulloqandovs, and others are the most important aspects of maqom as Bukharian Jewish music, de facto "ownership" regardless of the official line. As one prominent musician told me in casual conversation, after I asked him about these issues of ownership, "The Shashmaqom is Muslim music. Jews here [in the United States] say it's Jewish music, but that's wrong. But it's an important question. Maybe it is Jewish, because we were there 2,000 years [i.e., before Muslims]. But we need *proof* [*isbot*]." Of course, official discourse does not necessarily reflect the opinions of individuals—especially in the Soviet Union, where speech was heavily circumscribed. Apparently, at least one Uzbek musician found ridiculous the Soviets' political interventions into musical processes and preoccupation with national connections to repertoire. According to his son Alisher (personal communication), the maverick instrumentalist and teacher Turgun Alimatov used to enjoy telling people he was from different cities to undermine their chauvinism, and if talking to a particularly nationalistic Uzbek, would provocatively insist that the Shashmaqom was "Jewish music" due to the Bukharian Jews' well-known mastery of the repertoire.

The ideological matter of nationality and ownership so central to Soviet cultural politics does indeed continue to be an "important question" in the United States, as the Bukharian Jewish musician put it, especially in the public sphere. In New York, Bukharian Jews are reconsidering their relationship to maqom in terms of nationality, framed as ethnicity—a reflection of Soviet discourse as well as the kinds of questions that scholars and figures at cultural institutions ask when presenting maqom in multiculturalist contexts. The pressures to define themselves as a distinct *Bukharian* Jewish ethnic group emerges in such situations, including intracultural Jewish situations, and Shashmaqom naturally fits the bill; the use of Shashmaqom as a Bukharian Jewish ethnic music mirrors the earlier situation of Uzbeks and Tajiks drawing on the repertoire to define their identity when they were compelled to do so.

With a new opportunity to present Bukharian Jews' historic relationship to maqom, Bukharian Americans organize their own maqom concerts and symposia. For example, questions of the Bukharian relationship to the Shashmaqom figured heavily in a symposium celebrating the life and work of Isḥoq Mavashev, a Bukharian Jewish writer who recounted the accomplishments of Levi Bobokhonov in 1960 for the journal *Sharqi surkh* (Benyaminov 1992:73; Nektalov 2005). At the symposium, Zoya Tajikova announced, "Jews could not claim to *create* the Shashmaqom, but could claim to *preserve* it" (18 December 2005). At a performance in Imonuel Rybakov's class on Bukharian Jewish history at Queens College, Avrom Tolmasov asserted the Jewish ownership of the Shashmaqom. Of all my Bukharian Jewish interviewees, Ilyos Mallayev was the most outspoken in his belief that the Shashmaqom was the property of Bukharian Jews. Regarding his recording of Maqom Buzruk, *At the Bazaar of Love*, he told me:

> Actually, this maqom—the Shashmaqom—was brought into the world by Bukharian Jews. By *Bukharian Jews*. Uzbeks have their own maqom—the Chormaqom of Ferghana—this is not the maqom of Bukhara. The maqom of Bukhara, the maqom of Samarqand, has a very different style.[29] For this recording, it is all Bukharian Jews performing. There are no Uzbeks, no Tajiks. This maqom recording is very good—because the owners (*sohibon*) of the maqom performed it.

The national questions surrounding the Shashmaqom notations have also entered some internal Bukharian debates over nationality and authenticity. Some of the differences are regional, brought into sharp relief as Bukharian Jews from different cities mingle side by side in Queens. Roshel Aminov, for example, has strong attitudes about the canonical Shashmaqom, explaining that the Tajik maqom notated by Belyayev is the correct version, as opposed to Rajabi's Uzbek version.[30] Aminov also links the notations to performance style: the Tajik maqom is to be played in the Bukharan style maintained in Tajikistan rather than *Tashkentski* style, characterized in terms of playing position of the tanbūr (the instrument's body against the heart, rather than on the lap) and the plucking style (always starting in a downward direction, rather than upward).[31] Aminov's attitudes are clearly inspired by the nationalistic cultural policies of the Soviets and his family's personal relation to the notations. His father, Neryo Aminov, lived in Dushanbe (after moving from Samarqand) and studied with Shohnozor Sohibov, one of the main informants for Belyayev's edition. But Aminov's position expresses broader internal conflicts over authority, recognition, and performance opportunities. When it is useful, Bukharian Jews may themselves adopt nationalistic stances.

While Soviet attitudes regarding the relationship between nationalities and the Shashmaqom repertoire are represented in the notated editions, and while the questions of national ownership continue to occupy public forums such as symposia and concerts, it is difficult to assess the extent to which Soviet nationalist ideologies changed the ways people actually thought about, engaged, and interpreted maqom with respect to musical style and performance practice over the past one hundred years. For Bukharian Jews in New York, the definitive representation of the Shashmaqom is captured by a figure such as Levi Bobokhonov: the master musician and his or her professional life. The printed Shashmaqom editions serve primarily as symbolic *Denkmäler*, monuments to a nation's musical heritage. For example, Roshel Aminov keeps a copy of Belyayev's Tajik edition on his desk at his maqom academy, but he does not read music. Even if they read music (as in the case of Ari Bobokhonov and Roshel Rubinov), Jewish performers usually continued to learn maqom by ear through members of their families or from recordings.

For Bukharian maqomists, the performance practices accompanying the notations had a significant impact. The national conservatories cultivated a version of maqom that had little flexibility and variation from performance to performance. In Yunus Rajabi's maqom ensemble of Uzbekistan, the notations of the maqom were reproduced faithfully to such an extent that Levin characterized it as "frozen" music (T. Levin 1996:45–51). Bukharian Jews participated in the recordings made by Rajabi's ensemble, and many learned melodies from those documents; as noted, they also contributed most of the source melodies as informants. Regardless of an ability or inability to read music, Bukharian Jews can be extremely faithful to the notated versions in their performances, especially the Belyayev edition. Roshel Aminov, Roshel Rubinov, and others articulate a keen sense of a "right" version of the maqom melodies, although they encourage flexibility with respect to the texts. The canonical notations also serve as a general standard for whether or not a melody is strictly Shashmaqom, or merely classical-sounding music: Roshel Rubinov and Roshel Aminov, when asked specifically about certain pieces, would only refer to a composition as "Shashmaqom" if it were part of the canon.[32]

On the other hand, the nationalist monolingualism encouraged by the official notations and performances had very little impact on the overall repertoire of Bukharian Jewish maqomists. For example, Bukharian Jews perform Shashmaqom melodies with Persian and Hebrew texts and have also maintained classical pieces with Turkic poems as part of their repertoire. Several important figures and families moved, maintained careers, or studied in both Uzbekistan and Tajikistan. Nationalization efforts in Uzbekistan and Tajikistan following the Soviet Union seems to have had a stronger effect on the Uzbek and Tajik populations, who are more likely to sing maqom only in Uzbek or Tajik—although at least in Bukhara, the Shashmaqom continued to be sung in Tajik Persian (Djumaev 1993:48). Bukharian Jews' multilingualism has been an essential part of their professional profile and identity throughout the Soviet era up to the present day. And now, thanks to Ari Bobokhonov and Angelika Jung, an edition of the Shashmaqom with both classical Uzbek and Tajik poetry is available for the first time (Jung 2010).

Ari Bobokhonov's multilingual edition of the Shashmaqom exemplifies the relationship between Bukharian Jews' outsider status and the nationalization of the repertoire. Bukharian Jews continually adapted to Soviet cultural policies in public while disregarding them in private, and the Soviet borders had a limited impact on their self-conceptions. At an international Shashmaqom symposium held in Weimar in 2011 organized by Angelika Jung, tensions surfaced between persistent Soviet national-isms and Bukharian Jews' non- or anti-nationalist attitudes. Although the Uzbek, Tajik, and Jewish (Ari Bobokhonov, now living in Germany) musi-cians in attendance demonstrated extremely convivial, productive, and respectful relationships with each other, nationalist discourses dominated the more presentational sections of the symposium as some academicians from Central Asia continued to reinforce divisions between Tajiks and Uzbeks and sideline Bukharian Jews. Bobokhonov passionately called for a "liberation from dogma," and exhorted the participants to condemn the continued politicization of the repertoire, to look abroad, and to move be-yond "dead points." In New York as well, Bukharian Jews have a flexible and open-ended approach to maqom, rooted in their complex status as musical insiders and national outsiders.

Maqom on the World Music Stage

The nationalist attitudes applied to maqom during the Soviet era have made it an obvious choice for Bukharian Jews needing to present their own national music. Since emigrating from Central Asia to the United States (and Israel and Europe) Bukharian Jews have freely broadcast their community's links to the maqom repertoire, especially at cultural presen-tations and "world music" concerts. On world music stages, Bukharian Jews engage a multiculturalist environment where they not only *can* pub-licly announce maqom as "their" music to non-Bukharians, but in which they are encouraged to do so.

In the late 1990s and early 2000s, many of the world music concerts in which Bukharian groups participated were initiatives presenting cultural examples of Muslim–Jewish exchange and the Silk Road as a proto-multicultural environment. The most prominent of these situations for Bukharian Jews was Yo-Yo Ma's series of "Silk Road" ensembles and concerts, which presented a picture of a multicultural and globalized Central Asia characterized by trade and exchange. As described in a press release for the Smithsonian Folkways CD *The Silk Road: A Musical Caravan* (2002), the Silk Road "represented civilization's first great period of glob-alization and resulted in an unprecedented cross-pollination of art, tech-nology, fashion, and ideas," and in the liner notes, Yo-Yo Ma calls the Silk Road "a crucible for cultural intermingling." Literature for the 2002 Smithsonian Folklife Festival (*The Silk Road: Connecting Cultures, Creating Trust*) stated:

Following the events of September 11, it seems clear to us that it is ever so important for people and societies the world over to take account of their neighbors, to come to know them and learn of and from them, to engage them in positive ways. Insularity and xenophobia, the fear and dehumanizing of "others"—even one's own neighbors—are recipes for disaster in a complicated world. (Kurin and Parker 2002)

The Silk Road was a mercantile phenomenon and Yo-Yo Ma's project correctly frames multiculturalism within the economics of globalization. In other words, the Silk Road model raises the idea that multiculturalism is not just a matter of different cultures coexisting, like in a salad bowl or mosaic, but a matter of trading goods and collaborating to make, buy, and sell things. In Silk Road projects, Bukharian Jews participate as Central Asians with an important role in the region's mercantile history, having bridged regional, ethnic, and religious barriers. For Bukharian Jews, maqom is a precious good with exchange value, and tied to the repertoire's historical association with elite patronage. The high profile nature of many world music stages, such as Carnegie Hall or the Smithsonian Folklife Festival, further reinforces Bukharian Jews' decision to use maqom. Representatives of corporations (such as the Ford Motor Company and Citigroup, which sponsored the Silk Road Project), elected officials, scholars, and even general American audiences in such situations are maqom patrons, and Bukharian professional musicians explicitly address their maqom performances to the specific patrons and sponsors involved in each situation.

Bukharian Jewish ensembles performing on high-profile, mainstream New York stages are a constellation of similarly named and similarly constituted ensembles, such as Ensemble Shashmaqom, Maqom, and Shashmaqom.[33] For American audiences, Bukharian musicians' consistent use of "maqom" in the names of their ensembles arguably connects maqom with the Bukharian Jewish community and the diverse standard repertoire that they perform more than with Muslim Central Asia. Bukharian Jews greatly outnumbered the ethnic Uzbek and Tajik population in New York through the end of the 1990s, and they have certainly dominated the performance of maqom in the city.[34] The performance contexts, repertoire, personnel, and audiences of maqom ensembles are interrelated—as more work develops for these groups, more musicians assemble themselves and perform programs in such configurations; as audiences emerge for maqom groups, so do performances; and as maqom groups add items to their repertoire and perform them regularly, those items acquire the potential to be considered "maqom" by other musicians and audiences.

The trajectories of the two major ensembles on the world music stages, Ensemble Shashmaqom and Ensemble Maqom, reflect the tensions, pressures, and opportunities of the American multicultural environment. Both ensembles presented the community as a distinct ethnic group through a small repertoire of various maqom styles. Ensemble Shashmaqom, closely aligned with the Center for Traditional Music and Dance and its multiculturalist mission, emphasized the community's immigrant status. Ensemble

Maqom became a showcase for the star professional musicians of the community, who came to New York later, only after the push and pull factors of immigration became overwhelming. Ensemble Maqom's members were reframed as classical masters, with Ilyos Mallayev at the center. But the institutional support and patronage necessary for promoting maqom in its purest and most elite forms contrasted with the grassroots support for maqom as a diverse, folkloric presentational repertoire.

Ensemble Shashmaqom (also just Shashmaqom) was the first Bukharian Jewish ensemble on the New York scene, formed in 1983 in association with the Ethnic Folk Arts Center (now the Center for Traditional Music and Dance). At the time, the Soviet Union was still strong and the Bukharian Jewish community in New York was small, a few thousand people at most. The ensemble was formed by Firuza Yagudayeva, a well-known conservatory-trained dancer and dance instructor in Tajikistan who immigrated to New York quite early, in 1976. She opened a restaurant in midtown Manhattan called "Firuz" soon after, where she would dance daily at 4 pm. The restaurant was reviewed favorably by Alan Jones in the *New York Times* (25 October 1981), with a picture of her dancing, which brought her together with another émigré, Shumiel Kuyenov, a doira player who had driven a taxi and operated a jewelry business in Queens (Yagudayeva, personal communication). As immigrants continued to arrive through the 1980s, Ensemble Shashmaqom became an umbrella ensemble for musicians, dancers, and singers, all of whom had some sort of formal training and professional music career in Central Asia. For example, Yosef Abramov, a tor and soz player, and Abukhai Aminov, a singer, doira player, and teacher, immigrated in 1989 and began performing with the group soon after.

In 1991, the group released a landmark CD for Smithsonian Folkways, *Central Asia in Forest Hills, New York: Music of the Bukharan Jewish Ensemble Shashmaqam*. Theodore Levin, who had met Bukharian Jewish musicians during his fieldwork in Central Asia (see T. Levin 1984 and 1996), produced the recording, marking a new point in what would turn out to be a productive relationship between scholars, institutions, and Bukharian Jewish Americans. The repertoire represented on the CD reflected a typical concert program, drawing on a wide variety of maqom styles: two pieces from the Shashmaqom ("Talqini Bayot" from Maqom Navo and "Nasri Chorgoh" from Maqom Dugoh), and two well-known lyric songs (Neryo Aminov's "To Bodi Sabo," also called "Ba Guliston," and Hoji Abdulaziz Rasulov's "Ushshoqi Samarqand").[35] The album also featured a good deal of lighter repertoire, including folkloric wedding songs.

The consolidation of the presentational maqom repertoire found on *Central Asia in Forest Hills, New York* served the needs of Bukharian performers, who were already searching for common musical ground, having come from a variety of places and backgrounds, and served the needs of the Bukharian community, seeking to define itself through a clear heritage repertoire. Ensemble Shashmaqom's presentation also seemed to work well with non-Bukharian audiences, who had no familiarity at all with the music. Neither the Bukharian community nor the general public in New York was prepared to support any particular style on its own. Adding to the general appeal, Ensemble Shashmaqom dressed in beautiful formal jommas and zarduzis, their coats ornamented with menorahs, Stars of David, and ornate designs.

After the fall of the Soviet Union, major performing stars began arriving in New York, including Ilyos Mallayev and Muhabbat Shamayeva, Ezro Malakov, and Isak Katayev. Katayev performed with Ensemble Shashmaqom on their national tour in 1993 and 1994 sponsored by the Ethnic Folk Arts Center with a grant from the National Endowment for the Arts (see Figure 3.6). By 1997, Ezro Malakov, Shoista Mullojonova, and Tūhfakhon Pinkhasova were performing with the group.

Ensemble Shashmaqom, although it contained some "stars," was largely defined by the group's relationship to the broader Bukharian Jewish immigrant community, as captured by the album title *Central Asia in Forest Hills, New York*. The main mission of the Center for Traditional Music and Dance, which worked closely with Ensemble Shashmaqom, is to help immigrant communities maintain and pass on their unique traditions. As the Bukharian American community grew, it supported more ensembles for world music situations. The arrival of Ilyos Mallayev, Muhabbat Shamayeva, Tūhfakhon Pinkhasova, and Ezro Malakov presented a watershed moment for the New York community because of their celebrity in Central Asia, as well as the tight relationships that these musicians already had with American scholars of Central Asian music involved on the concert and recording scene, including Theodore Levin and Walter Zev Feldman. In particular, Mallayev's relationship to Levin (documented in T. Levin 1996) had a tremendous impact on maqom in New York. Mallayev and Levin shared many attitudes regarding the Shashmaqom, and Levin's promotion of Mallayev's art largely set the stage for Bukharian Jews' representation and participation in world music recordings and performances.

Ilyos Mallayev began leading a group with some overlap to Ensemble Shashmaqom in personnel, but with a different core: Mallayev, Shamayeva, Ezro Malakov, Tamara Katayeva, Yosef Abramov, Ochil Ibragimov, and Matat or Osher Barayev. This group also featured introductions in English by their manager, Svetlana Levitin; for the musicians, most of whom have limited English skills (or are uncomfortable speaking publicly in English), Levitin's introductions greatly assisted them in setting up performances and bringing their music to non-Bukharian audiences. By the beginning of the 2000s, when I started my research, Mallayev's group (Ensemble Maqom) performed most of the high-profile concerts for Bukharian Jews. For example, this group performed at Carnegie Hall as well as around the five boroughs in a series of sponsored neighborhood concerts in connection with Yo-Yo Ma's Silk Road Project, funded by the Ford Motor Company, Citigroup, and a number of city, state, and national governmental organizations.

THE BUKHARAN JEWISH ENSEMBLE

SHASHMAQAM

1993-1994 TOUR

A NATIONAL CONCERT TOUR FEATURING MUSICIANS AND
DANCERS FROM THE BUKHARAN JEWISH COMMUNITY
OF FOREST HILLS, NEW YORK

PRODUCED BY THE ETHNIC FOLK ARTS CENTER
WITH THE GENEROUS SUPPORT OF
THE NATIONAL ENDOWMENT FOR THE ARTS

Figure 3.6. Press materials for the 1993–1994 tour of Ensemble
Shashmaqom, sponsored by the Ethnic Folk Arts Center (now the
Center for Traditional Music and Dance). Top row (l. to r.): Yosef
Abramov, Yasha Kakuriyev, Isak Katayev, Borukhai Davrayev. Middle
row (l. to r.): Shumiel Kuyenov, Firuza Yagudayeva, Fatima Kuinova,
Abukhai Aminov. Bottom row (l. to r.): Merkhai Aminov, Mikhail
Abramov. Courtesy of Center for Traditional Music and Dance Archive
(www.ctmd.org). Reproduced with permission.

In contrast to Ensemble Shashmaqom's presentation as an immigrant
group, Ensemble Maqom was increasingly framed as a Central Asian classical chamber group, tied to the growing status of Ilyas Mallayev as a virtuoso maqomist. Mainstream media outlets such as the *New York Times,*
which profiled Mallayev in a milestone 1997 article, "A Virtuoso Far from
Home: Uzbeks' Classical Master Reclaims Role in Queens" (Dugger 1997),
bolstered Mallayev's reputation as a world-class maqom master. Mallayev's
1997 recording of Maqom Buzruk, *At the Bazaar of Love,* was subtitled

"Timeless Central Asian Maqam Music." As part of Yo-Yo Ma and the Silk Road Ensemble's three-night run of performances at Carnegie Hall in 2002, Ensemble Maqom (called the Ilyas Malaev Ensemble for these events) played "Classical Music of Bukhara"—selections from Maqom Navo—alongside an international, star-studded cast of players. The group's immigrant makeup was mentioned in a sentence in the program notes, but that aspect was not a defining quality in this context.

Ilyos Mallayev positioned himself as a maqom master in the United States by drawing on his deep knowledge of the classical repertoire and professional strategies he learned as a musician in the Soviet Union. In the USSR, Mallayev's maqom knowledge, gleaned mostly from studying records, was a minor part of his public performance life. His lighter styles, vaudeville routines, and imitations were his main attraction. In the United States, encouraged by supportive arts organizations, journalists, and scholars, Mallayev grasped the opportunity to flip this emphasis and perform Central Asian maqom, the music that was closest to his heart, on world music stages.

Mallayev's Ensemble Maqom navigated different performance contexts by drawing on multiple styles, a large repertoire, and considerable professional acumen. At Carnegie Hall, during the Smithsonian Folklife Festival, and on *At the Bazaar of Love*, Mallayev's group presented a dry, acoustic, "pure" sound and the performance of Shashmaqom in suites. On other world music concerts or at local community events, Ensemble Maqom focused on the same multifaceted repertoire performed by Ensemble Shashmaqom: a mixture of pieces from the Shashmaqom, folkloric tunes, and lyric songs. In these situations, the main difference between the groups was the inclusion of original material by Ilyos Mallayev and the celebrity quality of the performers.

Two recordings, *At the Bazaar of Love* and *Bukharian Jewish Folk Music*, provide a useful comparison of Mallayev and Ensemble Maqom's different approaches to maqom. *At the Bazaar of Love*, an acoustic rendition of a Shashmaqom suite, is nearly unique; in the twenty years since the Bukharian community arrived with *Central Asia in Forest Hills, New York*, nothing like it has been produced within the New York Bukharian community (with the sole exception of Roshel Aminov's *Bukharian Classical Shashmakom*, which differs in several respects).[36] The seventy-minute abridged recording of Maqom Buzruk begins with a brief instrumental introduction taken from the opening mushkilot instrumental subsuite. The bulk of the performance then takes place, the first vocal subsuite of the maqom, which can be outlined as follows: "Sarakhbori Buzruk" plus six *tarona*-s (songs which come between the "signpost" melodies of the suite), "Talqini Uzzol" (Audio Example 3.3🔊) plus two taronas, "Nasrulloi" plus four taronas, "Nasri Uzzol," "Ufori Uzzol" and the connecting "suporish" melody. *At the Bazaar of Love* concludes with the soqinoma and the ufor (and a thirty-second "suporish" coda) from the middle of the "Iroqi Bukhoro" subsuite, one of Buzruk's subsuites according to the Belyayev edition.[37]

At the Bazaar of Love clearly reflects the attitudes of Mallayev as well as his sponsors for the project, Theodore Levin and the Ethnic Folk Arts Center. The recording is presented as a return to a pre-Soviet musical style, with Mallayev's approach described in the liner notes as "[an] older and all-but-abandoned-style of performing the maqâm." And in fact, Mallayev's style is understood by other musicians in Queens, such as Ochil Ibragimov, as harking back to an older style (Ari Bobokhonov's virtuosic, heavily ornamented style on the Afghan rubob serves as a contrasting modern style). The instrumentation is limited to tanbūr (played by Mallayev), violin (played by Roma Narkolayev, in the manner of a ghijak), and doira (played by Osher Barayev), explicitly contrasted in the liner notes with the large Soviet maqom orchestras. Levin connects Mallayev's performance to only one Soviet innovation, the inclusion of women (Muhabbat Shamayeva is part of the ensemble, although she disappears after the third tarona and and is never featured as a soloist).

One remarkable aspect of *At the Bazaar of Love* as a Shashmaqom recording is the inclusion of Mallayev's poetry. Mallayev set his "Sūhbati Dono" ("Discourse of Wise People," Mallayev 1999:54) to "Talqini Uzzol" and his "Tamosho Kun" (Mallayev 1999:117) to the third tarona following "Nasrulloi." These are ghazals on sophisticated themes, composed in classical poetic meters and set in traditional ways. "Sūhbati Dono," for example, is a treatise on the benefits of associating with smart people, in the fifteen-syllable apocopated ramal meter:

> ‾ ᵕ ‾ ‾ ‾ ᵕ ‾   ‾   ‾ᵕ ‾ ‾ ‾ ᵕ ‾
> har ku-jo do-no bu-vad, mehr-u va-fo on-jo bu-vad
> ("everywhere wise people are, friendship and loyalty are there")

Mallayev's superb poetry underlines the CD's overall portrait of him as a rare keeper of the flame, a master of artistic styles and practices that were all but destroyed by Soviet policies and their enforcers.

Shown in Figure 3.7, the cover to the album continues the theme of Mallayev as a transplanted master of an exotic great tradition. Mallayev, clothed in jomma and zardūzī and holding his tanbūr, looks out from his balcony over the roofs of a Rego Park street. The image contrasts dramatically with the covers of locally produced CDs of any style, such as Roshel Rubinov's *Tamanno* (Figure 3.8), which typically figure local musicians in Western clothes superimposed onto a skyline or some striking New York landmark, such as the World Trade Center, or a well-known site in Central Asia, such as the Registan in Samarqand.

At the Bazaar of Love captures the New York musicians in peak form, demonstrating their mastery of the Shashmaqom, but it is a one-of-a-kind recording, and an album that does not coincide with the standard aesthetics and ideals of the community on the whole. As opposed to most recordings produced within the Bukharian community, the production aesthetic of the recording is remarkably dry and the voices unadorned. One of the performers reported that it took over a year to teach the abridged suite to the ensemble; it was not something that most of the

Figure 3.7. The Ilyos Mallayev Ensemble, from *At the Bazaar of Love* (1997). Photo by Theodore Levin. Photo and album cover reproduced with permission.

musicians on the recording already knew. Despite the occasional overtures to the importance of the Shashmaqom's suite form, Bukharian audiences and musicians have continued to support and present maqom as self-contained melodies in virtually every instance, with a focus on the relatively recent work of Jewish composers of the twentieth century. Of course, At the *Bazaar of Love* was also a commercial work and one of the more earnest forays of Bukharian Jews into the international world music market. Had Mallayev's CD made him an international star on the level of an Alim Qasimov, Bukharian Jewish ensembles might have gravitated to more performances of maqom in suites with similar production aesthetics.

The fact that *At the Bazaar of Love* is so unusual in retrospect conveys the general needs and preferences of the immigrant community, and the institutional and academic support necessary to maintain and present maqom as a pure classical form composed of large-scale suites. In both Soviet and post-Soviet contexts, the Shashmaqom's transmission and performance in suites is supported by governments and foundations. Later projects also directed by Levin, such as those he produced in connection with the Aga Khan Music Initiative in Central Asia (AKMICA), reflect a similar aesthetic. The Tajik Academy of Maqom's Smithsonian Folkways release of Maqom Rost, *Invisible Face of the Beloved*, also presents an

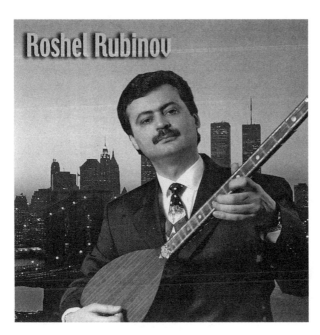

Figure 3.8. Roshel Rubinov, from *Tamanno* (2002). Reproduced with permission.

abridged suite following established canonical models (the performance exactly follows Belyayev [1954]) and women and men singing, sometimes in a mixed chorus. The CD also contains liner notes stressing practices and techniques described as pre- or non-Soviet (the ustoz-shogird system, the "study of *maqâm* as a musical cycle or suite," texts "redolent with symbols drawn from Sufism, the mystical dimensions of Islam" [Academy of Maqom 2006:15, 17]). The Shashmaqom's inclusion on the UNESCO Representative List of the Intangible Cultural Heritage of Humanity (inscribed in 2008, originally proclaimed in 2003), essentially tied to the countries of Uzbekistan and Tajikistan, further reinforce the repertoire's ties to nations and institutions.

In contrast to the approach represented on *At the Bazaar of Love*, Mallayev's Ensemble Maqom usually followed the same model as Ensemble Shashmaqom in recordings and performances, presenting a small assorted repertoire of Shashmaqom, light-classical, and folkloric melodies. Ensemble Maqom's self-produced CD *Bukharian Jewish Folk Music*, sponsored by Ezro Malakov and Mira Mushebayeva, conforms to the grassroots-supported Bukharian Jewish maqom aesthetics usually heard in New York. The instrumentation is rich, with tor, violin, synthesizer (using a nai sound), with reverb. The star vocal soloists are highlighted, with the featured singers listed with every selection; in contrast, none of the soloists' performances are identified in *At the*

Bazaar of Love. The female singers Shoista Mullojonova, Muhabbat Shamayeva, and Tamara Katayeva are prominently featured on *Bukharian Jewish Folk Music*. True to its title—"Bukharian Jewish Folk Music," not "Timeless Central Asian Maqâm Music"—the recording focuses on lyric songs and light-classical repertoire rather than one suite, with the Shashmaqom barely represented (just "Ufori Uzzol," listed as "Mahvashi Nozuk"). The focus on lyric songs allows the group to highlight a major interest for Bukharian audiences, the lyric contributions of the poets: Mallayev, Roshel Rubinov, and Mikhoel Zavul.

In concerts, Ensemble Maqom performed the same sort of repertoire. I heard some variation of this program dozens of times, and while it clearly went against strict definitions of maqom, it demonstrates how Bukharian Jewish musicians adapted the repertoire to the professional demands of the American multicultural context. The group would usually begin with the folkloric "Bukharian Jewish Wedding Song," which featured group singing alternating with dramatic solos. In the more high-profile concerts, they might begin with "Sarakhbori Navo," a slow introductory piece from the Shashmaqom. The next selection, "Georgian Miniatures" was an instrumental composition for the tor by Mallayev, played by his student, Yosef Abramov. This piece, connected to Mallayev's artistic ambitions, was unusual in several respects; in no other Bukharian Jewish performances of this type can I remember hearing a virtuosic instrumental piece announced as the product of a composer and unrelated to any preexisting maqom melody or classical poem. "Georgian Miniatures" (later "Eastern Melody") also exploits rare sounds and techniques for Central Asian maqom: an augmented second interval, which is supposed to sound exotic and evoke the Caucasus across the Caspian Sea (or the East, with the later title), and the strumming of the tor. The group would then feature the individual singers. Ochil Ibragimov would sing a selection from the Shashmaqom, such as "Ufori Savti Kalon" (from Maqom Rost). "Noz Noz" with a rubato introduction followed by a lively 6/8 melody was always an opportunity for Tamara Katayeva to get up from her seat and dance. Tamara Katayeva would then sing Neryo Aminov's "Ba Guliston" and Yakhiel Sabzanov's "Dilbar," snapping into the microphone or clapping to urge audience members to respond. Ilyas Mallayev would sing "Shirinjon," and the other singers would respond with the chorus from the sozanda repertoire, "soq-soq-i jon, piola pur may kun" (dear cupbearer, fill the cup with wine). Ezro Malakov would sing his signature tune, Neryo Aminov's "Zulfi Pareshon" (a resetting with Persian lyrics of Gavriel Mulloqandov's "Qurbon Olam"). Muhabbat Shamayeva, always introduced by Levitin as "the star of our show," would sing "O Khonum," which had overtones of Indian or Afghan music and an "alap"-esque introduction. The ensemble would always end with Mallayev's diasporic anthem, "Yalalum," in which the group sings about immigrating to America over an upbeat 6/8 rhythm.

Ensemble Maqom's program was an impeccably distilled one-hour presentation of Bukharian Jewish maqom for an American multiculturalist context. They would play one Shashmaqom selection and one folkloric Jewish melody, but the group focused on the contributions of Jewish musicians and composers from the twentieth century, including Neryo Aminov, Yakhiel Sabzanov, and Mallayev himself. The group also highlighted the "star" aspect of this particular ensemble, with stunning performances by Muḥabbat Shamayeva and Ezro Malakov that clearly translated to multiple audiences, eliciting spontaneous applause and standing ovations. The focus on individual virtuosos represented an arrival on the American scene, as the hofiz is a defining role in the community. By adapting maqom in these ways, Bukharian Jews found a mode to continue using it as the primary repertoire for intercultural interactions, and as an internal ethnic heritage music that spoke to the community's immigrant situation.

Maqom and Intercultural Encounters between Jews and Muslims

Maqom's legacy as the main repertoire for intercultural exchange between Bukharian Jews and Muslims continued after the post-Soviet era despite mass migration. Maqom's symbolic power as a representation of productive, long-running exchanges between Muslims and Jews in Central Asia proved to be a special niche in the United States. The Queens Council for the Arts, for example, noted the close proximity in Queens of Muslim and Jewish immigrants from Uzbekistan, Afghanistan, and Iran in their concert *Musical Bridges: Jewish and Muslim Traditions of Asia*. The 23 February 1997 concert, at Lincoln Center's Alice Tully Hall, featured Mallayev's Ensemble Maqom, Quraishi and the Tanin Ensemble (Afghan Muslims), and the Farrvardeen Ensemble (Iranian Muslims and Jews together). Ensemble Maqom and Roshel Aminov's ensemble also performed at Peter Norton Symphony Space on 19 February 2005 as part of the *Cultural World of Islam* series. Joining Ensemble Maqom that night was Rustam Khojimamedov (often called Samarqandi), an Uzbek American singer who sometimes performs with Jewish groups, and an Uzbek American dancer, Dilafruz Jabarova. I have been asked to help facilitate Jewish-Muslim ensembles for such initiatives. As part of a symposium entitled *Common Ground: Dialogue between Jewish and Muslim Worlds through Art* at the University of Virginia (3–4 March 2013), organized as a "bridge-building project" by the university's Jewish Studies Program, McIntire Department of Music, and Department of Middle Eastern and South Asian Languages and Cultures, I helped coordinate a performance by the "Shashmaqam Central Asian Ensemble," for which the long-standing Bukharian Jewish members of Ensemble Shashmaqom Shumiel Kuyenov, Firuza Yagudayeva, Abukhai Aminov, and David Davidov joined the Uzbek Americans Sobir Saïdov and Rustam Khojimamedov.

Figure 3.9. Advertisement for Uzbekistan Independence Day event in the *Bukharian Times* weekly, 2005. Reproduced with permission.

Maqom is also central to internal events geared to both the Bukharian Jewish American and Uzbek American communities. Occasions for such events include Uzbekistan's Independence Day (September 1) and Navruz (Persian New Year) celebrations. As shown in Figure 3.9, an advertisement for an Independence Day concert sponsored by the Uzbekistan-American Association and ASA College, music and dance unite the two diasporic groups. The paragraph at the bottom reads: "We have all kept the warmest feelings for the native land, the native language, our traditions, and so sometimes we need to come together. Let this meeting and banquet remain in your hearts for a long time. We will not be homesick, we will organize it here!"

Bukharian Jews also continue to interact through maqom with their former Muslim neighbors still living in Central Asia. Bukharian Jews remain connected to Central Asia, with musicians occasionally traveling to make recordings or give concerts, and with Uzbek and Tajik musicians sometimes coming to the United States. The Internet and the instantaneous circulation of audio and video has been invaluable in keeping New Yorkers and Central Asians networked. In one compelling instance of a post-Soviet musical encounter, in March 2006 Abduvali Abdurashidov brought an ensemble of five students from his Tajik Academy of Maqom (sponsored by the Aga Khan Music Initiative in Central Asia) to tour the United States, and during the evening before their concert at Columbia University's Miller Theater the group performed at a private engagement at a Bukharian Jewish restaurant in Queens. Ilyos Mallayev and Muhabbat Shamayeva, Ezro Malakov, Roshel Aminov, Roshel Rubinov, and Avrom Tolmasov were among those in attendance. Several of them knew Abdurashidov from Central Asia. The complex relationships between the immigrant Bukharian Jewish community in New York and the Tajiks were immediately apparent in their different approaches to interpreting maqom: the Tajiks with institutional support presenting maqom as a long classical suite with Sufi associations, the Jews highlighting their heritage as master musicians and a free, spontaneous approach to maqom as melodic springboards for virtuosic performance.

After eating a catered meal, Abdurashidov and his students prepared to perform. Roshel Aminov commented happily that Abdurashidov's group would be playing "naturally," without microphones. Abdurashidov in turn made a small "request," explaining that he and his students would be performing a suite in order to appreciate the "shape" and the "mystical [or Sufi] path" (*tariqi tasavvuf*) of the maqom, and reminding the assembly that they were playing on quiet, unamplified instruments. The group then performed the *nasr* (vocal section) of Maqom Dugoh. The instrumentation was lean (tanbūr, dutor, sato, and doira), and the timbres clear and unadulterated—no microphones, reverb, or large orchestrations. Most of the melodies and the texts were the same as those found in the Belyayev edition, although this performance contained more variations than the group's CD recording of Maqom Rost (Academy of Maqom 2006).

It was indeed impressive to hear such an expert, memorized rendition of Maqom Dugoh, especially knowing that the students had also made an equally excellent interpretation of Maqom Rost on their CD. Clearly, these students were passionate about the Shashmaqom and also had the opportunity to invest a serious amount of time in their studies. The performance of the full subsuite without interruption provided a striking contrast to the typical assortment played by Bukharian Jews in Queens. As Abdurashidov noted in the liner notes to *Invisible Face of the Beloved* and in his introduction to the night's performance, he is concerned with the spiritual qualities of the maqom's suite form and in highlighting the repertoire itself as a masterpiece of Muslim Central Asian heritage.

The Bukharian Jews in attendance demonstrated a great deal of appreciation and respect for the students' performance. Whereas Bukharian listeners in community settings tend to express their appreciation for performers physically, by singing or clapping along, dancing at appropriate moments, or by conspicuously rewarding the performers with money, for the most part they listened quietly and respectfully to the entire performance which lasted over an hour. (At the end of the sarakhbor Roshel Aminov began to sing along, and during "Nasri Chorgoh" Avrom Tolmasov did too, but that was all.) When people talked, they were generally shushed. The Tajiks received heavy applause and a standing ovation.

Several Bukharians made long toasts after the performance, an important aspect of any banquet or public event in which speakers are expected to welcome guests, praise hosts, and overtly show appreciation. These particular speeches, in Tajik Persian (not Russian) by Boris Katayev, Ilyos Mallayev, and David Mavashev (son of Isḥoq Mavashev), managed to express deep gratitude and recognition for Abdurashidov and his students while also taking advantage of an opportunity to place Bukharian Jews at the center of a conversation with Tajiks about Shashmaqom. Ilyos Mallayev commented that the Shashmaqom was "not only the treasure (ganj) of the Tajiks, but also the treasure of Bukharian Jews." Boris Katayev commented:

> Friends, many Bukharian Jews became world famous for this art. The same way of the Tajiks, in Bukhara, Samarqand, was once in the hands of Bukhara and Bukharian Jews: Levicha Hofiz, Yusefi Gurg … [at this point, others start saying names and Katayev repeats them:] Borukh Kalkhok, Dovidcha Inoyatov, Mūrdekhai Tanbūri, and others in the ensemble of Levicha Hofiz…. [He then names great deceased Tajik and Jewish masters who lived in Tajikistan:] Fazliddin Shohobov, Boboqul Faizulloyev, Shohnazor Sohibov, Neryo Aminov, Barno Isḥoqova, all lived here today, they were pleased. This happiness is here today in New York. The Shashmaqom Academy of Tajikistan came to be with [here Katayev points out people at the banquet:] Tolmasovs. With Mulloqandovs. With Ilyos Mallayev. With Ezro Malakov. With the son of Neryo Aminov, Rosheljon. With Shoista Mullojonova. The art of Uzbekistan and Tajikistan is a great pride. Thanks to you. Thanks to you for coming today, this is all from God. God does not want Tajiks and Bukharian Jews to be separated from one another. [Applause from everyone.]

Katayev also went on to praise the president of Tajikistan, Emomalī Rahmon, and the Aga Khan for their efforts to maintain the Shashmaqom. Typical of Bukharian Jewish speeches about the Shashmaqom, Katayev's speech focused on Jewish achievement and displayed a transnational attitude, as he mentioned Uzbekistan and Bukhara, Samarqand, and the masters of those cities. At the same time, Katayev made clear overtures to Tajikistan in support of the Academy of Maqom's national agenda.

Following these speeches the Bukharian Jews performed in a much different style. Impromptu groups of two and three musicians assembled to perform one or two individual pieces from the Shashmaqom or related maqom repertoires. The Bukharian Jewish performances reflected the deep familiarity those in attendance had with maqom, and even more, the importance of maqom as a musical space for Bukharians to appreciate and "perform" their community to each other and to the Tajik students present.

The songs themselves became vehicles to appreciate the hofiz, in many ways a more meaningful emblem of the Bukharian community than the repertoire alone. In the middle of one song, Roshel Rubinov passed his tanbūr to Avrom Tolmasov as a gesture of respect. At other times, particularly virtuosic or expressive gestures would receive words of encouragement. People would sing along at times, outwardly demonstrating their knowledge of the repertoire. In one of the most stirring performances of the night, Avrom Tolmasov (on tanbūr) and Roshel Rubinov (unusually, on doira) sang "Nasrulloi" from Maqom Buzruk with a standard poem, a ghazal attributed to Saïido (Audio Example 3.4⦿). In this example, the vocalizing at the end of each couplet, musical interludes between couplets, and ornamentation were major spaces for impromptu self-expression, rather than a presentation of the canonized melodies. At those moments listeners interjected "salomat boshad!," "ey!," or applause. In the next-to-last couplet, Ezro Malakov, sitting near them, began singing along loudly. The three singers then competed and complemented each other on the highest section of the piece, the avj, or culmination. The last couplet provided a return to the low range.

Between songs, musicians made more speeches about the history and friendship of Tajiks and Jews, as well as the distinct accomplishments of Jewish maqomists and the ancestors of important people at the party. On several occasions, most memorably during a freewheeling performance by Roshel Aminov of his father's "Ba Guliston," students from the Tajik academy joined the Bukharian musicians in performance, underscoring the general feeling of friendship and maqom's position as a shared vehicle for Jewish and Muslim expression. However, the performances also indicated a legacy of tension stemming from the Shashmaqom's attachment to Soviet national categories, and Bukharian Jews' attempts to undo their persistent marginalization.

Maqom and Intracultural Jewish Encounters

Jewish multicultural initiatives in the United States constitute a significant performance situation, where Bukharian Jews are presented as Central Asians who lived among Muslims, representing both "us" (Jews) and "them" (an exotic, unfamiliar other). Their history has made Bukharian Jews an appealing group for concerts and events at mainstream American Jewish institutions dominated by Jews who have lived in the United States for generations. These "American" Jews, usually of Ashkenazic backgrounds, have extended multiculturalism to an idea of Jewish multiculturalism, introducing synagogue programs and curricula that promote understanding of Jews from diverse backgrounds. An article on one such event stated, "Throw out your idea that Jewish music means only klezmer music. Bukharian Jewish music will remind you that the Jewish culture comes in many different looks and sounds" (Friedman 2005). Multiculturalism and globalization together create conditions in which exotic qualities are assets with considerable worth. In Jewish multiculturalist contexts, Bukharian Jews are especially valuable as a model for Jewish-Muslim interaction in a world that increasingly portrays members of the two religions as irreconcilable enemies from time immemorial.

The post-Soviet Jewish environment in New York is a particularly significant Jewish intracultural context for Bukharian Jews. New York was the locus for a vital transitional moment immediately following the end of the Soviet Union and the arrival of many Soviet Jews to the United States. To outsiders, it may have seemed that these Jews were all "Russian"—and Bukharian Jews did share in this experience as Soviet Jews—but the lives of the Bukharian Jews in the far eastern republics, under Muslim rule, were a mystery to most Soviet Jews hailing from western Russia, Ukraine, and the Baltic states. Western Soviet Jews sometimes are prejudiced against those from the East, who they consider to be "country bumpkins" with strange accents and an inability to speak Russian properly. In New York, all of these Soviet Jewish communities found themselves side-by-side and in situations where they collectively reflected on their pasts.

The *Nashi Traditsii* (Our Traditions) Community Cultural Initiative of the Center for Traditional Music and Dance is of special interest here (see Figure 3.10).[38] Designed to showcase the diversity of post-Soviet Jewish life in New York City, the Center created the program in partnership with scholars and performers with expertise in Yiddish culture, klezmer music, and Russian and Soviet traditions, including Michael Alpert and James Loeffler (a graduate student at the time). Bukharian Jews shared with Ashkenazic Jews and "Mountain" Jews (from Dagestan and surrounding areas) several stages throughout Manhattan, Brooklyn, and Queens, over a five-year period. The initiative demonstrated the new character of Bukharian connections to other Russian-speaking Jewish groups immediately following their immigration. Although Ashkenazic and Bukharian Jews lived side by side in Central Asia, and some Bukharian Jews did go to and from western Russia, the *Nashi Traditsii* initiative brought Mountain, Ashkenazic, and Bukharian Jews together under a distinctly American multicultural spirit of internal exchange and external presentation.

The groups shared their heritage folkways with each other. Other Jewish representatives from New York's long established Jewish Ashkenazic population, the clarinetists Andy Statman and David Krakauer, even collaborated with the post-Soviet groups, finding musical common ground. At one of the annual concerts, the "Crossing Bridges" concert of 19 May 2002 at Kaye Playhouse, Andy Statman performed a duo with the Bukharian Jewish singer Abukhai Aminov. They took turns; Statman played in the style of a doina, improvising in the *ahavah rabbah* mode (strongly

Figure 3.10. Postcard for the Center for Traditional Music and Dance's *Nashi Traditsii* initiative. Top row (l. to r.): Shumiel Kuyenov, Osher Barayev, Ilyas Mallayev. Bottom row (l. to r.): Roshel Rubinov, Firuza Yagudayeva. Courtesy Center for Traditional Music and Dance Archive (www.ctmd.org). Reproduced with permission.

associated with Eastern European Jewry), then providing a drone under Aminov while the Bukharian singer performed in the style of ashulai kalon. David Krakauer later joined the Mountain Jewish group, Ensemble Tereza.[39]

The *Nashi Traditsii* initiative brought the Bukharian Jews' marginal and exotic status into focus, both with respect to mainstream Jews in New York and to the Russian Jewish post-Soviet population. In the May 2002 Community Cultural Initiative Project Report, Tavriz Aronova from the Bukharian contingent is quoted as saying, "I started to translate the program text [into Russian].... Suddenly I saw that this was not only interesting, not only important, but our obligation. This was our only opportunity to announce loudly in public our culture among all the other cultures, to pass on something good."

Nashi Traditsii also illuminated some cultural conflicts, especially between the new immigrants on stage and the established Jewish Americans presenting them or listening to them in the audience. At the Kaye Playhouse concert, the nuanced descriptions in the program and multicultural presentation contrasted with the announcements from the stage, in which the Bukharian Jews were described "as if in a time capsule," with arresting overtones of exoticism. Similarly awkward was the announcement from the stage that the grandmother of Tereza Elizarova (from the Mountain Jewish group Ensemble Tereza) had performed for Stalin, which received a chorus of boos from the audience. In the United States Stalin is an unequivocally despicable figure almost on par with Hitler, but for those recently arrived from the Soviet Union, having performed for the leader of the nation is a point of honor and pride and typically mentioned when Soviet performers list their résumés.[40]

Soviet Jewry was an important umbrella context for Bukharian Jews adjusting to life in New York, and *Nashi Traditsii* conveyed the complexities of that post-immigration situation. But over the course of the first decade of the twenty-first century, the importance of the Soviet milieu gradually gave way to a nascent, distinctly Bukharian American culture, steeped in an overwhelming interest in developing and sustaining Jewish religious practice. The once taken-for-granted importance of the relationships between Bukharian Jews and their Muslim Uzbek and Tajik neighbors is also changing. The middle-aged and older members of the Bukharian maqom ensembles lived for decades in the Soviet Union, but now a whole generation of Bukharian Jews born in the United States, or who moved here as very young children, has come of age. Many of them have no first-hand experience of Central Asia. Maqom is becoming more symbolic and less participational, a cultural touchstone with increasingly limited uses. Accordingly, maqom transmission has moved into a cultural extracurricular heritage arena for Bukharian Jewish youth, where they experience maqom's symbolic value but ultimately do not pursue the repertoire with the long-term goal of becoming professionals or maqom masters.

The State of Maqom Transmission in New York

Although older Bukharian Jewish classical stars have found high-profile homes for their maqom ensembles in the United States, maqom has moved into a limited cultural heritage after-school enrichment space for younger musicians. It is crucial to remember that participation of Bukharian Jews in the Shashmaqom is intrinsically related to their role as professional musicians. Dwindling audiences, lack of significant patronage and sponsorship, disappearing knowledge of Tajik Persian, and an absence of opportunities for monetary rewards have all made the role of "professional master of Central Asian classical music" tenuous in the United States. As Roshel Aminov glumly (and accurately) put it, in the United States, "there's no money for music—only for war." Students in New York have almost no time to study this difficult repertoire, nor any real opportunities for practicing it in the long term.

As Roshel Rubinov explained,

> That [the time of the serious hofizes] was a previous time. Today it's become a different world. Today everything's changed. One singer comes, he puts on a minidisc, plays it back, learns maybe two or three songs, and everybody says, "Oh, he's a good singer, a very fantastic singer." Maybe he can sing one octave, [he has a] small

voice but a microphone—today is different. ... Because there isn't the extended periods of time today to study Shashmaqom, and here, people don't really want it.

Other maqomists have complained about a general lowering of standards. Roshel Aminov explained that the art of incorporating the precomposed variations called *namud*-s ("appearances") into a performance, the hallmark of a true expert hofiz, has been lost (on namuds, see Karamatov and Radjabov 1981).

To master maqom and become a great hofiz requires a tremendous amount of dedication and effort. With respect just to poetry, one of Roshel Rubinov's poetry teachers, Professor Abubakr Zuhuriddinov of the Mirza Tursunzoda Institute, told him, "every hofiz must know at least a hundred ghazals to a hundred rubo'is" (Rubinov 2002:7). When I asked him about this, he explained:

> Ghazals as well as rubo'is. Minimum, you must know one hundred ghazals minimum, one hundred rubo'is minimum. For one hundred situations, different situations. Different situations. When you are a singer, your level must be a little bit higher than that of regular people. Everybody will sit with you and talk with you, so you have to show your level.... Sometimes they will make you give a speech for the memorial day [i.e., anniversary of someone's death], something. You have to know these things by heart.
>   ... It is necessary to become a wise (*purdon*, lit. "full of knowledge") hofiz. *Purdon*. Do you know what it means, "purdon"? *"Yak khel odamon purdon, yak khel odamon nodon"* ["One kind of person is wise, one kind of person is ignorant"].[41] Purdon means you must be smart. Ignorant people are everywhere. They don't know what to do, they don't know even one ghazal or one rubo'i, they don't know how to learn.

One attempt to institutionalize maqom transmission in New York is the Traditional School of Bukharian and Shashmaqom Music, established by Roshel Aminov in honor of his father, Neryo Aminov, one of the most esteemed maqomists of the Soviet era, a noted composer, and a teacher at the conservatory in Tajikistan. The school is based on the sixth floor of the Queens Gymnasia, a Bukharian Jewish day school funded by Lev Leviev, the Bukharian Jewish billionaire diamond magnate now living in London. Aminov's school is symbolic for the Bukharian Jewish community, and public concerts of his students are well attended. At the school, the Shashmaqom repertoire is taught primarily in small classes, by rote, with Aminov singing and performing one line of poetry at a time, repeated by the students (see Figure 3.11). The only notations used are poetic texts, as is common practice among Bukharian Jews; students are not taught to read music. Thus, although the students are taught in a group class setting, the method of transmission is akin to that of a traditional ustoz-shogird

Figure 3.11. Roshel Aminov teaching a music class. Photos by the author.

system. I studied at Roshel Aminov's school too, but only in a one-on-one situation.

The repertoire taught at Aminov's academy is typical of the small heterogeneous repertoire played by contemporary maqom ensembles in New York, a combination of Shashmaqom, classical songs by composers (such as his father's "Ba Guliston"), khalqī music ("Chuli Iroq"), and lighter "folklore" (such as "Mahvashi Nozuk" and "Shastu Shastu Chor"). When I studied with him, I learned "Savti Navo" (from the Shashmaqom) and "Chuli Iroq." He typically teaches "Sarakhbori Navo" to the group classes as an introduction to the Shashmaqom.

The concert programs he presents also reflect standard New York maqom practice, with a variety of maqom selections performed individually, rather than organized in suites. The young students perform one or two maqom compositions ("Sarakhbori Navo," "Zulfi Pareshon") along-side features by Ezro Malakov, Tamara Katayeva, and Roshel Aminov's own ensemble. The recitals focus on ideas of transmission and self-representation, reinforcing maqom's symbolic importance to the community, and the sense that Bukharian youth are learning their heritage music.

At a book launch for Aminov's collection of classical Persian poems, *Sitorarezhoi adab* (2011), Aminov's student Virginia Zavolunova gave a speech in English that excellently expressed the role of Aminov's academy:

> Hi, my name is Virginia, I'm a student of Mr. Roshel Aminov and I've been going to him ever since I was maybe 14, and I'm 20 now, so a while it has been going on. We learned a few songs and he teaches me Bukharian, the Bukharian language, it is the traditional language of my culture. I was born in Dushanbe, Tajikistan, and I came here after immigrating first to Austria, Vienna, and it's been hard for me to learn the language that my parents speak, so Roshel Aminov has been teaching me these songs as a way to link my barrier between English, Russian, and Bukharian....
>
> Thank you to Roshel Aminov. He helped me to give me more respect for my culture, to kind of connect back with my culture. I love the songs that we sing in folklore. It's very emotional, and through this emotion I can feel the words, and with the words I can understand a little bit of the context of this language.

Like Virginia, most of Aminov's students learn only a handful of maqom compositions. The students are not there at all to become professional maqomists; indeed, I did not find any children or parents interested in such a path, which would be untenable in the United States. Their time in the Shashmaqom academy is a relatively short-term investment in order for them, as Americans becoming quite removed from the Central Asian milieu of their parents, to learn some of their heritage music and become more aware of Bukharian Jewish culture. Aminov's school is analogous to Bukharian heritage institutions for other aspects of culture, such as Malika Kalontarova's dance school, where mostly young girls learn a small repertoire of standardized "folk" dances, and Imonuel Rybakov's "Bukharian Jewish language" classes. Younger musicians are pursuing other professional routes, as is natural, without any significant support for maqom in the United States.

Roshel Rubinov expressed concern over the state of maqom transmission during my lessons. Rubinov graciously taught me but rightly identified that our ustoz-shogird relationship, at least in terms of tanbūr technique and maqom repertoire, was for a limited time. He noted that he needed a Bukharian student, who held maqom "close to his heart." During the period while I was taking lessons, he did begin teaching some students from the community, but for them too, demands on time and the limited opportunities for maqom performance constrained their interactions. But because of maqom's pride of place in the Bukharian Jewish community, Rubinov and others are working to find solutions for invigorating and continuing the tradition for the community's future.

Updating the Classical Repertoire

Maqom among Bukharian Jews in New York now lies at the nexus of two conditions: increased opportunities to showcase maqom as an international "world music" and the waning role of maqom within the community. At this crossroads stand individuals who are committed to the maqom repertoire and the Bukharian Jewish role in it, but who also make their living as professional musicians in the community. Two of these figures, Roshel Rubinov and Avrom Tolmasov, straddle the two worlds of Soviet Central Asia and the United States.[42] They both grew up and studied music in Soviet Central Asia. Having learned from the masters of the previous generation, they brought to the United States a sense of maqom's importance and a thorough, complete understanding of the classical repertoire. Yet they are also young enough that they think about their American careers in the long term, and they are keenly aware of their role as inheriting the mantle of the high-status position of Bukharian hofiz. They shared the role of Levi in *Levicha Hofiz*—Rubinov as the young Levi and Tolmasov as the mature Levi—capturing their symbolic importance in the community and the expectation that they will carry the torch. Rubinov and Tolmasov take their roles seriously, and they continually search for ways to update and adapt the maqom repertoire to keep the traditional viable for the multigenerational diasporic population in Queens.

Rubinov and Tolmasov work constantly, playing weddings, bar mitzvah celebrations, and community events. While I was studying tanbūr with Rubinov, he would often work five nights a week. They intimately know the wedding scene and the community's needs and desires. They are deeply committed to the maqom repertoire, but they wrestle with the questions of when to play maqom and how much to play. As professional musicians, Rubinov and Tolmasov must usually be judicious with maqom at a wedding. Avrom Tolmasov commented that this dilemma is hardly unique to Bukharian Jews:

> It's not easy to play a tūī. It's hard. Because there's five hundred people there. Five hundred, many people, each one wants to hear something different. Today people don't sing these songs that people don't understand. Every nationality (*milla*) has their classic music, but today people don't listen to it. Iranians [also] don't listen to it, they don't understand their true [or spiritual] music (*muzykai haqqiqa*).... Eighty percent don't understand classic music (*muzyka klasik*).

Roshel Aminov remembered a golden age in 1960s Tajikistan, of a wedding where hundreds of knowledgable listeners sat in rapt attention while a small ensemble of his father, him, and his brother sang nothing but maqom with just tanbūr and doira. But such a scene is a far cry from contemporary New York. I asked Roshel Rubinov the possibility of such a wedding today. He told me, "You want to play a wedding with just one tanbūr and one doira? Good luck to you! … They'll say, 'get out of here, what are you doing here?'" Another day he elaborated further:

RR: Today, people don't really study Shashmaqom. People here don't really want it. They want pop music; they want to dance. Today everything is completely changed. [An older person born in Central Asia might come to the party and] ask me, please, sing one song, … Uzbek song, Tajik song, Bukharian song.[43] … Listen to me. I'm a businessman. I see two hundred people, young people, young guys—for one [person] I'm going to lose two hundred customers? What do you think?!? I'm very smart … I know what to do. I tell him, "all right, wait, I'll sing"—

ER: —Near the end.

RR: Near the end, if I have room, if it's possible, three or four minutes, "for this guest, for Evan Rapport, God bless him, 'Sayora' [a classic Uzbek lyric song]." You know?

ER: Do only old people want it?

RR: They understand, they want it, they listen to it, but not only old people. People that grew up over there. Those that were born in Uzbekistan, Tajikistan, they like this music, maybe they're about 40 years old, 50 years old, 45 and up, people from Samarqand, Bukhara, Shahrisabz, Navoi, Kattakurgan[44]…

ER: At a tūī, pop songs for dancing are the most popular?

RR: Yes, for young people. Sometimes we play a party, like a wife and husband that are 60 or 70 years old, nice people, we'll play differently, all Bukharian songs, classic songs, Shashmaqom.

A young maqom enthusiast and an aspiring singer, Yosef Munarov, commented on the state of maqom among his generation. For him, maqom is fading because it has associations with serious or sad events, and because young people are losing the ability to understand the Persian poetry:

Maybe this is only going to last two more generations, maybe all this maqom stuff will disappear. In New York, not in Uzbekistan. But even in Uzbekistan, it's the same thing. Maqom is more or less older. You won't hear a tanbūr or tor playing in a restaurant. We're losing a lot. We like [maqom], but people don't like to hear it. They say, "why are you singing this, we're not at a cemetery right now, you're crying." When you sing maqom, it's more calm music. If you want to remember bad things, it makes you remember your Mom who passed away and things like that. So younger people don't want to hear that. They say, "stop singing that." But they're saying that because they don't understand the words.... Even though I understand Bukharian, it's sometimes very hard for me to understand because it's poetry.... I try to explain this to my friends who don't understand poetry. I think if they understood, they'd enjoy it, but because they don't understand, they hate it. I think that if they understood it they would like it.

In order to address the current situation, Tolmasov, Rubinov, and some other musicians have adopted certain strategies for keeping the maqom repertoire vibrant and a living tradition. These include writing new poems and melodies, making novel settings of preexisting poems and melodies, changing instrumentation, and creating new arrangements of traditional tunes. Such innovations are especially important, as locally supported performance contexts have proven to be more reliable than the government-funded or institutionally supported world music opportunities on mainstream stages, especially after Ilyos Mallayev's death. Projects such as *At the Bazaar of Love* require great time and effort with little financial reward, while Bukharian Jewish celebrations and the local cottage industry of CDs help sustain the immigrant musicians' livelihoods. Furthermore, updating the maqom repertoire pushes Rubinov, Tolmasov, and other musicians to the best of their abilities and satisfies their desire to constantly grow as artists. Rubinov reserved his harshest criticisms for those that he felt "only copied," "just repeated," or imitated without putting their own stamp on the repertoire, and he constantly stressed to me the importance of an artist finding his or her own path.

A straightforward form of updating is to alter instrumentation. The tor, clarinet, and accordion were already adopted for maqom performance in Central Asia. In New York, instead of tanbūr, contemporary maqomists may favor the guitar; however, the guitar is played in an adaptation of tanbūr technique, with melodies played on one string and the use of similar types of ornamentation. The doira has remained a very popular instrument, and musicians have added more drum solos and opportunities for flashy technique. Groups have added percussion, including the davul, darabukka, and electronic drum samples. Keyboards figure prominently, mirroring the guitar or other melody instrument, or in a departure from the older Central Asian style, superimposing some chordal harmony. Indian instruments are popular with Bukharian musicians; Ilyos Mallayev and Avrom Tolmasov both used the Indian sitar for maqom and Roshel Aminov has experimented with the sarangi.

On the subject of composing a new arrangement, Rubinov explained about "Tamanno," a ghazal by Ilyos Mallayev that he set to a classic melody:

It's the same music, but a new arrangement. A new arrangement, a new style. Something new. People need something new for their ears. You know, all the time, it's the old style, tanbūr, doira, now young people need something new. With keyboard, guitar, and clarinet, if you play classic music they are going to listen. If you play all the time with one tanbūr and one doira, they'll say, "get out of here." That's why I change.

Rubinov's album *Pesni Moeĭ Dushi* ("Songs of My Soul," 2007) exemplifies his approach to new arrangements, featuring a variety of maqom melodies (Shashmaqom, Chormaqom, lyric songs, and new compositions) performed with chordal keyboard accompaniment, electronic percussion arrangements, synthesized flute, violin, and contemporary production values. His arrangement of "Soqinomai Bayot" (Audio Example 3.5🔊) uses a classical poem by Navoi (in Chaghatay), the traditional melody (from the Chormaqom, not the Shashmaqom), and the standard 4/4 *soqinoma* rhythm, but with interspersed contrapuntal melodies and a bass line that implies harmonization. Although the bass line largely mirrors the melody, the couplets often begin with a I chord in first inversion and they resolve with a V–I authentic cadence. Near the end of the arrangement, the entire ensemble modulates to the IV chord for a couplet, and transitions back to the original tonic over the course of the next couplet. The end brings a surprise change in rhythm as part of the final descent (*furovard*).

The composition of new poetry is another important starting point for innovation. Ilyos Mallayev's poems have provided Bukharian maqomists with a fount of new material, and as mentioned with respect to *At the Bazaar of Love*, Mallayev himself set these poems to preexisting maqom melodies. Mikhoel Zavul's poems have also been set and entered into the maqom repertoire. Roshel Rubinov is exceptional among the younger performers in that he has followed in Mallayev's footsteps, composing and setting new poetry in classic meters. Ochil Ibragimov's album *Ohangi Dil* ("Heart Song," 2008) contains a number of maqom melodies with poems by these three Bukharian poets. For two examples of Shashmaqom melodies, "Talqinchai Savti Kalon" provides the basis for one Mikhoel Zavul's poems, and "Navruzi Ajam" for one of Roshel Rubinov's. Avrom Tolmasov's *Giriya* (1997) includes a setting of Mallayev's "Ohista, Ohista" (Slowly, Slowly) to "Chapandozi Ushshoq" from Maqom Navo.

Not only are new poems by Bukharian poets in classic Persian ʿarūz meters, but they are suitable for maqom settings because they teach morals and tackle spiritual and elevated themes. To briefly discuss two of Rubinov's poems, in "Panj Panja Barobar Nest" ("The five fingers are not the same"), for example, Rubinov extols those who do not compromise their integrity in exchange for bribes or favors with the line "I never eat a meal out of obligation" (*az oshi puri minnat hargiz nakhuram albat*), explaining that it is preferable to live simply and humbly, "It's better I eat bread and water" (*behtar bari man yavghon*). He praises those who refrain from gossiping and speaking too freely, writing, "Silence is golden and blabbing is feeble-minded" (*Khomushī adab astu purgūī kamaqlī ast*). He reminds people of their brief time on earth, explaining, "Everyone in the world is a guest, God is the host" (*hama ba jahon mehmon / kholiq ba jahon mezbon*). In his "Har Kas Ba Khud Ovora" ("Everyone is busy with themselves"), he decries the way people run around losing their way, worrying and being dissatisfied, without ever resting and taking time for the important things in life.

Because Rubinov composes his poems in classical forms and meters, he can successfully set them to a variety of preexisting melodies. He set his poem "Pedar," for example, to a melody by the Uzbek singer and composer Fattakhon Mamadaliyev. "Panj Panja Barobar Nest" is a ghazal written in the classic meter *hazaji musammani akhrab* ($--\cup\mid\cup---\mid--\cup\mid\cup---$), and a setting to a new melody composed by Tolmasov (Audio Example 3.6◓) has entered the maqom repertoire. The recording features clarinet, doira, guitar, and keyboard, and in between couplets of the ghazal, the instruments provide flourishes and brief improvisations. Production values are also crucial for updating maqom, and as is evident on this recording, almost all contemporary recordings employ audible studio elements, such as reverb and echo. Through explicit studio sounds, Bukharian Jews represent maqom as adaptable to technological innovation. Similarly, as discussed in contrast to *At the Bazaar of Love*, maqomists represent themselves in suits and urban settings on the covers of their locally produced recordings.

The changing circumstances of immigration have resulted in another notable change: young women are notably absent from contemporary maqom recordings and performances. The pressures of balancing life and career have always been especially strong for female musicians; Tamara Katayeva, for example, remarked to me that she put her career on hold while she raised her children. In New York, women face the same difficulties as men in pursuing a career in maqom, in that it requires a great amount of training and investment, along with the fact that the United States presents an unprecedented situation for female educational advancement, job opportunity, and occupational mobility. Women have the extra challenge in that religious authorities in New York have dissuaded the Bukharian community from having female performers entertain at mixed events. As mentioned, no women performed at Carnegie Hall in 2011 for a high-profile tribute to Turgun Alimatov that featured Bukharian Jews and Uzbek musicians from Central Asia. I have personally only met one young woman, Virginia Zavolunova, who has spent time studying maqom with Roshel Aminov, but like other students of his, she was learning a few songs as a way to connect to her heritage, and not as a career choice.

* * *

The maqom repertoire has remained a touchstone for Bukharian Jews in New York. Immigration has presented serious challenges to the continued development of the maqom tradition among the Bukharian community, but the roles of maqom and the hofiz as cultural symbols and defining points of pride for the Bukharian community have made maqom a resilient and useful repertoire. The innovations of musicians such as Roshel Rubinov and Avrom Tolmasov have allowed maqom to remain a viable option for professional musicians, a vital part of Bukharian life supported by the people. New poetry, new arrangements and settings, and even completely new compositions have entered the maqom repertoire, in response to demands and desires of Bukharian audiences.

While intracommunity developments are the most essential pieces in the continued growth of maqom as a living tradition among Bukharian Jews, mainstream opportunities have proven to be tremendously effective. World music stages, multicultural initiatives, and folklore programs of the Center for Traditional Music and Dance and other institutions continue to be important. Externally generated circumstances for maqom performance can exert profound influence on the choices of professional musicians and the approaches they take to performing, teaching, and otherwise engaging the repertoire.

In New York's multicultural landscape, maqom and its hofizes have served as the community's representatives and emissaries. Bukharian Jews responded to the pressures of multiculturalism by drawing on their historical attachment to maqom as well as their persistent outsider status, both of which have become professional assets to the immigrant musicians finding their place in the American multicultural landscape. Yet while maqom has great symbolic meaning, it does not express or represent the gamut of the contemporary Bukharian Jewish American experience. To understand the Bukharian Jewish community's attitudes regarding Judaism and Jewish life, as well as the cosmopolitanism that best captures the community's self-image, we must now turn to the religious and party repertoires.

4

Religious Repertoire

"Like Mushrooms after the Rain"

First of all, America is a *free* country (*davlati free*). Whatever one
wants to do, to write—if one wants to study Torah, if one wants to
take religion and piety seriously, the government permits it. It is
free here. I wanted to study Torah and to master ḥazzanut ... to do
it out in the open. *We came here for this,* from the difficult political
situation in the Soviet Union. For me, this is a very good place. The
American people are not opposed to me doing all of this religious
work.... In Uzbekistan [religion] was in secret. We didn't show it,
we had fear. It was difficult. We did all of these things in secret. We
were scared, so we did things in the houses. No one saw or spoke
because we were scared.

—Ezro Malakov

For Ezro Malakov, religious freedom and the lack of anti-Semitism in
the United States are the essential keys to understanding the emigration of Bukharian Jews following "2,000 years" of life in Central Asia. The
community's growth and the importance of religion and religious institutions are immediately apparent in the numerous synagogues for Bukharian
Jews in Queens. In New York, Bukharian synagogues are proliferating
"like mushrooms after the rain," according to Ochil Ibragimov. In addition
to many smaller synagogues, two major Bukharian congregations emerged
after en masse immigration. Congregation Beth Gavriel on 108th Street
was established in 1996, and the impressive Bukharian Jewish Community
Center building opened in 2005 near the 71st St.-Continental Ave. hub in
Forest Hills. Bukharians have also revitalized synagogues such as Tifereth
Israel in East Elmhurst and are worshipping in congregations

established by other communities, such as broadly Sephardic synagogues and nearby Iranian Jewish congregations.

Ochil continued, connecting the explosion of Bukharian religious institutions to the now familiar theme of Jewish community life separate and out of the public sphere. Like Ezro Malakov, Ochil underscored the necessity of hiding Jewish practice during the Soviet era.

> Every year, there's a new synagogue. Thank God, people are coming back to our religion. In the Soviet Union, there was no God, in Russia. In kindergarten, from the beginning, they cut religion from our minds. But our Bukharian people, they took two ways. At home is the religion. Not Orthodox, but they know the tradition. Mother lights the candles, Father makes kiddush on Shabbat, the children see. But going to kindergarten, [they say] "yes, yes, no God, right." *Two ways.* At home, they wear a kipah around the home.... But in New York, mostly the young generation, 25 years old, 30 years old, all of them come to religion.

The public/private dichotomy remains salient in that Jewish religious repertoire has stayed in the synagogue and internal community settings while maqom continues to be the public repertoire of choice. However, newfound religious freedom in the United States and the tenets of American multiculturalism have dramatically shifted the role that Jewish religious music plays in defining Bukharian identity. Now out in the open, Bukharian religious music is undergoing tremendous change as Bukharians infuse their traditions with stylistic variety and innovation. At the same time, the fears of assimilation and loss accompanying immigration have sparked a preservational and reconstructive impulse, with religious repertoire acquiring explicitly ethnic and nationalist associations.

Religious repertoire is arguably the most dynamic area of expression for Bukharian Jewish men. Religious music has in many ways become more restricted for women, revealing some complexities of the concept of "freedom." The freedom to do "whatever one wants to do" is contingent upon one's relation to the community's more general adaptations and adjustments. It should be noted that freedom and restriction are not mutually exclusive. In the case of many religious Bukharian Jews (of any gender), freedom means the ability to choose what restrictions one places on oneself, from dietary laws to gender-specific limitations.

Closest to some of the Bukharian Jewish community's highest priorities, Bukharian religious music is the most intense embodiment of the many complex relationships between Bukharian Jews and other Jewish communities. More than maqom or the party repertoire, Bukharian Jewish religious music reflects the Jewish intracultural dilemmas facing Bukharian Jews after immigration, especially the competing pressures of (1) integration as part of a singular Jewish people, which often requires abandoning or changing familiar Bukharian ways and (2) developing distinctiveness in order to thrive in a Jewish multiculturalist atmosphere.

Defining the Religious Repertoire

In the simplest terms, religious repertoire refers to the singing of specifically Jewish texts. Unlike the texts of the maqom and party repertoires, these texts are not shared with non-Jewish neighbors. Jewish texts include Hebrew texts from the Bible (*Tanakh*), Aramaic texts from the Zohar, and other Hebrew or Aramaic liturgical and paraliturgical texts such as the poems called *piyyutim*. Bukharian Jews also use Persian translations of any of these, and they have a distinct repertoire of texts on specifically Jewish themes in Hebrew, Persian, or both languages, set to maqom melodies. These settings, part of the wider repertoire simply called *shiro* (Heb. "song," "singing"), are especially noteworthy because they combine the serious qualities of both the maqom and religious repertoires within an exclusively Bukharian Jewish area of creativity.

Religious repertoire performances tend to be restricted to internal community events. Liturgical texts are usually sung in the synagogue and paraliturgical texts are performed for specific holidays, sacred meals, weddings, funerals, and other religious occasions. Since the fall of the Soviet Union, recordings have also become a major outlet for religious repertoire. The context determines the performance style, which is wide ranging in the case of religious repertoire: a cappella synagogue singing, maqom styles played on tanbūr and doira, and the use of upbeat dance rhythms and wedding-band instrumentation.

Religious repertoire is a male-dominated area of performance. Although individuals practice varying levels of observance, on a general community level Bukharian Jews today adhere to the codes of international Orthodox Judaism, which prohibits men from hearing women's voices according to rabbinic dicta generally referred to as *qōl ishāh* ("woman's voice"), first established in the sixth century but debated and variously interpreted over the centuries (for a historical overview of qōl ishāh, see Koskoff 2001:126–34). Before emigration, Bukharian Jewish women had more opportunities to perform religious repertoire in mixed or public settings, and women's singing is a volatile post-immigration issue. Women's repertoires are performed at women-only events, such as women's parties after the late Saturday night meal on a Shabbat associated with a wedding, when the singers and performers teach the bride values and help prepare her for her new life. Women also sing at Rosh Ḥodesh (new moon) gatherings, or at occasional women's parties organized at the synagogues, such as the Mother's Day party held at Beth Gavriel.[1]

The Reform, Conservative, and Reconstructionist movements have not made significant inroads to Bukharian Jewish life. Originally developed in Europe and North America by Ashkenazic Jews, these varieties of Jewish practice were unknown in Central Asia. These forms of Judaism all differ greatly from Orthodox Judaism in their approach to prayer structure, the Hebrew language, the use of musical instruments, and above all, their approach to the sexes, as they permit women and men to sit together, and allow women to participate as prayer leaders and singers in mixed environments. Orthodox Judaism per se is also a European and North American invention, originally a response to secularization trends, the Jewish Enlightenment (*haskalah*) and Reform movement in Central Europe (Silber 1992; Gilman 2006:55–56), but it mapped most closely to Bukharian Jewish practice. In New York, Bukharian Jews generally view non-Orthodox varieties of Judaism as agents and symbols of assimilation. The self-conscious rejection of these forms of "assimiliation," so unlike the rapid embrace of these forms by earlier Jewish Americans, underscores the impact of multiculturalist ideas that encourage separateness and distinctiveness. I did meet one younger Bukharian man during my research who told me that he had recently started attending a Reform or Conservative synagogue in Manhattan, saying that he preferred its mixed gender choir. He also asked me not to tell anyone, demonstrating that he recognized it would be regarded as a rejection of Bukharian values.

Synagogue Styles and Roles

Beth Gavriel Synagogue was established in 1996 to accommodate the expanding Bukharian Jewish population in and around Forest Hills. Located on 108th Street, "Bukharian Broadway," Beth Gavriel typically serves over five hundred worshippers on Saturday (about 350 adults and 150 in youth services). Especially on Saturday morning and major holidays, Beth Gavriel is a central meeting place for Bukharian Jews to worship together, socialize, and catch up on important community matters. Ezro Malakov serves as Beth Gavriel's ḥazzan alongside Daniel Pinḥasov and Rabbi Imonuel Shimonov, helping congregants participate in one of the most vibrant forms of their community's spiritual life.

At Beth Gavriel, as at every other Bukharian synagogue, repertoire is performed a cappella, by men, following standard Orthodox Jewish practice. Ideally, Jewish prayer takes place communally, with a quorum of at least ten men over the age of thirteen (a *minyan*). Orthodox interpretation of Jewish law prohibits the playing of instruments on the Sabbath, Rosh Hashanah, Yom Kippur, fast days, and certain other holidays. The prohibition against instruments squares well with the Bukharian definition of *muzyka* ("music"), which refers to the use of instruments; a cappella singing is described as *be muzyka*, or "without music." Women attend services, especially on Saturday morning, but they sit apart from the men in a dedicated section and do not sing. At Beth Gavriel or other small synagogues, a screen (*meḥitsah* or *parda*) is used to separate the men from the women; at larger synagogues, such as the Bukharian Jewish Community Center, women sit in a balcony above and behind the main area.

The service is a common structure that links Jews throughout the diaspora, the "one prayer" of Roshel Aminov's "one God, one prayer, one Hebrew language" definition of the Jewish people. There are three obligatory daily services for Jews: morning (*Shaḥarit*), afternoon (*Minḥo* [*Minḥāh*]), and evening (*'Aravit* [*'Arvit*]), and the basic structure of worship is the same throughout the entire Jewish world. The central prayer for each is the *Amida* ("standing"), also called the *Shemoneh 'Esreh* ("Eighteen [Benedictions]") or just *tfilo* (*tefillāh*, "prayer").[2] Biblical passages and later expansions precede and follow the Amida. Shaḥarit services start with morning benedictions and the "verses of song" (a collection of Psalms, other biblical passages, and poems), which serve as a warm-up for the central points that follow: the *Shema* (Deuteronomy 6:4–9, 11:13–21, and Numbers 15:37–41) and its benedictions, and the Amida. The Amida is first performed silently, or almost silently, by those present (it is required of the men), and then repeated by one or more of the prayer leaders on behalf of the congregation as a whole and for those who might not be able to perform the prayer properly. After the Amida on certain days there is a Torah reading. More prayers end the service as a mirror image of sorts to the opening "verses of song." Different forms of the Aramaic *Qaddish*, the "Call to Worship," and various biblical passages and hymns serve as transitions or introductions.

The overall structure of the service is subject to changes, adjustments, and variations. Services for some days, especially major holidays, are lengthened by adding prayers and selections to the core structure, or an additional service (called *musaf*). On Friday night, the beginning of the Sabbath, the Minḥo and 'Aravit services are connected with a special section of Psalms and songs called *Qabbalat Shabbat*, a custom started in the seventeenth century by Rabbi Isaac Luria and the mystics of Safed (Summit 2000:28–31). Other changes are determined according to the time of day; for example, in the Minḥo service, the Shema is not recited. The service might have variations in the sequence of particular items or in non-obligatory (but still standard) sections, depending on the rite that the congregation uses.

The most well-attended weekly service at Beth Gavriel is the Shaḥarit service on Saturday morning, which features the Torah reading, preceded by the opening of the Ark (which holds the scrolls) and a procession. At Bukharian and Sephardic synagogues, the Ark is in or against a wall while the reading takes place from the *bimah* (pulpit) in the center of the room (in Ashkenazic synagogues, the bimah and the Ark are both in front of the congregation). The room fills with a chaotic and electric excitement when the Torah is removed, as congregants get as close to the Ark as possible when it is opened and cluster around the Torah, touching it during the procession. Before the Torah is read, the screen dividing the women's section is raised, and many women make a sweeping motion with their arms toward their eyes. Once the Torah reading begins, the screen is lowered.

The *gabbai* (beadle) of the congregation announces each person called to bless the Torah. The honoree's time on the pulpit is an opportunity for him to have blessings said for specific people, and sometimes he will himself announce the ones in the congregation he wishes to honor—typically, he will announce families ("mishpaḥat Malakov, mishpaḥat Elishayev, mishpaḥat Abramov") and then extend his blessing to "kol ha-keniso" ("the whole synagogue"). He blesses the Torah while touching his prayer shawl to the Torah's case. Following the blessing, someone trained in cantillation lifts the fabric covering the words of the Torah and chants a section of the weekly portion. The fabric is replaced, the Torah is blessed again, and more prayers are said for the honoree, at which point he sits on the pulpit until after the next blessing. On his way back to his seat, congregants shake hands with him and acknowledge his honor.

At Beth Gavriel an auction for various honors (in Persian, Hebrew, and English), led by a respected community member named Mullo Avrom, precedes the Torah reading. When one successfully bids on an honor, he is blessed by Mullo Avrom, the rabbi, Ezro Malakov or another ḥazzan, or any combination of the above. The auction is one of the more controversial parts of the service, reflecting divergent opinions about assimilation and adaptation. Although auctioning honors is a widespread practice among Jews, in many "American" congregations donations are made in private and some Bukharian Jews have remarked that they are uncomfortable with the conspicuous nature of the donations. Others say "it goes on too long" or "at that synagogue, it's always money, money, money." Still others think the money, or at least some of the money, should be spent on other things for the community. However, most appreciate the public auction for two reasons. First, the public nature of the donation seems to encourage people, especially wealthy people, to give more, as it reflects well on their prestige if they give and looks bad if they do not. And second, it provides additional opportunities for blessings by the rabbi or ḥazzan, which Bukharian Jews greatly value.

The auction is followed by a sermon (*sukhan*), given by the rabbi in Tajik Persian and related to topics presented in the current Torah portion. Other individuals may also be invited to give speeches; many of these will be in Russian. Rabbi Shimonov's decision to give the sermon in "Bukharian" adds to Beth Gavriel's reputation as a synagogue strongly invested in Bukharian tradition. At the Bukharian Jewish Community Center, where Rabbi Yitshak Yehoshua presided until 2010, sermons are in English. Younger congregants at both Beth Gavriel and the Bukharian Jewish Community Center often do not understand Persian.

Performance styles in the synagogue run the gamut from repetitive melodies sung in rousing collective sing-alongs to barely audible murmuring and loud, spoken recitations. Whereas Jewish congregations vary little in their core approach to texts and structure, melodies are extremely varied and diverse. Textual homogeneity and musical heterogeneity reflect the two currents or paradigms in Jewish life: toward unity and centrality (texts), and toward a recognition of cultural diversity (melodies).

Worship performance styles include *nusaḥ* (Heb. "style," "version," "manner"), *nigunim*, and *ḥazzanut*. Jews worldwide use the term *nusaḥ* to capture the understanding that music is distinct from community to community, congregation to congregation, and even person to person; Bukharian Jews much more frequently use the term *roh* or *tavr* ("way," "path"). (Following Bukharian parlance, I use the English word "way," which captures roh and tavr.) In the Bukharian Jewish lexicon, the terms *nusah, roh,* and *tavr* overlap with *nigunim* (or sometimes *pizmonim*), the word for "melodies." In much the same way that Bukharian Jews understand maqom in terms of specific melodies rather than springboards for improvisation, Bukharian Jews think of religious performance styles as melodies and not as modal improvisations. *Hazzanut* is an expert rendition, by the ḥazzan, of any of the prayer styles.

The simplest performance styles in the Bukharian Jewish way are melody types combined with various cadential formulas. Audio Example 4.1◐ is an example of Menaḥem Malakov performing the Borukh She'omar prayer in an example of a foundational Bukharian "simple melodic recitation on few notes without much melodic elaboration" (Frigyesi 2002:122), the way it might be chanted on Saturday morning. In this style, the ḥazzan or prayer leader chants most of the prayer on a single tone, emphasizing certain syllables with dynamic contrasts and by moving to a different tone, usually a half-step up. Cadential patterns mark the ends of phrases. Certain syllables or passages (such as the first "Borukh Ato Adonai") are treated with more melodic variation.

On well-attended occasions, liturgical and paraliturgical texts are typically treated with more elaborate versions of the recitational style heard in Menaḥem Malakov's rendition of Borukh She'omar, or as "quasi-strophic" (Frigyesi 2002:122) melody types with a strong overall melodic outline. Singers subject these melody types to variation, treating them as foundational melodic contours and guides for cadential phrase endings. The amount of variation depends on the ability of the singer and performance context: a ḥazzan on a major holiday might use the melody type as a basis for tremendous elaboration and proceed through two octaves, while an average singer may stick to an ambitus of a fifth to one octave, repeating the melody type in the quasi-strophic style with little elaboration over the course of the performance. Even though the melodic formulas can be rearranged, applied to different words from version to version, or treated with various amounts of ornamentation and elaboration, Bukharian singers describe these melody types as specific melodies that are "the same" from performance to performance. Example 4.1 compares two performances of a common melody type and cadential formula, used by Moshe Leviyev for the piyyut "Khudovando (Goali, Goali)" and by Ezro Malakov for Israel Najara's piyyut "Yo Ribun Olam" (Malakov's performance is transposed for comparative purposes). Although these two poems are paraliturgical texts, the melody type appears in liturgical situations as well.

Prayer styles also reflect regional differences within communities. In New York, Bukharian Jews from different cities sometimes worship side by side, and sometimes congregate in synagogues where they are surrounded by the people and melodies from their homes. Example 4.2 shows Ochil Ibragimov's demonstration of the slight differences in the Shahrisabz and Bukhara melody types for the opening of the "Nishmat" prayer.

In fact, every individual can be said to have a specific way, and the combination of each individual's style in a true heterophonic texture is a hallmark of synagogue performance.

Example 4.1. Comparison of "Khudovando" and "Yo Ribun Olam" melody types. Transcribed by the author.

Example 4.2. Ochil Ibragimov, comparison of Nishmat according to Shahrisabz and Bukhara ways. Transcribed by the author.

The ḥazzan, or singer of ḥazzanut, is a crucial figure in the synagogue. However, strictly speaking, a ḥazzan is an extra element in Jewish worship, as it is the obligation of every Jewish male over the age of thirteen to perform the central Jewish prayers, in a quorum of at least ten (a minyan). The ḥazzan is a grassroots-fueled role (Slobin [1989] 2002:3–8), providing a correct and aesthetically pleasing performance of the prayers, creating an enhanced worship experience for those present, and acting as a proxy for those men in attendance who are unable to perform the prayers accurately. Ochil Ibragimov and Ezro Malakov are two professional singers who are both hofiz and ḥazzan in New York, a natural move considering the tremendous growth in synagogue life and the decline in opportunities for Central Asian classical music in New York. Roshel Aminov, Roshel Rubinov, and Ilya Khavasov and other hofizes have also served as ḥazzans, and as seen in Figure 4.1, their talents are attractions for major holidays. At Beth Gavriel, Malakov specializes in certain sections of the service that the congregation likes to hear in an exceptionally loud voice with a broad range, while other portions of the service are sung by Daniel Pinḥasov

Figure 4.1. Advertisements for High Holiday services featuring Roshel Aminov, Roshel Rubinov, and other prominent singers, *Bukharian Times* weekly, 2009. Reproduced with permission.

(another ḥazzan), Simḥa Elishayev (the synagogue's sponsor), Imonuel Shimonov (the rabbi), and other congregants. The ḥazzan is also an important religious figure, role model, and community leader. Following the Jewish custom of making new meanings out of words by turning them into acronyms (a method called *notarikon*), Ibragimov described the ḥazzan as aspiring to be *ḤaZaN: ḥakham*, wise, *zaken*, sage, and *nā'im*, nice, which he elaborated as "not just a nice voice, but having a nice character."

Melody types with more virtuosic ornamentation, a wider range, and more expansive performances such as Ezro Malakov's rendition of the Nishmat prayer on Saturday morning (heard on Audio Example 4.2◐) are firmly in the sphere of ḥazzanut.[3] Over the course of a melodic treatment of a religious text, Bukharian singers slowly expand their range, climbing to a culmination (avj) and then descending, following the same contour as a piece from the Shashmaqom. In some dramatic moments of the service, such as the performance of the Nishmat prayer at Beth Gavriel, two or more lead singers will trade passages back and forth in rising tessituras until reaching the avj, culminating in a duet or trio. This singing style, reminiscent of ashulai kalon (the "great song" style), seems to be an old one in Bukharian synagogues; compare Henry Lansdell's account of a visit to a Samarqand synagogue, published in 1885 (also instructive as to the relative nature of aesthetics and taste):

> We went then to the synagogue, allowed to the Jews of Samarkand only since the Russians came, where the best chorister in the region was that evening to sing. The crowd was dense, and in a short time two singers appeared; the "*primo*," a delicate, modest-looking man, who blushed at the eagerness with which his arrival was awaited, whilst the "*secondo*" was a brazen-faced fellow, who carried his head on one side, as if courting attention, and with the assurance that he should have it. They were introduced to us, and began at once, that we might hear. The singing, so called, was the most remarkable that up to that time I had ever heard. The first voice led off in a key so high, that he had to strain for some seconds before he could utter a sound at all. After this he proceeded very slowly as to the number of words he sang, but prolonged his notes into numerous flourishes, screaming as loud as he could in falsetto. The second voice was an accompaniment for the first; but as both bawled as loudly as possible, I soon voted it anything but good music, and intimated that it was time for us to go. The congregation, moreover, were crowding round, without the smallest semblance of their being engaged in divine worship. (Lansdell 1885: 592; see also Genshtke and Vaganova 2004)

The active participation of many congregants and lay leaders alongside the guidance of ḥazzans, rabbis, and professional singers together make for a diverse amalgam of styles and melodies as congregations balance individual and collective expression in the course of performance.

Example 4.3. "Yigdal," melody sung at Beth Gavriel. Transcribed by the author.

Yig - dal E - lo-him ḥai   ve - yish - ta - baḥ   nim - tsa ve-en ʿet el   me - tsi - u - to   E -

ḥad ve - en yo-ḥid   ke - yi - ḥu - do   neʿ - lom ve-gam ein sof   le - aḥ - du - to

Example 4.4. "ʿAnenu" melody sung by Iraqi and Bukharian Jews. Transcribed by the author.

ʿA - ne____ nu   e - lo - he____ Av - ro - hom____ ʿa - ne____ nu

Although the congregation mostly proceeds with the service together, it is crucial that each worshipper be free to elaborate the melodic patterns as he sees fit, which means that individual styles cannot be legislated or forced. Congregations need to arrive at a consensus when singing responses and strophic songs. However, ḥazzans and prayer leaders do have many opportunities to display their own personal style and vision of the community's way.

Congregational performance styles also include collectively sung hymns. One example of a collective song is the "Yigdal" prayer that ends Friday night services. The tune (shown in Example 4.3) is ideal for group participation, repetitious, and in a narrow range. Most of these collective metrical tunes seem to be borrowed from other Jewish communities. One example is the "ʿAnenu" melody (Example 4.4), which is shared with Iraqi and other congregations (cf. Kartomi 2007, track one). The distinctive Bukharian Jewish melodies, especially those borrowed from the maqom repertoire for the shiro songs discussed later, are difficult to master and do not lend themselves as easily to group participation.

Religious Repertoire Outside the Synagogue Service

Music is an essential part of living a Jewish life, and Bukharian life in New York is completely organized by the Jewish calendar, Jewish law, and Jewish practice. Food choices, daily activities, and gender roles are governed by the Jewish religion. Religious repertoire is an expression of Bukharian Jewish life in the synagogue and beyond, at weddings, funerals, holiday celebrations, bar mitzvahs, and Sabbath meals, providing music for festivity and remembrance.

The primary contexts for shiro ("songs"), including Jewish texts set to maqom melodies, are celebrations and events beyond the strict standard synagogue service, where they function as paraliturgy (in the synagogue, shiro are generally sung to celebrate special events such as circumcisions or bar mitzvahs). At meals following Shabbat services on Friday night and Saturday afternoon, Bukharian Jews participate in exuberant and joyous group singing of shiro. Accompanied by vodka and traditional foods such as *osh plov*, the traditional meal for Saturday afternoon, laypeople and professional singers alike take the opportunity to express themselves with the maqom settings and other paraliturgical songs viewed as particular manifestations of Bukharian Jewish identity. Other festive holidays, such as Rosh Hashanah, Purim, and Pesaḥ (Passover), also have associated repertoire and mealtime opportunities for singing.

Simḥat Torah (Sefar Tūĭ) is perhaps the most musically celebrated holiday, featuring professional singers and instrumentalists performing at free large parties given for the entire community. This holiday is an important internal event for Bukharians to represent themselves and take stock of the community's situation. The repertoire played at the Sefar Tūĭ is diverse, comparable to the amalgam of styles and songs presented as maqom or folklore in a concert by Ensemble Maqom. The musicians combine traditional shiro for the holiday ("Simkhu No," "Halleluyo"), old and new maqom with religious or ethical texts ("Qurbon Olam," "Ushshoqi Samarqand," "Panj Panja Barobar Nest"), and new songs in a light style, such as poet Nison Niyazov's "Chi Ajab Umri Javoni" (set to "Ufori Iroqi Bukhoro") or Avrom Tolmasov's "Ajab Ajab" ("Amazing, Amazing"). Audio Example 4.3🔊, an excerpt from the 2007 party, demonstrates.[4] The track begins with Mullo Avrom completing an auction sale, followed immediately by "Simkhu No," Roshel Rubinov singing the first two stanzas and then Ezro Malakov. Mullo Avrom continues to make announcements in the instrumental breaks. The instrumentation is electric guitar and keyboard/drum machine. Mullo Avrom leads another auction, raising money for a new synagogue. The band then goes into "Halleluyo" in a 6/8 rhythm, again in alternation with the auction. Ezro Malakov, in this instance, was the winner of the auction. Rabbi Shimonov blesses him with the Priestly Benediction and a few improvised lines. Another sale is completed, and the band goes into "Ajab, Ajab," sung by Roshel Rubinov.

The range of styles and songs at the Sefar Tūĭ mirrors the kind of mixture heard over the course of Shabbat, but at even more audible extremes. A Sefar *Tūĭ*, with its *tūĭ* wedding-party atmosphere, gives musicians and participants the opportunity to perform some of the new Jewish religious repertoire finding its way onto CD recordings, with instruments and the dance rhythms typically associated with *sabuk* "light" party music. Dancing, food, and alcohol all contribute to a festive atmosphere for Bukharian Jews (again, especially men) to celebrate their religious freedom and status as proud Americans.

On the other end of the spectrum, paraliturgy plays an important role in the music of remembrance at memorial events. In addition to funerals, Bukharian Jews hold memorial events such as the *haftruz* (meal following the first week of mourning), *seruz* (meal following the first thirty days of mourning), and one-year anniversary meal, where singers sing excerpts from the Zohar and a memorial genre with Persian texts called *haqqoni* (from *haqq+khoni*, Truth/God + singing/chanting/praising). Like celebrations and Jewish prayer, mourning is both a communal and individual matter. Haftruz and seruz memorials can be well attended, and events for popular figures can draw huge crowds. Ilyos Mallayev's seruz was attended by hundreds of people.

Bukharian Jews also sing memorial songs at the cemeteries of their ancestors. Heard on Audio Example 4.4◐, at the grave of his older brother Avrom and his mother Yeshuo in Tashkent, Ezro Malakov begins with a selection from the Zohar (Potaḥ Eliyahu Hanavi, from the end of the second introduction to the Tikkunei Zohar or Tikkunim). Like Jewish prayer, the performance of haqqoni and funerary paraliturgy is communal, with a conventional and public quality to it. Stylized weeping, collective Qaddish recitation, and blessings for the participants make memorial practices group events. Skilled public mourners such as Ezro Malakov are also called upon to perform memorial genres for others. Audio Example 4.5◐ is an example of Malakov singing at a haftruz banquet held at Da Mikelle Palace in Queens on 2 May 2011.

Women's voices are notably absent from paraliturgical contexts. Public mourning used to be an important role for women called *gūyanda*, including Ezro's mother Yeshuo Borukhova. Gūyandas would sing haqqonis at the *khonagoh*, a building for worship at the cemetery. Increasingly, Bukharian rabbinic authorities have discouraged this context for women singers, as well as other paraliturgical and entertainment situations where men would hear women's voices. Even where Bukharian Jews are expanding their distinctive religious repertoires, celebrating their heritage as a group with their own culture and melodies, they have curtailed women's genres as a community in accordance with Orthodox and especially Hasidic codes.

Religious Recordings

Recordings have become an essential and fast-growing medium for religious repertoire. Ezro Malakov's *Musical Treasures of the Bukharian Jewish Community*, a monumental effort of seven CDs and accompanying notations, is but one example of the many CDs with religious content recorded and released within the Bukharian community. Commercial or produced recordings of Jewish religious music were impossible in the secretive atmosphere of the Soviet Union, explaining the explosion of creativity found on these recordings. Recordings are proving to be useful pedagogical tools and an important basis for worldwide exchange of repertoire across the Bukharian diaspora. Bukharian Jews have recorded nearly every piece of their contemporary religious repertoire, from a cappella renditions of biblical texts and paraliturgy to new settings of Jewish texts and new poems written by Bukharian poets on religious themes. And although it is extremely rare, recordings also provide one of the only contemporary circumstances for women today to participate vocally in religious expression alongside men; one example is Tamara Katayeva's performance of "Ozod kun Khudoyo" on one of the recordings of settings of Nison Niyazov's poems.

Bukharian religious recordings are unified by textual content but display a remarkable diversity of musical style, an internal expression of the general Jewish principle of textual homogeneity and musical heterogeneity. Away from the stylistic limitations and requirements of the synagogue or other sacred contexts (such as the restrictions on instruments), recordings allow musicians to exploit both heavy and light musical settings for religious texts. These recordings showcase Bukharian musicians' versatility and Bukharian audiences' appetite for variety. Often commissioned by religious institutions and given away at holiday events, recordings such as *Erets Isroel* (Beth Gavriel 2003) and *Az Qudrati Khudovand* (2003) are designed to bring the religious repertoire to a large audience.

Toward Jewish Centers

With religious repertoire, Bukharian Jews engage the twin impulses of conforming to general Jewish practice and keeping their community's culture separate and distinct. The relationships between Bukharian Jews at the margins in relation to various centers have been consistent issues in Bukharian history, the encounters or "conversations" between Bukharian Jews and various Jewish others being the main topic of Cooper's monograph (2012). The addition I wish to offer to Cooper's discussion is how these encounters manifest musically, and how Bukharian Jews strategically use marginality in a multicultural environment.

Women's Silence and Ultra-Orthodoxy

In New York, the process of integration is heavily mediated by a hierarchy in which Bukharian ways are positioned at the margins of a central authority characterized by global Hasidic and "ultra-Orthodox" customs.[5] The ultra-Orthodox Judaism that has coalesced among Ashkenazic and Sephardic rabbis in Israel, dominated by Ashkenazic ideas, has adherents among Bukharian religious authorities such as Rabbi Yitshak Yehoshua, who was born and raised in Tel Aviv, and Rabbi Imonuel Shimonov from Samarqand (Cooper 2012:187–89). The spread of Lubavitcher Hasidic ideas in particular (Habad) from their Ashkenazic roots to the entire Jewish world, including Sephardic communities and their authority figures, has had a significant reception among Bukharian Jews. Furthermore, Lubavitcher Hasidim had a presence off and on in Central Asia beginning in the 1890s, and played a significant role in Central Asian Jewish education following World War II (Ro'i 2008:71). The billionaire Lev Leviev, who supports many Bukharian educational and cultural institutions, is a follower of Habad (Chafets 2007); this becomes immediately apparent when, upon walking into the Queens Gymnasia day school Leviev supports, one is greeted by an enormous picture of Leviev staring into the eyes of "The Rebbe" (Menaham Mendel Schneerson). Many Bukharian Jews have at least a portrait of the Rebbe in their house.

The most significant musical impact of Hasidism and ultra-Orthodoxy on Bukharian Jewish religious repertoire is the silence of women, especially in the paraliturgical genres. The tensions resulting from accepting differences and general societal conformity, encapsulated here by the debates over women's voices, are more generally indicative of the friction at the limits of multiculturalism (Murphy 2012:84–95), when a community's religious laws or moral standards (such as those pertaining to circumcision rituals, dietary laws, head coverings, and freedom of speech) conflict with those of the mainstream or majority.

The *shayd ovoz* genre, now a heavily discouraged funerary practice sung by women and men with instruments, came up in a discussion between Theodore Levin and Ilyos Mallayev, as documented in *The Hundred Thousand Fools of God* (T. Levin 1996):

> "Here they're trying to change all our traditions," Ilyas continued.... "There was a tradition called *shayd-e âvâz*,[6] which means 'farewell,' or 'epitaph.' It was like when dervishes begin to chant rhythmically the name of Allah in crazy intonations. It's a Bukharan Jewish tradition. One person begins with a solo, and another person answers. Men and women did it together in the home of the deceased person. If the dead person hadn't lived to see his children married, they buried him to the accompaniment of the wedding drum. Here instruments are forbidden in the synagogue, and so is lamenting. And God help you if a woman should show herself during prayers in the same hall as the men [in the Bukharan Jewish synagogue]." (T. Levin 1996:276)

Many Bukharian Jews, however, do not share Mallayev's discomfort about losing this particular tradition, especially since they are inclined to believe rabbinic authorities who explain that such practices are forbidden. Ezro Malakov and his wife Bella Khaimova explained that it "wasn't good" that women were being told not to sing, but Ezro added that it "wasn't allowed" according to the Torah. I asked Roshel Rubinov his thoughts about Mallayev's comments, as related in Levin's book, and we had the following exchange:

> ER: In this book, Mallayev said that it's difficult in New York because important people such as rabbis are introducing new rules. For example, shayd ovoz, he says that in Central Asia—
>
> RR: —women's singing. In New York, the rabbis say it's not permitted. In Central Asia, when someone died, the musicians would come with tanbūr, kamancha, ghijak, and they would sing shayd ovoz songs. Songs of mourning (*motamī*), an

elegy (*marsiya*). They would sing (*tarannum mikardan*) for the appearance of the person who died.[7] Over here, they say it's not permitted.

ER: So, Mallayev says that's unfortunate. And you?

RR: No.

ER: No? It's not necessary?

RR: They sing over here too, you know, a little bit, before everybody comes together, women sing a little bit for the women's party. Our Torah says that men and women must not sit together.

ER: I understand.

RR: For me, whatever the rabbi says, I want to implement (*ijro kardan*). This is my opinion. Whatever the rabbi says is important to me, because he knows Torah. The words of the Torah are good, and the rabbi knows more Torah than me and you.

The conversation between me and my teacher highlights the authority that rabbis have among Bukharian Jews, for whom adherence to religious law is quite fraught. Religious practice is not considered a lifestyle choice but an obligation of cosmic significance. Furthermore, some ideas about Judaism that might be painted by other American Jews as superstition or premodern are critical to some Bukharian Jews—for example, the importance of ritual for ensuring the protection of angels (*malakhim*), bringing financial rewards (*parnasa*), or giving birth to the preferred first-born son rather than a daughter. Breaking religious laws, on the other hand, may cause misfortunes; for example, driving one's car on Shabbat can result in an accident. Such considerations, while they go against some of the mainstream conceptions of Judaism in the United States, are significant factors when considering the decisions that Bukharian Jews often make with respect to religious life. Furthermore, when such attitudes among Bukharian Jews conflict with mainstream American Jewish ideas, the complexities of "freedom" and multicultural pluralistic tolerance are brought into sharp relief.

Intracultural Borrowings

Bukharian Jewish religious repertoire contains Ashkenazic and Sephardic melodies, another indication of a desire to integrate with broader varieties of Judaism and as well as a shared pan-Jewish multiculturalist interest in global Jewry's diversity. The service at Beth Gavriel, as at most congregations, is a hodgepodge of melodies, constantly in flux. "Some Yerushalmi, some Bukharian, something by a Tajik composer," as Ezro Malakov said. Hazzans, lay leaders, and average worshippers draw on freedom of melodic expression to retain their distinctive melodies but also address innovations taking place throughout the Jewish world. As they strike this balance they also further their goal of blending in with other Jewish communities.

Some Bukharian repertoire is "Yerushalmi" (Jerusalemite), brought back and forth between Palestine/Israel and Central Asia for at least a century.[8] For example, Ezro Malakov's grandfather Mullo Obo Deroz studied in Palestine from 1887 to 1889 and brought melodies back to Central Asia before he emigrated for good in 1933. Bukharian ḥazzans sometimes lead their congregations in a Jerusalem-Sephardi style. As Ezro Malakov explained, Yerushalmi melodies have been a part of the Bukharian way for generations:

> For example, there is a ḥazzan in Erets Isroel, Eli Balkhi. He is a Yerushalmi ḥazzan [i.e., a cantor in the Jerusalem-Sephardi style]. And he also sings Bukharian style. Why is this? Because his father, one hundred years ago, went to Israel to live. In Israel he put together maqoms and also our Torah melodies (niguns) from Central Asia. And he taught his son, Eli Balkhi. He sings very well.

Malakov has Balkhi's cassettes, among other recordings of cantors from throughout the Bukharian diaspora. Ḥazzans typically share repertoire this way, staying abreast of new melodies and updating their own performances with melodies they like.

Bukharians born or raised in New York are also drawn to Ashkenazic melodies, which might be more familiar to them through their education. Yeshiva-educated young people who can read from the Torah often have an Ashkenazic interpretation of the te'amim (symbols that indicate melodic formulas for cantillation). Young Bukharians also think Ashkenazic melodies "sound happier" than Bukharian tunes (E. Malakov, personal communication). This sentiment was a common theme in my research: that distinctly Bukharian melodies sounded "sad" or "like crying" to Bukharian youth. Regarding the strong influence of Ashkenazic melodies in New York, Malakov quite simply said, "There are a lot of Ashkenazic Jews here [in New York], and not many Bukharian Jews."

The Sephardic Liturgy and the Persistent Isolation Narrative

The Sephardic establishment exerts a strong pull as a "center" on Bukharian Jews. Bukharian Jews are not technically Sephardic Jews in that they do not descend from those expelled from the Iberian Peninsula, but Bukharian Jews sometimes refer to themselves as "Sephardic Jews" because they practice the Sephardic liturgical rite. Some Bukharian Jews also employ the general sense of "Sephardic" as referring to any non-Ashkenazic Jews, and their participation in such events as the Sephardic Music Festival adds to this binary understanding of world Jewry.[9] Bukharian Jews may prefer to pray with other non-Ashkenazic Jews at general Sephardic synagogues such as the Sephardic Jewish Center in Queens, and the religious repertoire incorporates a great deal of pan-Sephardic melodies and prayer styles. The Sephardic identity was key for the few Bukharian Jews who arrived in the United States before the 1990s, before there were enough

Bukharian Jews to enable community-supported, Bukharian-specific synagogues, schools, and other institutions.

The old and intense dynamics between Bukharian Jews and Sephardic Jews date back at least to the end of the nineteenth century in Palestine. Central Asian immigrants in Jerusalem established the "Society of Bukharia and her outskirts" in 1889 (under a longer name) as a fundraising response to the Sephardic establishment, which had taken responsibility for all non-Ashkenazic groups and wanted to direct funds to groups, such as Yemenite Jews, that they felt had a more immediate need (Cooper 2012:129–34).[10] The new society helped the Jews from Central Asia raise funds for their own community and avoid being subsumed under the Sephardic category. These attempts to distinguish themselves from Sephardic Jews in Jerusalem, in fact, created Bukharian Jewry per se, as a unified group (Cooper 2012:128). Today the tension remains between Bukharian Jews existing as their own group or falling under a larger Sephardic umbrella. For instance, Bukharian Jews maintain their own governing bodies, such as the World Bukharian Jewish Congress, and also come under the purview of organizations such as the American Sephardi Federation.

The Bukharian Jews' adoption of the Sephardic liturgical rite in the late eighteenth or early nineteenth century is a good example of the multiple ways that the relationship between Bukharian and Sephardic Jews can be read. On one hand, the Bukharian embrace of the Sephardic rite is evidence of the community's long-standing engagement with worldwide diasporic Jewish developments and their consistent maintenance of Jewish religious practice. The Central Asian Jews seemed to have adopted the Sephardic rite as part of a widespread interest throughout the Eastern Jewish communities (Nosonovskiĭ 2005); Iranian Jews may have also adopted the Sephardic rite around the same time, "perhaps as late as the early nineteenth century" (Loeb 2000:36). The shift toward the Sephardic rite would not be unprecedented or surprising, as interest among Central Asians in innovations originating in the Sephardic world extends back earlier. For example, in the beginning of the 1700s, the Bukharian poet Yusuf Yahudi translated into Judeo-Persian some of the poems of Israel Najara (ca. 1555–ca. 1625), the poet who revitalized Hebrew poetry throughout the Ottoman Empire.

On the other hand, portrayals of Bukharian Jewish history usually shift agency away from the Bukharian Jews in accordance with internal Jewish hierarchies. In these narratives, the Bukharian Jewish adoption of the Sephardic rite is framed as the work of Sephardic authorities discovering and reeducating Bukharian Jews after a period of isolation and religious decline. According to many published narratives by both Bukharians and non-Bukharians, Bukharian Jews adopted the Sephardic rite after a Moroccan-born emissary named Rabbi Yosef Mamon Moghribi came to Bukhara from Palestine in 1793 and enacted a number of reforms among the "virtually isolated" community, including the "replacement of the Khorasani rite with the so-called 'Spanish rite'" (Zand 2000:535; see also

Altschuler and Müller-Lancet 1971:1474; Wahrman 1991:10; and Cooper 2012:62). In the typical telling of the Mamon story, the isolation and religious deterioration of the Jews in Bukhara is often linked to their strong relationship to their generally Muslim surroundings. Joseph Wolff (1795–1862), the converted Christian missionary who traveled to Central Asia in 1828 and 1843–1845, wrote that before Rabbi "Mooghrebee" arrived "The Jews of Bokhara ... did eat the meat of the Musselmans indiscriminately" (Wolff 1835:187; Cooper 2004:103). Wolff's comments and stories echo those of Samuel bar Bisna, a Babylonian *amora* who visited Margwan (Mary) in the fourth century and refused to drink the wine and beer there, "doubting their ritual cleanliness" (Zand 2000). In a more recent article discussing Mamon, not only do the Central Asian Jews whom Mamon meets eat the same meat as the Muslims, but they, like Iranian Jews, are more interested in the poetry of the "Persian mystics" than Torah and kabbalah (Puzhol' 2004).

Alanna E. Cooper drew our attention to the historical inaccuracies of the Mamon narrative (2004, 2012:35–66). Mamon is largely a composite creation of a historian named Avraham Yaari "woven together from a few fragments of unreliable sources that contradict one another in significant ways" (Cooper 2004:80). Indeed, for just two examples among many, Elkan Adler (1898) mentions "Abraham Mammon," not Yosef, and the nameless "Rabbi of Bokhara" in Baron von Meiendorf's edition is from Algiers, not Morocco (Meiendorf 1870:35). Nevertheless the story persists, with Mamon, the Sephardic representative, typically cast as a savior or father figure.[11] The chapter on Mamon in Ochildiev's history, a book by a lay historian widely circulated and read in the Bukharian Jewish community, is entitled "Crisis and Salvation: Religious Reforms of Iosif Mamon Magribi" (Ochildiev 2005:46–52).

The theme of isolation, decline, and rescue found in the Mamon narrative is cyclical, applied to Bukharian Jews in subsequent encounters with other Jewish groups. For those furthering a story of a perpetual and renewable bond between a religious center and an atrophied periphery, the Mamon story is "the story of Jewish diaspora history writ large" (Cooper 2012:52). In the present day, Bukharian Jews are typically characterized as having undergone yet another period of decline and isolation under the Soviets, with rescue and reeducation by Ashkenazic or Sephardic authorities following the mass migrations from Central Asia (Cooper 2012:8). In the twentieth and twenty-first centuries, Habad missionaries often take the role of the rescuers due to their high level of activity in the transitional period surrounding the fall of the Soviet Union (Ro'i 2008:71; Cooper 2012:185–202). Some young Bukharian Jews in New York, educated in Ashkenazic-run yeshivas and adopting Hasidic practices, say they "know more than their parents" (see also Cooper 2004:94).

But the power that the isolation narrative has for Bukharian Jews themselves demands more attention. The Mamon narrative, for all of its inaccuracies, is repeated by Bukharian Jews as much as the more dominant groups who are in the position of rescuers. In a multiculturalist environment, the theme of isolation and the Bukharian community's position on the periphery actually raises the value of the community's culture, already marked as exotic and other. The isolation narrative can be flipped to support the Bukharian Jews' uniqueness as a particular ethnic group, with an authority defined by an imagined link to ancient Israel. It is this current, toward intensifying the distinct Bukharian Jewish culture, that we must now consider.

Toward Bukharian Jewish Distinctiveness

While narratives of isolation support clear hierarchies between Bukharian Jews and Ashkenazic and Sephardic Jewry, the theme of isolation also adds to an exotic aura and distinct brand of authority for Bukharian Jews, linking them to an imaginary pre-exilic ancient Jewish past.[12] Bukharian Jews are even sometimes associated with the so-called Lost Tribes of Israel. Bukharians have their own origin story tracing their community to the tribes of Issachar and Naphtali, and they claim that Central Asia is the Habor of the Bible. In an article titled, "A Lost Tribe, Found in Queens," the popular Bukharian singer Yuhan Benjamin was quoted as saying, "The Bukharan community is the closest to what original Judaism is.... Only Bukharian Jews follow the Old Testament" (Wishna 2003).

Bukharian Jews draw on the isolation narrative to support claims about the uniqueness of their community. Uniqueness is a particularly salient identity point in the contemporary United States as communities strive to find their own voices in a multicultural atmosphere. In an online chat on the subject of Bukharian history, one editor of BukharianJews. com (Peter Pinkhasov) presented Central Asia not as part of the globalized mercantile Silk Road, but as isolated and remote, and without making distinctions between the cities—where Jews lived—and the rest of the vast region:

> [The] Central Asian region is bordered by deserts and mountains which were very difficult to cross before the modern means of transportation. That is why Bukharian Jews have a totally unique culture, ways apart from other Jewish communities.[13]

The website of Beth Gavriel Congregation states, "Among many Jewish communities in the world there is one that for more than 2,000 years has survived and preserved its religion and national identity in almost total isolation from the rest of world Jewry. Jews of that community have developed their own distinct culture, while at the same time adhering to Jewish principles and hoping some day to return to the Land of Israel. These Jews are called Bukharian Jews."[14]

Music is a key indicator of Bukharian uniqueness: when I asked Ezro Malakov to tell me what he thought was the most important thing for me to include in the book, he responded, "Bukharian Jews have their own completely unique music, unlike any other Jewish ethnic group (*millat*)."[15] The strongest musical expression of Bukharian Jews' distinctiveness in relation to other Jews is the shiro repertoire, specifically the songs unique to the Bukharian Jewish community that combine Judeo-Persian texts and maqom melodies.

The Shiro Repertoire: Jewish Texts and Maqom Melodies

Most shiro song texts are drawn from the shared Jewish repertoire of piyyutim (religious poems), which have been set in particular local ways by various Jewish communities. These piyyutim include "Deror Yiqrā" by Dunash ben Labrat (10th c.), the earliest known adapter of Hebrew to Arabic 'aruz poetic meters, to "Yo Ribun Olam" and "Yom le Yom Odeh le Shimkho" by Israel Najara, who reinvigorated Hebrew and Aramaic poetry throughout the Ottoman Empire with the publication of his *Zemirot Yisrāēl* in 1587. Bukharian Jews also sing Persian translations of these poems—either on their own or in alternation with the Hebrew text—and Hebrew and Persian poems written in Najara's spirit, such as "Shaday Ḥokets/Moro Zi Khobi Ghaflat" by the noted Bukharian scholar Shimon Ḥakham (1843–1910).[16]

Najara's collection was innovative in that he explicitly based his new poems on Turkish and other melodies and gave the non-Hebrew incipit as a musical direction for the singing of the hymn (Avenary 1979:186–90; Seroussi 1990; Shiloah 1992:123, 153; Tietze and Yahalom 1995:14). Although controversial among religious authorities at the time, his goal in applying religious texts to secular melodies was to encourage his fellow Jews to praise God with familiar tunes. Najara's approach, like Dunash ben Labrat's, spread quickly among the people of the Jewish diaspora, providing the foundation for numerous contrafactum repertoires, including the Syrian Jewish *pizmon* in which Hebrew texts are set to secular Arab melodies (Shelemay 1998), and the use of borrowed melodies in many different genres of Judeo-Spanish song (J. R. Cohen 1990).[17]

For Bukharian Jews, local melodies used for Jewish texts are essential defining characteristics for each Jewish "ethnic group" (millat), and the maqom melodies are their particular property. Roshel Rubinov commented, "Moroccan Jews take Moroccan melodies, Ashkenazic Jews take Russian melodies, Bukharian Jews take Central Asian melodies. That's it. We have permission, because we were born over there." The difficult nature of maqom melodies requires the abilities of a hofiz, but just as with melodies in other religious contexts, there are ways for both laypeople and professionals to sing these settings. Roshel Rubinov explained that those with average voices might start with the maqom melody, but not perform the melody exactly right over the course of the setting. Malakov indicated that alternative ways are available to those who do not have the ability to execute a high, loud culmination (avj), as he does.

The Bukharian practice of setting Jewish texts to maqom melodies reveals the impact that Central Asian classical music has had on the way Bukharian Jews interpret Jewish texts. Bukharian Jews understand maqom as a set of tunes, predetermined melodies, and not as a collection of intervallic resources, melody types, or scales. Hence, Bukharian contrafacta using maqom involves the use of tunes as melodic resources, rather than the use of modes or scales that guide spur-of-the-moment melodic elaborations. Whereas Syrian Jews, for example, understand maqom along a modal spectrum ranging from tunes to scales, which they use for tune-based pizmonim and metric songs as well as for scale-based cantillation and more improvisatory unmeasured sections of prayer (Shelemay 1998:104–34; Kligman 2009), Bukharian Jews use a separate set of melody types and intervallic resources for cantillation and unmeasured prayer, and use maqom for tune-based settings of piyyutim.

Maqom settings require a strong internally developed sense of the rhythm of ʿaruz poetic meters. Maqom singers nearly always exploit the durational relationships between short and long syllables for rhythmic effect. Even with Jewish texts that are not based on ʿaruz meters, Bukharian Jews will interpret them as such. When setting Jewish texts that can be scanned according to ʿaruz meters, such as many of the Hebrew piyyutim that use the hazaj foot, Bukharian Jews align the texts to maqom melodies and rhythms that are typically associated with those poetic meters.[18] For example, "Yehalel Niv," which conforms to a sixteen-syllable hazaj meter, is set to "Nasri Chorgoh," following the convention that "the verse meter of all shuʿbes of the nasr type is … hazaj muṯamman sālim [ᴗ – – – ᴗ – – – ᴗ – – – ᴗ – – –]" (Karamatov and Radjabov 1981:112).[19] As shown in Example 4.5, in Ezro Malakov, Roshel Rubinov, and Matat Barayev's setting of Israel Najara's "Yom le Yom Odeh le Shimkho," Najara's poem is treated as a fourteen syllable variant of a ramal meter (– ᴗ – –), coordinated with "Mūghulchai Dugoh" in a five-beat mūghulcha rhythm.

<pre>
  –   ᴗ   –   –   –   ᴗ   –   –   –ᴗ –   –   –   –
Yom le yom o- deh le shim-kho el a-ni   ʿav- de-kho
Qol be shir ho-dosh ve ze-   mer e-ʿe-rokh neg-de-kho
</pre>

The practice of setting Jewish texts to maqom melodies is of uncertain age. It is quite possible that it began or grew in earnest even as recently as the early twentieth century. But Bukharian Jews in New York consider the setting of Jewish texts to maqom melodies to be a very old tradition, connected to their long presence in Central Asia and their self-conception as a historical, ancient Jewish community with a culture developed in isolation from the rest of world Jewry. Roshel Rubinov said:

> It's very old. Once, Bukharian Jews knew the Hebrew language by heart. Over time, we lost our mother tongue. Because it was a long time. And for 100 years, 300 years, 400 years, we learned Central Asian melodies, and we learned Uzbek, Tajik, Shashmaqom

Example 4.5. Ezro Malakov, Roshel Rubinov, Matat Barayev, "Yom le Yom" set to "Mūghulchai Dugoh." Transcribed by the author.

melodies. But, we set Torah and the Hebrew language together with the Central Asian melodies. More than 500 years. We were in exile (*golut*) 2,000 years, right? We came to Uzbekistan, Tajikistan, Central Asia, from Iran, from Persia. And Bukharian Jewish cemeteries are over 400 years, 500 years old, the tombstones are over 500 years old.

Regardless of the practice's age, the setting of Jewish texts to maqom melodies must also be understood as a reconstructive effort and as a product of recent creativity due to the underground nature of Bukharian Jewish religious life during the Soviet Union. Bukharian Jews have been expanding this area of creativity dramatically since leaving the Soviet Union, turning it into one of the cornerstones of contemporary Bukharian Jewish life.

Ezro Malakov, more than anyone else, has spearheaded the effort to remember and reconstruct the music of his grandparents' generation, with a focus on the shiro repertoire. He described the process of recovering the Bukharian melodies: "I knew these things before. I knew Bukharian melodies, everything. After [I became ḥazzan at Beth Gavriel] I sang over and over, and I remembered. Again and again they came to my memory, it became good. [Together] with my older brother [Menaḥem]." At a recording session for one of Ezro Malakov's projects, Malakov, Rubinov, and Matat Barayev worked out a new setting of "Chu Sanjid" (a Persian paraphrase of the piyyut "Yehalel Niv") to the Shashmaqom melody "Navruzi Sabo" (Audio Example 4.6💿). Malakov indicated that this version was old (*qadim*), and that he remembered it from the elders at the synagogue. In comparison with other versions of this composition, "qadim" aspects seemed to be an increased emphasis on non-diatonic intervals, including microtonally flat-tened scale degrees 2 and 6 in addition to the more familiar pitch variability on scale degrees 3 and 7, a more liberal use of wide vibrato, especially in the lower range, and a slower tempo (the association of "qadim" with "slow" can also be found in the slow zarb of sarakhbor, often called zarbi qadim). He also explained that these settings were the work of both professionals and laypeople; he attributes the settings of "Chu Sanjid" to "Navruzi Sabo," "Nasrulloi," and "Talqini Bayot" to "folk musicians." "Professional musi-cians would not have made these particular settings, but since they exist in folk practice, I decided to preserve them," he wrote (Malakov 2007:11).

Malakov's efforts also involve completely new settings. His most recent project is the ambitious setting of all 150 Psalms (Tehillim), which he is undertaking with his colleagues, including Roshel Rubinov, who is re-sponsible for many of the settings. This project is explicitly innovative, as the matching of Psalms to maqom melodies is something new for Bukharian Jews. Furthermore, he is drawing on the *instrumental* maqom melodies (from the mushkilot sections of the Shashmaqom and instru-mental pieces by classical composers), which are a new repository for set-ting Jewish texts. As mentioned earlier, the usual maqom resources for such settings are familiar melodies such as "Chapandozi Gulyor," "Mūghulchai Dugoh," "Mūghulchai Segoh," and "Nasri Bayot," matched with Hebrew and Persian poems in classical ʿaruz meters (or meters that can be easily approximated or understood in ʿaruz terms) coordinated in standard ways with the rhythmic patterns. The Psalms have no such con-sistent rhythmic meter and the instrumental melodies have no conven-tions for text setting, so the Psalms project is challenging in unprecedented ways. Malakov described his setting of Psalm 10 to "Chapandozi Bayot" (Audio Example 4.7💿) as incredibly difficult, due to the challenging push and pull of the *chapandoz* rhythm (similar to talqin) and the absence of rhythmic patterns in the text. The difficult and innovative nature of the Psalms project positions it as original creative work for professional musi-cians, not a preservational or reconstructive attempt geared toward aver-age people. At the same time, for Malakov it is a continuation of the old tradition of setting Jewish texts to maqom melodies: his religion matched with his culture, both being his birthright and property.

Another area of growth has been the composition of new Persian-language religious poems for maqom settings. Historically speaking, Jews in Central Asia are a branch of Persian Jewry, and they share a Judeo-Persian literary heritage with Jews of Iran and Afghanistan. Bukharian Jews are passionate about the Persian language, which they consistently shared with their neighbors as part of a general Persianate or multilingual environment in urban Central Asia. Persian remained the main elite and literary language in most of Central Asia through the beginning of the twentieth century,[20] and the general population in the region is fond of poets such as Hāfez, Omar Khayyām, and Sa'di, just as in Iran.[21] Bukharian Jews view the literary heritage of Iran and Central Asia as their own, regardless of the religion or retrospective "ethnicity" or "nationality" of the authors. Ochil Ibragimov described Hāfez and Rumi as "holy." As Persian dwindles as a mother tongue, it is increasingly viewed as a link to the Bukharian past, with spiritual and even sacred overtones. Persian-language texts on Jewish themes may even rival Hebrew-language texts in terms of cultural value.[22]

In New York, the symbolic power of the Persian language has grown considerably, and young people are taught to sing in "Bukharian" in order to keep their heritage alive.[23] Ilyos Mallayev did the most to expand the Persian-language religious repertoire, having composed more than twenty new Persian poems in classical meters intended to be sung to maqom melodies (Mallayev 2003).[24] The growth of Jewish religious life since immigration has made religious projects fertile ground for creativity and innovation, and like Ezro Malakov and Ochil Ibragimov, Mallayev diversified to include religious repertoire as an important aspect of his professional profile in New York. Most of these poems have been recorded, both the poems and the recordings having been commissioned by Rabbi Hillel Hayimov and the Ateret Menaḥem Organization in Israel. In these poems, Mallayev addresses the appearance of the Torah ("Vasfi Tūro"), the coming of the Messiah ("Omadani Moshiaḥ"), Jewish holidays ("Idi Purim," "Idi Pesaḥ"), and the city of Jerusalem ("Yerushalayim"). In some cases, a particular maqom melody is specifically indicated in the text, and he explained to me that he composed those poems with the melody in mind. In cases such as "Idi Purim," set to "Qashqarchai Rok" (from Maqom Buzruk), the meter of Mallayev's poem matches the meter of the Persian poem typically sung to that tune, a ghazal by Avzah in the *muzore'* meter ($- - \cup | - \cup - - |$ $- - \cup | - \cup - -$). As shown in Figure 4.2, below the title, Mallayev indicates "ba ohangi Qashqarchai Rok" (to the tune of Qashqarchai Rok), and Ezro Malakov's copy indicates how he and the other musicians have agreed on the setting of the poem, with arrows indicating different sections of the piece by range, and where to place choruses (*pripev*) and instrumental breaks (*pauza*).[25]

The burst of creativity among professional musicians surrounding the practice of setting Jewish texts to maqom melodies speaks to the diverse needs of the contemporary Bukharian Jewish community, and the ability of religious music to speak to the group's condition. As a distinctly Bukharian practice rooted in the Central Asian past, it is an ideal repertoire for Bukharian Jews as they cultivate a unique identity, and it is a way for professional musicians to continue their long, intimate relationship to maqom now that they are geographically removed from its source. In many ways, the Jewish religious sphere is where the maqom tradition is most alive among Bukharian Jews, expanding and transforming with new

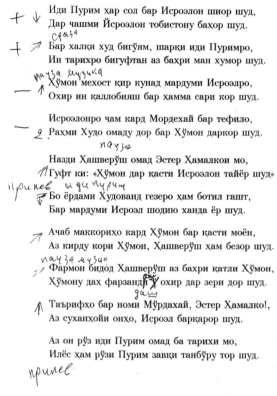

Figure 4.2. Ilyos Mallayev, "Idi Purim" (Ezro Malakov's annotated copy). Reproduced with permission.

creativity while maqom in the classical sphere becomes increasingly symbolic and presentational. Simultaneously, the vibrancy and innovative spirit with which Bukharian Jews have approached this repertoire exemplifies their impressive adaptive abilities and their call, especially as professionals, to continually move forward and engage their tradition as a process.

Bukharian professionals see innovation and adaptation as depending on—not in opposition to—antiquity and distinctiveness. Their self-conception as members of an ancient community in fact gives them a position of authority to explore whatever innovations they see fit. Ezro Malakov and Roshel Rubinov, invoking the "2,000 years" of Jewish life in

Central Asia, flip the limiting power of nationalist ideology on its head. For example, some of the backing tracks for the Psalms project are recordings made by the Uzbek Radio and TV Orchestra about thirty years ago. Malakov asked permission to use the recordings, and was greeted with confusion by one Uzbek professor over why he would want to use Uzbek melodies for his religious music. Malakov told me the explanation he gave the professor:

> Bukharian Jews lived in Uzbekistan for 2,000 years. For 2,000 years Bukharian Jews, Uzbeks, and Tajiks sang Shashmaqom together. I asked him, "Bukharian Jews helped Uzbeks notate the nasr [vocal sections] of the Shashmaqom, right?" He answered, "Of course." "OK," I said, "if we helped you with the nasr, isn't it likely we helped you with the mushkilot [instrumental sections]?" "Of course," he said. [I said:] "The Psalms of King David, the Qur'ān of Muhammad, the Torah of Moses, the Gospel of Jesus. These belong to the whole world. All people sing 'Halleluya.' 'Halleluya' comes from King David. He made his music for the whole world. He was the first to create music for the people of the world." "Of course," he said. "The same music you have for your mushkilot, that Jews helped with, I want to set King David's Psalms to these same instrumentals." So he decided, "Set our music to your words," and gave me permission.

For Bukharian Jews, Jewish texts and maqom melodies both predate limiting modern nationalisms. Their "2,000 years" of life in the region gives them a position of authority and "permission" to engage maqom resources and Jewish texts creatively as part of an ongoing tradition. They see their contemporary religious works as part of a wide and deep continuum that stretches back across the generations, a diasporic music that transcends time and space. The combination of maqom melodies and Jewish texts effectively expresses the paradoxes at the core of Bukharian Jewish diasporic identity: the discourse of isolation, separation, and distinctiveness combined with a reality of constant contact, exchange, and cultural synthesis.

Bukharian Diasporic Consciousness: Combining Senses of Belonging and Otherness

Bukharian Jews, Iranian Jews, and many other "Mizraḥi" ("Eastern") groups hold a deep sense of rootedness in their diasporic homes, in contrast to the collective memories of mass expulsions and wanderings that characterize the Ashkenazic and Sephardic past. In general, Bukharian Jews consider the centuries in urban Central Asia leading up to the Russian conquests as relatively stable and part of an overall Persianate environment dating all the way back to the earliest Jewish diaspora from Babylonian-ruled Judea to the Persian Achaemenid empire (ca. 770 BCE to

330 BCE), extending through subsequent Persian empires including the Sassanians (third to seventh century) and Samanids (ninth to tenth century). Even under Timur, who made Samarqand his capital in 1371, and the Turkic dynasties that followed him, Bukhara and Samarqand remained centers of Persian culture (Rowland et al. 1992).[26] Although Bukharian Jews do recognize periods of migration and turmoil, until the post-Soviet period they do not share such a traumatic moment of rupture as the Iberian expulsions (not even the devastating Mongol invasions in the thirteenth century, which led to substantial migration), and their existence was not destroyed during the Holocaust, as it was for European Jews.

Thus, despite a history of many indignities and discrimination, Bukharian Jews often look back on Central Asia as another homeland almost equal to the Land of Israel, with a double sense of diaspora that strongly appears in Bukharian music and literature, and which is evidenced by continued travel back and forth to Central Asian cities. Back visiting his home of Samarqand, an Israeli *mashgiah* (supervisor of kosher law) explained to me that Samarqand was second only to Jerusalem. Israel and Central Asia can be poetically merged, as in Ilyos Mallayev's "Pazmon Shudam": "Your [Israel's] bread is like the bread of Samarqand / Your dates like the dates of Bukhara" (*Nonat misoli noni az Samarqand / Khurmoi Tu chu khurmoi Bukhoro*). Longing for the Central Asian homeland is also expressed through the traditional genre of the *gharibī*, the plaint of a wanderer or stranger (gharib) away from one's home; Mallayev's "Boghi Gharibi" ("Foreign Garden," Mallayev 1999:165) begins "In a foreign garden, there is no jasmine or sweet-smelling flowers...." (*Dar boghi gharibi guli khushbūiu suman nest*). The many layers of diaspora and homeland in Bukharian Jewish life generate what Jonathan Boyarin has called "multiple experiences of rediasporization, which do not necessarily succeed each other in historical memory but echo back and forth" (quoted in Clifford 1994:305).

Studies that seek to understand diasporic communities in terms of ideas of "hybridity" following the work of Stuart Hall (1990), James Clifford (1994), and Paul Gilroy (1993) (Dufoix 2003:24–25) may miss the reality for the members of those communities who explicitly reject such a notion, or who seem paradoxically to perpetuate both hybrid and essentialist attitudes simultaneously. Bold resistance to assimilation and a self-conscious embrace of one's "senses of otherness" are just as likely to be found in today's diasporic groups, encouraged by globalization and multiculturalism, as explicit hybridization or acculturation. In the case of Bukharian Jews, one must acknowledge the singular sense of belonging to the Jewish people that sustained them as a subjugated minority population while considering their adaption to new environments. Turino's suggestion regarding contemporary diasporic group identity is extremely applicable to the Bukharian Jewish case: "the earlier essentialist, homogeneous views of identity, and more recent ideas about identities being fluid, constructed, and multiple, must both be held in mind simultaneously in order to understand identity in relation to expressive cultural practices" (Turino 2004:9).

Bukharian Jews have a variety of stylistic, linguistic, and poetic resources available to them to express different aspects of their diasporic conditions. Shared Jewish texts espouse ethical and religious ideas, including the "classic" diasporic formulation in which the Land of Israel is the Homeland (Elazar 1986; Aviv and Shneer 2005:3–4), and exile a "punishment for failure to fulfill God's command properly" (Rosman 1997:38). By setting all of the Psalms, Ezro Malakov is engaging some of the most famous expressions of the exilic Jewish diasporic consciousness, such as Psalm 137, "By the Rivers of Babylon," or Psalm 80 ("Restore us, O God; show Your favor that we may be delivered").[27] Settings of these Psalms to maqom melodies that conjure old Central Asia, such as the combination of Psalm 80 with "Nasri Segoh," directly reflect the combination or conflation of the two homelands in the Bukharian imagination.

The evocation of diasporic homelands can also be heard in the new religious poems set to maqom melodies. Ilyos Mallayev's poem "Qurbon ba Tu Man Yerosholayim" (Mallayev 2003),[28] sung to "Ufori Mūghulchai Segoh" (Beth Gavriel 2003) is but one example:

> Peshvoi shariati jahon Tu,
> Sa'nu sharafi Yahudiyon Tu,
> Sarchashmai umri jovidon Tu,
> Qurbon ba Tu man, Yerusholayim
> Ey shahri muqaddasi charoghon,
> Mardum zi rukhi Tu shodu khandon,
> Har kuchai Tu chu boghu buston,
> Qurbon ba Tu man, Yerusholayim
>
> . . .
>
> Mushtoqi jamoli Tu budem mo,
> Ey pokizai tamomi dun'yo,
> Chashme narasad ba Tu Iloyo,
> Qurbon ba Tu man Yerusholayim
>
> [Translation:]
> You, leader of religious laws of the world,
> You, honor and glory of Jews,
> You, source of everlasting life,
> I am Your sacrifice, Jerusalem
> O holy, brilliant city
> From Your countenance, people are happy and cheerful
> All Your streets like gardens,
> I am Your sacrifice, Jerusalem
>
> . . .
>
> We yearn for Your beauty,
> Oh pure of all the world,
> May the evil eye not reach You Oh God,
> I am Your sacrifice, Jerusalem.

The word *mushtoq*, meaning "yearning, longing," found at the beginning of the third stanza ("we yearn for Your beauty"), captures a quintessential Jewish diasporic stance. Central Asian signifiers come through in the maqom setting, as well as the poem being composed in a classical meter (the hazaj variant $--\cup\cup-\cup-\cup--$) and form (the *murabba '*), and performed with the traditional instrumentation of tanbūr and doira.

The traditional Jewish diasporic status suggests more than just dispersion and a longing for an ancient homeland. A controversial and complex topic that often goes unaddressed in scholarship perhaps due to uncomfortable political realities, "diaspora" as a Jewish formulation is often linked to messianism, deliverance, redemption, and justice or vengeance. The Psalmist, for example, writes of the destruction of the Jews' enemies accompanying return as a form of justice and the arrival of the Messiah, what Stuart Hall famously alluded to and negated in "Cultural Identity and Diaspora": "diaspora does not refer us to those scattered tribes whose identity can only be secured in relation to some sacred homeland to which they must at all costs return, even if it means pushing other peoples into the sea" (Hall 1990:235). Psalm 137 is not just "how can we sing a song of the Lord on alien soil" but also "Fair Babylon, you predator; a blessing on him who repays you in kind what you have inflicted on us; a blessing on him who seizes your babies and dashes them against the rocks!" Psalm 59 (set by Ezro Malakov to "Soqinomai Savti Kalon") asks God to "In Your fury put an end to them [Israel's foes]; put an end to them that they be no more; that it may be known to the ends of the earth that God does rule over Jacob."

Bukharian Jews often hold a strong belief in messianic ideas and dispersion in exile as an unwanted condition that awaits redemption through supernatural acts of God. But Hall's implication of the Jewish diasporic conception as "the old, the imperializing, the hegemonic, form of 'ethnicity'" (Hall 1990:235) neglects the mystical and religious essence of diaspora for Jews, which may or may not coincide with attitudes toward the Israeli nation-state or geopolitical events. However, Bukharian Jews' long and productive history in Central Asia does exist in tension with religious and mystical perspectives, with life in any location no matter how extended or deep essentially a "sojourn" in exile. New Bukharian Jewish shiro poems typically impart a deep sense of otherness reflecting biblical language, and may take a messianic, antagonistic, or vengeful stance. For example, Ilyos Mallayev's "Khanuko" (Hanukkah) set to "Ufori Tulkun," commemorates a story much closer to the anti-assimilationist narrative in the apocryphal book of Maccabees (see Satlow 2006:99) than to the story of rededicating the Temple and triumph over impossible opposition that supports the gift-giving "Jewish Christmas" holiday in the United States (Sklare and Greenblum 1967; Joselit 1992). Mallayev's poem reads, for example, "Tyrant and enemy burn in the fire of Hanukkah" (*Dar otashi khanuko sūzand zolimu dushman*). The historical "tyrant" and "enemy" of the Hanukkah story do not refer to any specific contemporary people, but Mallayev's poem connotes a general, persistent sense of otherness that constitutes an essential Jewish condition of life in diaspora as exile.

Music provides a means of representing the complex interweaving of classic pan-community Jewish diasporic formulations, expressed primarily through Jewish texts, and the distinct Bukharian post-immigration longing for the secondary homeland of Central Asia, expressed with maqom melodies. These two attitudes coexist, sometimes uneasily, like the twin trajectories of moving toward a general Jewish identity and toward a unique Bukharian American identity. Rather than recognize cultural hybridity, a concept that often goes against Bukharian Jewish attitudes and understandings of diaspora, Bukharian Jews are more likely to use different musical repertoires and signifiers to capture the multiple senses of belonging and otherness that accompany their multiply diasporic condition. In religious repertoire (as opposed to the party and maqom repertoires, where other notions of diaspora dominate), Bukharian Jews reinforce an exilic diasporic formulation—not only the elevation of Israel as the eternal Jewish Homeland, but an antagonistic stance that portrays Jews in contrast to the non-Jews surrounding them. In a complicated way that resists resolution, this sentiment is combined with music that harks back to the people and places that they physically miss and remember from before immigration. The characteristics of persistent Jewish "otherness" are blurrier in the United States, where Jewish identity is not fundamentally opposed to American identity, but where Bukharian Jews must still draw lines around their identity as an "ethnicity." Bukharian Jews are drawing on their religious repertoire, with its complex associations of both belonging and otherness, to express the paradoxes of ethnic multiculturalism in New York.

Religious Repertoire as Bukharian Ethnic Music

The multicultural environment of the United States has compelled Bukharian Jews to define their "ethnic" music. Maqom has provided some of the basis for that national repertoire, but while it has proved an excellent repertoire on American "world music" stages for external representation, the discourses of nationalism surrounding maqom, maqom's role as Uzbek or Tajik music, and the marginalization of Jewish participation in the repertoire have made it an imperfect music for self-representation. Internally, Bukharian Jewish men have found the religious repertoire to be a more complete vehicle for defining Bukharian ethnicity, as it encompasses a particularly Bukharian Jewish take on maqom as well as the melodies and genres specific to religious life.

The Sefar Tūĭ in New York is an excellent representation of the intersection of American identity and Bukharian Jewish ethnicity. In the first decade of the 2000s, I witnessed the growth of the Sefar Tūĭ party from Beth Gavriel's main sanctuary to larger catering halls; in 2009, with Beth Gavriel no longer able to contain the crowd, the party was moved to the

Figure 4.3. Sefar Tūĭ at Elite Palace, 2009. Photo by the author.

Elite Palace catering hall (Figure 4.3). The event, also attended by Mayor Michael Bloomberg and local congressman Anthony Weiner (pre-scandals), was surrounded by much public display of Bukharian Jews' established place in the New York social landscape. The *karnai* (long trumpet) and *naghora* (small kettledrum), typically associated with processions and events requiring fanfare, were in abundance. Simḥa Elishayev, Beth Gavriel's vice president, is shown in Figure 4.4 wearing a jomma with an American eagle on the back and Stars of David, rather than the usual abstract designs sometimes flecked with Jewish symbols. As in years past, the party featured some of the community's most prominent performers: Avrom Tolmasov, Roshel Rubinov, and Ezro Malakov (Figure 4.5).

Ezro Malakov's *Musical Treasures of the Bukharian Jewish Community* is another demonstration of contemporary Bukharian Jewish identity, but with global ambition and scope. This watershed seven-CD, 450-page collection is a recuperation of nationalistic ideals in terms of Bukharian religious music, heralding the Bukharian Jewish community's arrival on its own terms. Malakov's collection seeks to define Bukharian "ethnic music" from a religious standpoint, drawing on the models of the nationalist monuments meant to define "people's" music, such as the canonical editions of the Shashmaqom that helped establish Uzbek and Tajik music in the Soviet Union. Malakov compared his work to Rajabi's collection and canonization of the Shashmaqom in Uzbekistan, which he greatly admires (personal communication).

Figure 4.4. Simḥa Elishayev wearing jomma adorned with American eagle and Stars of David. Photo by the author.

Musical Treasures of the Bukharian Jewish Community, like the Shashmaqom editions, serves many purposes. It attempts to address the multiple thematic streams of Bukharian history, as it is filled with a huge range of materials from a wide variety of sources, all presented as ancient and unique in the interest of defining a distinct contemporary Bukharian Jewish identity. The collection includes rearranged melodies with modern instrumentation to a cappella recordings mirroring cantorial solos, cantillation, and prayer-leading in the synagogue. The songs range from those purported to be centuries old to Mallayev's brand-new poems newly set to maqom tunes, as well as melodies borrowed from other Jewish communities (such as the melody for "Anenu" mentioned previously). It covers the major days of the Jewish calendar; in addition to nearly three full discs of Shabbat shiro (including eight of Mallayev's poems), *Musical Treasures* includes melodies for Shabbat morning and Havdala (the end of Shabbat), the Brit Millo (circumcision), Hanukkah, Purim, Pesaḥ, Shavuot, Selikhot, Rosh Hashanah, Yom Kippur, Sukkot, and Simḥat Torah. The collection also contains almost one hour of passages from the Zohar for various uses as well as some Bukharian Jewish folklore, including wedding songs (Ensemble Maqom's recordings, the only recordings in the collection that feature both male and female singers), and borderline maqom genres such as ashulai kalon and yakkakhonī (the latter sung by Ezro, not by a woman as would be traditional). Malakov presents the collected Jewish repertoire as the product of a unique Jewish ethnic group, despite its heterogeneity.

Figure 4.5. Ensemble performing at Sefar Tūĭ. From left to right: Nerik Kurayev (keyboard), Solomon Barayev (doira), Avrom Tolmasov (vocals, guitar), Roshel Rubinov (vocals, guitar), Ezro Malakov (vocals). Photo by the author.

Like so much of Bukharian American culture, *Musical Treasures* is an international diasporic accomplishment, capturing the local situation in the United States in relation to a global network. While the edition reflects Malakov's adjustment of Soviet ideas of ethnicity and nationality in terms of American multiculturalism, it was notated by Ari Bobokhonov in Germany, assembled with the assistance of several people in Uzbekistan, and contains many recordings of friends and colleagues in Israel, such as Amnon Davidov and Yosi Niyazov. Malakov actually assembles much in his international projects by physically picking up and dropping off recordings over the course of his frequent travels to Israel, Europe, and even Central Asia.

The collection seeks to preserve distinct Bukharian melodies for future generations and to encourage the use of Bukharian melodies in everyday practice. For Ezro Malakov, *Musical Treasures of the Bukharian Jewish Community* unifies Bukharian Jewry by providing a defining tangible document of their culture. In another view, as Rafael Nektalov commented, Ezro Malakov's collection gives Bukharian Jews the chance to "clear [their] memories," to curb the use of Ashkenazic and Sephardic melodies and to reintroduce distinct Bukharian melodies. Nektalov rhetorically rejects hybridity or assimilation, although embracing Malakov's collection implicitly requires recognizing such factors as key components of the religious repertoire. Bukharian religious music is the product of a perpetual history of exchange, making Nektalov's goals of purification impossible, just as it proved impossible to purge Turkish of Persian- and Arabic-derived words (see, e.g., Lewis 1999). This issue is compounded as everyday worshippers, like everyday speakers of languages, continue to draw on musical elements from any source that they see fit. Jewish religious practice is especially open to musical change, with its history of "orality as a religious ideal" (Frigyesi 2002) and the idea that every worshipper can bring his or her own musical interpretation to the texts. However, Malakov is able to reinforce his conception of the Bukharian way beyond *Musical Treasures* through his role as ḥazzan at Beth Gavriel and at other religious occasions.

Musical Treasures stands at the crossroads of preservation and change in the United States. By collecting and publishing Bukharian Jewish religious music in the form of national classical music—the model of the canonical Shashmaqom editions—Malakov is suggesting a change in attitude from an individual oral ideal for religious melodies, in which everyone can pray in a different way, to the standardized ideal reserved for classical music, in which musicians strive to perform the melodies in one correct way in every circumstance. Roshel Rubinov, one of Malakov's major collaborators on the project, described the importance of *Musical Treasures* while reasserting the oral ideal:

> [*Musical Treasures*] is necessary. Before him, people didn't know these things. They don't know niguns. He knows them, because his mother sang them. That's why he knows more. But, people are also singing other ways. They [Malakov and Ari Bobokhonov] took [the melodies] and wrote them in musical notation, but maybe tomorrow I want to read (or "pray") in a different way. Maybe—there's no need for dogma.

As a ḥazzan, Ezro Malakov experiences the multiple styles and changes in the Bukharian community firsthand, especially as a generational divide.

> Now all the young people are going to other ways, they are not singing our way very much. People only sing our way a little bit now. They only sing the Ashkenazic way. They sing the Sephardic way, the Jerusalemite (*Yerushalmi*) way.
>
> Young people sing the Ashkenazic way. We [Ari Bobokhonov and I] made the book [*Musical Treasures*] for them, so that it would be said that in all of the places that Bukharian Jews lived in the provinces of Russia, Uzbekistan, and Tajikistan, they sang the same way. But young people aren't singing this way. Because the Israeli Jerusalemite way is very strong in the world. Many children, youth, and teachers are singing the Jerusalemite melodies. In the Bukharian synagogues there is a little bit of singing the Bukharian way. Old people sing it. Perhaps it [the Bukharian way] will continue, perhaps not, the old singing of Shahrisabz or Bukhara or Samarqand.

While Ezro Malakov is concerned with preserving Bukharian melodies, he is also actively pushing the tradition forward and pursuing innovations such as the Psalms project. The two impulses are not opposed to each other; rather, the dynamic coexistence of multiple styles within a religious context expresses the contemporary Bukharian Jewish condition.

Bukharian Jews pride themselves on their ability to draw on different styles and to create something new. For all of his concern over the loss of Bukharian ways, Malakov's religious projects are not particularly dogmatic, instead relating the attitude that Bukharian Jewish religious music is distinct in its combination of particular Bukharian melodies and interpretations of melodies drawn from various sources but reinterpreted in a Bukharian style. For example, in the Psalms project, Ezro Malakov has included a number of settings to completely new melodies, some drawing on explicitly Bukharian elements (such as the use of tanbūr), and many borrowing from styles of other Jewish communities. "Avrom [Tolmasov] is playing the tanbūr, a little bit Arabic style, a synthesis," said Malakov. To him, this is all part of the Bukharian approach. As he explained, "All of the Jewish ethnic groups (*millat*) have their own way of singing the Psalms, and they only sing them one way. Ashkenazi Jews always sing the Psalms one way. For me, there are 150 different Psalms, I want to sing 150 different ways."

This bold and in many ways surprising statement suggests a paradigm shift in thinking about tradition, repertoire, and the ways that discursive categories determine understandings of music. Modes of preservation, reconstruction, innovation, and adaptation are not seen as mutually exclusive by these Bukharian musicians. In fact, Ezro Malakov sees new settings of the Psalms and other Jewish texts as a traditional and preservational endeavor, since it is the *process* of engaging these materials in particular ways that define Bukharian music as much as it is the old tunes he remembers. Malakov's intentions with *Musical Treasures of the Bukharian Jewish Community* were to preserve particular Bukharian melodies for future generations while also pointing the "way" and "path" for these future Bukharian Americans to continue creative and distinct spins on their own heritage, as the abilities to develop a personal style and introduce fresh ideas are seen as requirements for Bukharian professionals. Malakov also intended for the document to serve as a landmark summation of the Bukharian Jewish community's heritage and ethnic music, and a celebration of their religious freedom following the hidden and secretive nature of Judaism under the Soviet Union. The embrace of a range of attitudes and approaches to Bukharian Jewish repertoire, and in turn, the constitution of the Bukharian Jewish community's ethnic identity, is manifested in the diverse collection and wide net of *Musical Treasures of the Bukharian Jewish Community*.

Resistance to assimilation and reinforcing cultural boundaries, as well as synthesis, innovation, and adaptation, are all various modes that Bukharian Jews put to different uses as they define their ethnicity in the post-Soviet era. The Jewish religious repertoire expresses Bukharian Jews' own multifaceted and complex relationships with other Jews, and the competing pressures of promoting distinctiveness and conforming to non-Bukharian Jewish ways. Maqom, on the other hand, is the primary presentational repertoire and expression of intercultural exchanges between Bukharian Jews and non-Bukharians, especially Muslim Central Asians. But neither maqom nor the religious repertoire fully expresses the facet of Bukharian Jewish identity that explicitly and outwardly celebrates heterogeneity and Bukharian Jews' self-conception as cosmopolitans. This side of Bukharian identity is best expressed in the party repertoire, which due in large part to the pressures of multiculturalism is confined to internal community events.

5

Party Music

Expressing Cosmopolitanism

storia World Manor is one of the catering halls where Bukharian Jews in New York hold their wedding parties (tūĭs, also *bazm*-s "banquets"), along with Leonard's of Great Neck, Elite Palace, Da Mikelle Palace, and several others. In the upstairs ballroom, Mazal Tov performs loud amplified music for several hundred people. Roma Narkolayev, the keyboardist, plays both melodic riffs and drum rhythms on his synthesizer. Ariel Karshigiyev and Yakov Rubinov are the two percussionists: one alternates between an electronic drum pad and a cylindrical drum balanced on one knee, angled toward the ceiling, the other plays small conga drums and a red Latin Percussion "jam block," and they both occasionally switch to doiras. The band has four vocalists—Ilya Khavasov; Albert Narkolayev, who also plays clarinet; Roshel Rubinov, also on guitar; and Galina Paliy, the cantorial student at Hebrew Union College-Jewish Institute of Religion who invited me to the event. Galina was raised in Kiev and immigrated to the United States in 1995, and at the time she is performing on and off with the group.

Although this is my first Bukharian Jewish event outside of staged folkloric perfomances, I recognize Roshel Rubinov and Ilya Khavasov from the *At the Bazaar of Love* recording. Here, however, there are no tanbūrs, no maqom, and the band isn't wearing jommas or "traditional" clothing, but white sport jackets over black pants and shirts. Galina is wearing a dress and high heels. On occasion, four young, flamboyant dancers accompany the musicians, performing elaborate routines. They stand out with their blonde hair (I later find out that they are "Russians"—in other words, not Jews). Men and women are dancing on the floor together, but they are mostly in sex-segregated circles and clusters; there is a range of

133

outfit styles and head coverings, with a few men wearing black hats or kipahs, most not.

After a few numbers, the dance floor clears and fog drifts in. The bride and groom slowly approach each other from either end, then perform a tightly choreographed dance to a light show and a CD of soft rock. Small flares go off at each table when the groom gets on his knees and spins.

All of the announcing is in Russian, but the songs are in Persian, Hebrew, and English. The master of ceremonies leads the celebrants through a ritual hand-washing and blessing over the challah. Back to the dancing, Mazal Tov plays the Eagles' "Hotel California," over which the band, in rhyming Russian poetry, gives well wishes to the bride and groom, their families, and everyone in attendance. "Hava Nagila," a Georgian song, a Russian disco song, an Israeli ballad, and several top-forty US hits (Christina Aguilera's "I Turn to You," Ricky Martin's "She Bangs," Jennifer Lopez's "Let's Get Loud") fill an hour or two, the music constant and the dance floor packed.

The second half of the evening is dominated by 6/8 Bukharian dance tunes, including original and cover material I recognize from the performers' albums: Roshel Rubinov's "'Arūsi Zebo," Albert Narkolayev's "Shirin Jon," and Ilya Khavasov's "My Samarqand" (a cover of a hit by the Uzbek singer Nasiba Abdullayeva). The symbols of Central Asian heritage are getting stronger. The percussionists are showcased with virtuoso doira solos. At one point, members of the reception dance in their jommas, adorned with Stars of David, to powerful drumming and the dramatic blasts of the long karnai trumpets. Galina comes over to me and points out a few things: the Narkolayev brothers had classical educations, she tells me, and I notice Roma's perfect hand position. I ask her what the lyrics are about. "Various places," she tells me. "Tashkent, Samarqand, Jerusalem." She points out the nationalities and backgrounds of all the songs: Romanian, Indian film music, and an Italian song with an "Oriental" keyboard part that the band particularly likes.

At that point, the bride's sister comes out and does a belly dance number to an Israeli song. Next, the professional dancers return in red and silver outfits topped by giant sombreros, and they dance to a Spanish-language song. I later notice a song that sounds as if it is in the Arab *bayāti* mode, with its characteristic 3/4-tone split minor third. This is surprising to me, as Bukharian music—classical, pop, or otherwise—is diatonic, and does not typically use these quarter-tone–based intervals associated with Arab, Turkish, and Iranian music. People start to eat from the sweet table. Galina tells me that normally the band would play a few Shashmaqom selections while people eat, but because the party was delayed on this evening, the band had to skip it.

At 1 am the music and dance are going full speed ahead. The band has hardly taken a break for almost four hours, and the drum machine seems to be going constantly. Even while the room is being cleaned at the end of the night, the band goes on playing and the party continues. When the party is finally over, the band eats and drinks and socializes for a while.

On my way home, I am trying to make sense of what I just witnessed in comparison to the maqom and religious recordings with which I had started to become familiar. There had not been one note of Shashmaqom. Instead, I heard a dizzying assortment of styles and languages, from the standard Jewish American wedding repertoire I had performed myself as a professional saxophonist to the exciting karnai-accompanied jomma dance, and all the Israeli, Spanish, Russian, and Indian music in between. Of course, this was not a demonstration of Bukharian ethnic heritage to outsiders, but an internal event where the young couple and their friends and families wanted to hear their reality represented with music. Explicit symbols of Central Asia were displayed at specific points as reminders, but for those at this particular party, it seemed that being Bukharian Jewish American was about celebrating the ability to adapt, to thrive as urban cosmopolitans, and to do it all in a modern and contemporary fashion.

Defining the Party Repertoire

Party repertoire is the diverse collection of dance music and international melodies heard at events such as weddings and bar mitzvah parties (following the religious ceremonies) and secular community celebrations such as birthday parties for important individuals. Party music is well represented in a thriving cottage CD industry and on videos that musicians upload to YouTube. Party music is the most prevalent repertoire at internal celebrations but largely absent from intercultural multicultural presentations, where maqom dominates, and from most religious ceremonies, where religious repertoire naturally holds sway.

Party music has precedents in traditional celebratory music, including some upbeat sections of the maqom, repertoire performed by the female wedding entertainer sozanda, and other wedding tunes now classified as "folklore." These repertoires all have a strong connection to dance and emphasize a marked 6/8 drum rhythm to which vocals are coordinated in a specific way. Roshel Rubinov referred to the standard rhythm for party music as *shest vosmykh*, "6/8," instead of a term such as *zarbi ufor*, which describes the same basic pattern in the Shashmaqom.[1]

Before the Soviet era the sozanda ensemble was an essential part of the Jewish and Muslim wedding in Bukhara, essential for women-only gatherings, and this entertainment remained an important wedding staple during the twentieth century. Similar roles and ensembles were found in other cities, including Kermina, Samarqand, Shahrisabz, and Kattakurgan (Djumaev 2008:58). In Bukhara the sozanda was an especially important role for Bukharian Jewish female musicians (Fātemi 2005:227–29). The sozanda had to be skilled at improvising praises and compliments. She also guided ceremonies for both Muslims and Jews, including birth celebrations, circumcisions (misvo-sa'udo for Jews, *sunnat tūi* for Muslims), Jewish tfillin-tying celebrations for a bar mitzvah (*tfillin bandon*), Muslim turban-binding rites (*salla bandon*), and rites without music and dance such as the *arvohi pir* (elder's spirit, a banquet to commemorate an apprentice's graduation or celebrate good luck) and *oshi bibiyon* (grandmother's meal, also known as *Bibi Seshanba* [Grandmother Tuesday], another way of paying tribute to one's elders) (Djumaev 2008). The sozanda repertoire is percussive music, as the sozandas accompany themselves solely on doiras, *qayroq* (stone clappers), *zang* (bells), and *piyola* (tea cups, clanged together), a legacy heard in showy doira solos and the percussion-heavy quality of contemporary wedding bands.

The specific role of the sozanda has seriously diminished among Bukharian Jews in New York. Sozanda music and dance is still an important part of the women's only wedding party following Shabbat, but much of the sozanda music in New York is heard at staged presentations of heritage music, part of a transformational process that began during the Soviet era. As the established contexts for performance began to disappear, the sozanda repertoire became more of a folkloric art or a form of stage entertainment, epitomized by the stardom achieved by the group "Nozanin," led by the most celebrated sozanda of the twentieth century, Yafo Pinkhasova, known as Tūhfakhon (b. 1928, Bukhara–d. 2010, Denver) (Levin and Matyakubov 1991; T. Levin 1996: 119; Djumaev 2008:59).[2] Even Tūhfakhon did not entertain at weddings very much after her emigration in 1995, although she did perform with Ensemble Shashmaqom.[3] Today, the sozanda's repertoire is mostly an object of scholarly research and preservation. However, the music and the role largely made their way into the repertoire of the contemporary party entertainer, and the sozanda legacy may account for the continued importance of the popular entertainer as a viable role for Bukharian Jewish women, along with the fact that women are unable to move into the professional roles for religious singers the way men have.

The sozanda repertoire consists of suites or medleys that proceed from medium-slow to fast (on the sozanda suite, see Nurjanov 1980; Fātemī 2005:241–60; and Reikher 2005–2006, the latter of which contains a description of a recreative performance in Israel by Nina Bakayeva and Nina Tillayeva). A full performance of a sozanda suite is said to last between one and two hours (Levin and Matyakubov 1991); however, as is the case with the Shashmaqom, in practice sozanda repertoire is typically performed as individual songs or in shorter suites. The only suite upon which performers and scholars consistently agree is the *bukhorchai zang* ("Bukhara-style music with bells"), portions of which are still commonly heard at weddings and concerts (Fātemī 2005:242–47).

The ends of sozanda performances feature fast 6/8-based songs, called *ufor* as in the Shashmaqom and *ufori tez* ("fast ufor"). Dancers make it clear that the basic drum pattern is heard in two groups of three, marking the first and fourth eighth-note pulse with their wrists, hands, arms, and feet. However, singers also exploit the feel of superimposing three groups of two with the prosodic rhythm of the lyrics. This rhythmic approach is a typical feature of both maqom and sozanda ufors, often heightened by call-and-response refrains. Examples 5.1 and 5.2 provide a useful

Example 5.1. Tūhfakhon Pinkhasova and her sozanda ensemble, "Soq-soqi-jon" refrain (from *Bukhara: Musical Crossroads of Asia*). Transcribed by the author.

Example 5.2. Ilyos Mallayev Ensemble, beginning of "Lalilabat" refrain at end of "Ufori Uzzol" of Maqom Buzruk (from *At the Bazaar of Love*). Transcribed by the author.

comparison. The first example is from a recording of an abridged sozanda suite on *Bukhara: Musical Crossroads of Asia* (1991); the line given is a repeated ensemble response to the calls of Tūhfakhon: "Soq-soqi jon, piyola pur may kun" ("Winebearer, fill the cup with wine"). Example 5.2 is the beginning of the "Lalilabat" refrain at the end of "Ufori Uzzol," with the same rhythmic coordination. A key element in both examples is the low "bum" stroke that hits on the fifth eighth note of every measure, which acts as both a syncopation of the even two groups of three, and as a sort of

Example 5.3a. Roshel Rubinov, "'Arūsi Zebo" (verse) from *Tamanno* (2002). Transcribed by the author.

Example 5.3b. Roshel Rubinov, "'Arūsi Zebo" (chorus) from *Tamanno* (2002). Transcribed by the author.

"pickup" stroke back into the hard "bak" on the one of the next measure. As a "pickup," the bum stroke pulls in the direction of hearing three groups of two (a "3/4" feel), and the rhythmic treatment of the words in both cases can also be grouped in that manner. But again, the movements of dancers on the first and fourth eighth notes make it abundantly clear that the three groups of two (the "6/8") is the dominant meter.

A contemporary party tune, Roshel Rubinov's "'Arūsi Zebo" ("Beautiful Bride") employs the same rhythmic relationships (Audio Example 5.1◖). In the verses, two lines of which are shown in Example 5.3, the vocals emphasize three groupings of two over the fast 6/8. In the chorus, Rubinov adjusts the rhythmic treatment of the words to fall squarely in the 6/8 meter, but his choice to sing the words "'a-rūs-i" and "do-mod-i" across barlines keeps the rhythm exciting and avoids a heavy-handed emphasis on groupings of three.

Perhaps the most distinguishing aspect of the party repertoire is also the most obvious: the texts. Maqom is most characterized by classical Persian and Turkic poetry, and even fast maqom numbers (such as "Ufori Uzzol") are vehicles for classical poems in ʿaruz meters. Religious repertoire is defined by its Jewish texts. Party repertoire, again in line with its sozanda precedent, is about wedding celebrations, brides and grooms, food and alcohol, and the event taking place in the moment. For example, take the verses of "ʿArūsi Zebo":

> Ba shabi bazmi tarab ʿarūsu domod oyad
> Bo gulu sunbuli tar hamma peshvoz baroyad
> Bio ʿarūsi zebo, bio ʿarūsi zebo
> Bio domodi barno, bio domodi barno

> Translation:
> The bride and groom come to the joyous wedding banquet night
> Greeting and bearing wet flowers
> Come beautiful bride, come beautiful bride
> Come handsome groom, come handsome groom

The party repertoire is also a continuation of the *estrada* ("stage") tradition in Russia and the Soviet Union, "electrified, Western-derived music" or "pop music" (Spinetti 2005:205). Also called *sho* ("show") music, estrada is accompanied by lots of glitz, elaborate choreography, and eye-catching costumes. As variety performers, estrada musicians are known for their versatility and their self-conscious incorporation of new and foreign elements. Estrada music, like other pop entertainment, typically contains love songs, songs about having a good time, and ballads.

The show environment retains some legacy of the boy dancer, or *bacha*, who historically entertained at all-male gatherings instead of female entertainers (T. Levin 1996:89, 120; Fātemi 2005:231–32). The bacha often dressed as a female (*zan-push*) and performed popular genres. The bacha legacy might be indirectly responsible for aspects in the style of the celebrated dancer Artur Gulkarov, son of "People's Artist" dancer Malika Kalantarova and doira player Isḥoq Gulkarov, who wears makeup and dresses androgynously (Williams 2010).

For the outside observer used to the Orthodox mores of the religious repertoire and the spiritual associations of maqom, the revealing outfits and seemingly overt sexuality of party repertoire can come as a surprise. Perhaps the separation of the party repertoire from the religious and maqom repertoires allows party performers to skirt the gender and sexuality restrictions that have affected the other repertoires. However, gender and sexuality conventions and attitudes are highly variable and culture-specific. The bacha tradition, for example, was described by Western observers as "lascivious" (Schuyler 1877:135), "immoral," and "obscene" (Olufsen 1911:437)—a symbol of the "degenerate Muslim" in Orientalist writings (Shay 2009:295)—but in fact, the tradition of males dancing for males in strictly sexually segregated societies is internally viewed as a moral alternative to men watching women dance. I was interested when a fellow audience member observing Gulkarov's routine at an important community celebration criticized it as bordering on immoral, not for the cross-dressing or suggestive movements, but because, as she put it, he was doing a "Buddhism dance" (presumably his India-inspired moves and soundtrack), and "Buddhism is not accepted by Jews."

Many Jews flourished as estrada performers, dovetailing with their reputation as cosmopolitans and cultural brokers. Ilyas Mallayev and Muhabbat Shamayeva were primarily stage entertainers in the Soviet Union, Mallayev a member of the Folk and Estrada Orchestras of Uzbekistan Radio from 1956 to 1962 and the Symphonic Estrada Orchestra of Uzbekistan Radio from 1962 until his emigration in 1992. Mallayev's cosmopolitan aesthetic is captured by his version of "My Favorite Things" played on the sitar and his admiration for Indian film stars—Mallayev and Shamayeva's children Raj and Nargis are named after Raj Kapoor and Nargis Dutt.

Unlike the roles of hofiz and ḥazzan, the role of stage entertainer has not required a major transformation in the United States. The party repertoire has stayed a consistently viable sphere for Bukharian musical professionals, who have kept the cosmopolitan aesthetic of the repertoire and expanded it to include more and more elements as they adjust to the changing needs of Bukharian audiences. It is an especially important avenue for female singers, who are dwindling from the ranks of maqom singers and prohibited or discouraged from participating in the religious repertoire, but who are thriving as stage entertainers in the United States. For example, unlike Mallayev, who overhauled his profile to pursue classical music and his religious and poetic interests, Shamayeva continued to sing and develop her diverse estrada repertoire, including Russian-language ballads and dance songs, alongside her maqom activities. Mallayev and Shamayeva's children, Raj, Nargis, and Violetta, have followed in their parents' footsteps, continually adapting the role of the Bukharian stage entertainer in contemporary New York. Raj is an accomplished guitarist with a heavy jazz and jazz-fusion inspired style, and all three are successful vocalists with eclectic repertoires. Other musicians went the opposite route from Mallayev, such as Roma Narkolayev, the classical ghijak master and former director of the Tajik State Radio and Television maqom ensemble, whose keyboard playing and arranging for Mazal Tov has subsumed his maqom activities.[4]

The estrada heritage accounts for the large presence in the party repertoire of music that is not rooted in the sozanda music or traditional wedding styles. Most estrada songs are still in Russian, but an insatiable appetite for new and foreign aspects is apparent in a wide variety of languages and styles found in Bukharian party contexts. Ilya Khavasov's album *My Samarkand* lists each track with its associated language

(Russian, Tajik, Turkish, Azerbaijani, Armenian, "Afgani" [Dari] and "shiru shakar"—"milk and sugar," traditionally referring to bilingual poems that alternate Persian "milk" and Turkic "sugar" verses), and has songs by Mallayev, Nasiba Abdullayeva, and İbrahim Tatlıses. Estrada is a "popuri" (CDs often contain a track combining excerpts from the album and titled with this variant spelling), evidenced by songs such as Robert Shin's "Castanets" on *My Samarkand*, a Russian-language song to a Latin-flavored melody. Bukharian party music in the estrada style contains 4/4 dance rhythms, Bollywood songs and belly dance numbers, and pop songs from the greater Russian-speaking world.

Central Asians have deep affinities with music from the Caucasus, and party music is a primary place for them to maintain and express those links. Bukharian party repertoire is filled with Armenian and Azerbaijani stylistic tropes and melodies. The clarinet, tor, and accordion, staples of Bukharian party ensembles, are all primarily associated with Caucasian music. Albert Narkolayev, the clarinetist and leader of Mazal Tov, is a major proponent of Caucasian music, recording melodies such as "Zhonushka," a song by the Armenian estrada singer Boka (Boris Davidyan, born in Baku, now living in Los Angeles).

The most recent component of the party repertoire is the explosion of English-language and Spanish-language songs, a growing piece of the repertoire as Bukharian Jewish Americans become increasingly situated in the New York environment. Nargis Mallayeva's *Desert Rain* (2001) is almost entirely in English, and her "Ayelet" contains a rap. Many popular CDs contain "remix" versions of songs from the album, and DJing (D.J. Mike Alayev is the most prominent) is a rising role for party entertainment. Young Bukharians listen to rap music (50 Cent was a huge favorite through the 2000s), top-forty hits, and electronic dance music. At one event honoring the Bukharian Jewish contribution to the Shashmaqom, I spoke with several teenagers and young adults about their opinion of maqom. One man in his twenties commented, "It's not really my music. I like ambient, electronica. In New York City, you hear everything."

To address the eclectic tastes of Bukharian audiences and their desire to hear themselves represented as urban cosmopolitans, diversity and versatility are necessary for the Bukharian Jewish professional musician hoping to make a living from performing. Bukharian Jewish professionals have diversified in terms not only of repertoire but also of performance contexts, and in addition to live performances, a cottage industry of locally produced CDs has emerged in Queens, with musicians such as Yuhan, Nargis, Ilya Khavasov, and Roshel Rubinov distributing their popular repertoire on high-quality, slickly arranged recordings. Variety also enables Bukharian professionals to play for non-Bukharian parties: Bukharian wedding bands play for Iranian Jews, Russian Jews, Uzbek and Tajik Muslim immigrants, and others. Roshel Rubinov says:

> Today, to make a living (*non khordan*—literally, "to eat bread") from one's art is extremely difficult. Why? Because even when you turn on

your telephone, there's going to be nice music. Right? Today, it's not easy to live on music. It's very difficult work. . . . That's why I like any kind of music. Chinese music, Uyghur music, Persian, Turkish, Arabic, symphonic orchestras, Demis Roussos, you know, everybody's good for me. If you're a musician, you have to listen to everything. *Everything*. Now I'm singing Arabic songs, I'm singing Turkish songs, Persian songs, Russian songs, you know? If you don't listen, how are you going to sing? It's not easy.

The choices of the Bukharian professional party musician compare with those of other Jewish professional musicians, shedding light on the archetypal qualities of the Bukharian American immigrant situation. The European professional musicians (*klezmorim*) who immigrated to the United States in the early twentieth century, for example, also adjusted their repertoires to include more and more "American" styles to address the changing tastes and self-conceptions of their audiences. And like the Bukharian professional, the American klezmer was continuing a process of change, as the klezmer repertoire in Europe was already a diverse collection of dances and styles that could be played for a variety of audiences in different places (Feldman 1994). Many klezmers or those from klezmer families remade themselves into American popular and jazz musicians or focused on "society" work (such as Lester Lanin's band) (Netsky 2002a:19, 2002b:66–67).[5] Bukharian party musicians are mostly performing within their community, but the precedent of the Jewish professional musician in the United States would suggest that over time, Bukharian professionals will increasingly participate in mainstream secular American genres. A crucial point of difference when comparing the Bukharian professional and the early twentieth-century klezmer is the impact of multiculturalism, and the significant internal and external pressures on the Bukharian musician to self-consciously retain signifiers of ethnic identity.

Cosmopolitanism and Bukharian Jewish Identity

Bukharian Jews define themselves in large part by their cosmopolitanism, expressed in party repertoire by the ability to appreciate and perform the music of others—but in the manner of multiculturalism, each group is kept distinct and defined by a representative kind of music. This is their own process of othering, an adoption of multicultural cosmopolitanism from the standpoint of Bukharian subjectivity, a Bukharian center. Ilyos Mallayev made cosmopolitanism and multilingualism a major point of distinction between Bukharian Jews and other "nations": Uzbeks have one language and one music, and Bukharian Jews speak more than one language and know more than one music. Roshel Rubinov agreed:

Indian, Arabic, Uzbek, Russian, Kyrgyz, Tajik, [Bukharian Jews] like all music. Actually, I don't see any other people (*khalq*) like Bukharian

Jews, because Bukharian Jews...like different [kinds of] music. Uzbek, Tajik, Indian, Turkish, Russian, different, different. Some people only like their own music. *Finito*. Today they'll only sing English songs, that's it, or only Russian songs. Bukharians are different....Whatever music is nice, if it's good, they like it.

Ezro Malakov applied this attitude to Jewish repertoire when he explained that unlike members of other Jewish ethnic groups, who only want to sing the Psalms in their particular way, he wants to sing them in "150 different ways."

Roman Tolmasov thought that the talent for learning, mastering, and enjoying other people's music was a particular feature of Jews worldwide, and not just Bukharian Jews. This attitude among Bukharian Jews relates to the Jewish minority status within Soviet ideology. While Uzbek and Tajik nationalities were represented in terms of monolingual canonized versions of the Shashmaqom repertoire, Jews were defined by their cosmopolitanism and alleged rootlessness. This view still seems somewhat taken for granted in post-Soviet writings. Alexander Djumaev wrote, "One of the features of the historical-cultural mission of the Jewish people [or 'nation'] is to preserve the cultures of other peoples [or 'nations']" (Djumaev 2004:84, original in Russian), and this is meant to be complimentary, introducing his article dedicated to Jewish musicians' contributions to Central Asian musical life.[6]

Cosmopolitanism can be a double-edged sword for Jewish professional musicians. The idea that Jews are particularly good at learning a wide variety of musical styles has increased their mobility and professional opportunities, making them in demand for parties of many different ethnic groups. On the other hand, the long-standing pejorative notion of the Jew as the quintessential performer-mimic and the reputation of Jewish musicians as skillful chameleons were used by anti-Semites (most famously Richard Wagner) in claims that Jews had no music of their own and could only imitate the music of other people (Gilman 2008; Loeffler 2010:113–19). Joseph Stalin infamously enlisted the phrase "rootless cosmopolitan" in his campaigns against Jewish intellectuals beginning in 1948; since Jews were world citizens, they were disloyal, unpatriotic, anti-Russian, and anti-Communist. Even the seemingly innocuous description of Jews in diaspora as living in "host countries" implies at best a guest status and at worst a parasitic relationship, in which Jews take culture and sustenance from others where they live, without giving back, and without fully integrating into the general society. Party repertoire is a space for Bukharian Jews to enthusiastically proclaim their cosmopolitanism in the supportive environment of the United States, as opposed to the ambivalence and even persecution with which "cosmopolitanism" was treated in the Soviet Union.

Bukharian Jews do not express negative associations with cosmopolitanism or their reputation for making the music of other nationalities their own. It is a point of pride, and displaying this aspect of Bukharian Jewish identity is one of the main characteristics of the party repertoire. Party musicians broadcast their cosmopolitanism as part of their résumés. According to Avrom Tolmasov's student Shlomo "Stas" Kalontar, a rising party musician in his own right, Tolmasov was "the first person to put in Bukharian music Persian, Afghanian [*sic*], Azerbaijanian, Armenian, everything. After him everyone started to sing it, before it was only Shashmaqom— that's it. All the different nationalities he put, India, everything." Yuhan Benjamin, one of the most popular party musicians in Queens, explained in an email exchange that because Bukharian Jews are not limited to one nationality, "[we are a] unique people possessing knowledge of world music styles and poetry. In our particular Bukharian folk music, you will find colors of India, Iran, Afghanistan, Arabia, Uzbekistan, Tajikistan, Azerbaijan, Spain, and even China…[and] I just created a new sound of Russian salsa to show the world [our] knowledge of Latin culture."

Bukharian cosmopolitanism resonates strongly with American multiculturalism, and the Bukharian attitude toward diversity, like multiculturalism, addresses larger concerns about how people of different backgrounds can or should coexist and learn from each other. Yuhan Benjamin is explicit about the utopian potentials of an eclectic repertoire on his website, www.yuhanny.com, which opens with a Flash animation sequence of a Star of David followed by a Cross, Crescent moon, and statue of Buddha. He positions his all-embracing approach as an inheritance of Central Asia as a multicultural crossroads:

> …[Yuhan's] father would name his new born son, Yuhan, "Peace Maker" in hopes it would instill a kind of legacy for peace for them and their neighbors.
>
> Growing up, Yuhan could hear it from house to house, within its streets, those seductive "mugam" Middle Eastern melodies spilling out of clarinets. 6/8 dance rhythms pulsating from round "doyra" drums, oriental echoes emanating from the southeast, romantic flamenco and Italian music heard at local parties, pain filled Russian songs, and Turkish folk singers whose strong hypnotic influence would later be heard on his unique vocal style. But at age eleven, for the first time, Yuhan listened to the renowned sounds of "The Beatles," following; Stevie Wonder, George Benson, Gino Vanelli, Billy Joel, Deep Purple, Pink Floyd, and UFO that in an instant, would envelop him completely.
>
> …By the time he reached the age of twenty-one, [he] had already toured most southwestern Russian Republics, including appearances on radio and television. An unusual accomplishment, to sing to rooms full of obvious cultural differences, but by now, he amassed the in-depth knowledge and natural instincts needed to combine and perform those styles successfully.
>
> Arriving in New York City, in what he calls "the best city in the world," Yuhan wasted no time. Has over the years established a large following touring with an incredible orchestra backed by toxic beats,

tantalizing show equipped with exquisite dancing, and uplifting vocals sung in streams of languages. (Yuhan 2006)

Bukharian Jewish cosmopolitanism draws on the language of multiculturalism in that diversity is constituted in terms of singular nations with representative cultures: Armenian, Azerbaijani, and others. Similarly, American multiculturalism and the "salad bowl" or mosaic metaphor defines the United States as a mixture of peoples defined by distinct cultures. Multiculturalism is dependent on a paradoxical subjectivity: "we" are always heterogeneous, whereas "they" are always homogeneous. Even in his influential endorsement of global cosmopolitanism, Kwame Anthony Appiah proposes starting with "individuals—not nations, tribes, or 'peoples'—as the proper object of moral concern," but must use the vocabulary of nationalities to describe Kumasi's diversity: "English, German, Chinese, Syrian, Lebanese, Burkinabe, Ivorian, Nigerian, Indian: I can find you families of each description" (Appiah 2006a). In the contemporary world, identity and nationality are inseparable, even as diaspora and transnationalism increasingly become the status quo; with respect to a global notion of "world music," Bohlman writes, "the nation is an ontological fact of life in the study of world music, even in an era when nationalism has increasingly become a dirty word" (Bohlman 2002b:94).

Bukharian Jews understand their distinctive national culture as eclectic, as opposed to other nationalities, members of which, in their experience, define their national culture in terms of one repertoire, language, and stylistic approach. The distinguishing factor in Bukharian cosmopolitanism is that the "we are eclectic and they are not" formulation is rooted in their complex historical situation as a minority population in environments in which they were excluded from the dominant nationalist logics. As opposed to the eclectic blend at a Bukharian wedding, when Mazal Tov plays an Uzbek wedding, the party-goers "only want to hear Uzbek music, nothing else" (Roshel Rubinov, personal communication); Muhabbat Shamayeva was stopped while singing a Russian song for an Uzbek audience in New Jersey (personal communication). Party music, which expresses cosmopolitanism better than any other Bukharian repertoire, dovetails with their notion of the United States—and New York in particular—as a mixture of different "nationalities" or "peoples." Bukharian Jews are excellent spokespeople for a global urban cosmopolitanism, consistent with their lives in the global cities of Central Asia and their historical roles as merchants, from the beginnings of the Silk Road to the present.

The irony of the Bukharian Jewish pride in their cosmopolitan identity is that in the landscape of the United States and the Jewish world, an intense minority and ethnic status strongly positions Bukharian Jews as a homogenous "them" and not a heterogeneous "us." In fact, multicultural situations exert a pressure on Bukharian Jews to keep their cosmopolitan party repertoire to themselves and to publicly participate in the cultural democracy with a singular ethnic repertoire, which Bukharian Jews have astutely identified as maqom. The loud amplification, pop hybrids, and linguistic Babel of the party repertoire can find no home on the "world music" circuit, although both ostensibly celebrate diversity.[7]

In world music situations, American audiences affirm their own cosmopolitanism and sophistication by assembling and then consuming a salad bowl of singular cultural products; Bukharian Jews do the same thing at their own parties. As Peterson and Kern theorized (1996), omnivorous musical taste may have replaced snobbery as a mark of "highbrow" sophistication and class status. However, the dichotomous standing of the party repertoire complicates this thesis. The rejection of party repertoire by world music audiences suggests that omnivorous taste remains highly subjective and concerned with value and aesthetics, with absolute ideals of choice, freedom, and democracy taking a backseat to issues of self-representation. Party repertoire's overtly Western and globalized qualities mark it as inauthentic and perhaps even lowbrow for world music audiences who want to reaffirm their own sophistication with "open-minded" appreciation for the music of the exotic other; party music, too much like Western culture, sullies this taste culture. Meanwhile, those same qualities are exactly the marks of omnivorous taste that Bukharian Jews employ internally to represent themselves as sophisticated and modern. Bukharian professional musicians are versed enough in addressing different audiences that they have adapted the different repertoires to the appropriate contexts.

A Generational Crossroads

The party repertoire sits at a generational crossroads, expressing two sides of the immigrant divide. On one side are the Bukharian Jews who decided to immigrate and on the other side, their children. For many of the middle-aged adults who grew up in the Soviet Union, Russian is their first language and estrada is their music. Estrada songs of the 1960s and 1970s pull at their heartstrings, sometimes in spite of their ambivalence with respect to the USSR. For their children, Central Asia is a distant memory or not a memory at all. In an English poem published in the Bukharian Jewish Organization of Youth magazine, Hanna Fazylova writes of "nostalgia," "childhood pictures," "forgotten trees and lands," and "I fear that my heart will never tire / Of longing for the past I've yet to meet." They do not know Central Asia, and most have never visited it (and some say they do not care, Israel having a greater pull). English is most likely their first language instead of Russian. This generation looks to party musicians to sing English-language songs and mainstream American hits.

The party repertoire is the primary place for Bukharians to sing in Russian. Russian-language songs provide a space for celebratory and sentimental remembrances of Central Asia, and the Soviet Union more generally. At parties, Ilya Khavasov's cover of Nasiba Abdullayeva's "My Samarqand" is a staple, painting a romantic picture of the city that transports those who lived there or who have been there, evoking a mysterious aura for those who have only heard stories about it:

> Ancient azure minarets
> Aromatic tea, engaging conversations
> Voices of friends and noisy weddings
> I remember my beloved Samarqand.
> Enchanted fairy tale!
> Appears in front of me, my Samarqand.
> How I love you, my city Samarqand.
> The years of my youth flew by
> As I took pleasure in the city's ancient beauty.
> My talisman, my motherland, my soul
> You will always be, my love, my Samarqand.
> Eastern song, sing with your soul.
> My Samarqand, how I love you, my city Samarqand.
> Tasty plov, flatbread
> Magical nights, dear ancient streets
> The distant roads won't separate us
> You are always with me, my beloved Samarqand.[8]

Performers who were major stage performers in Central Asia might still sing patriotic Russian songs, capturing a nostalgic mood for those whose diasporic experience includes the pain of migration and the memories of their geographic homes. For example, on her album *Yallalum* (2003), Muhabbat Shamayeva included "My Russia," a song made famous by the estrada diva Ekaterina Shavrina as "Glyazhu v ozera sinie" ("I Look at the Blue Lake"). Although this song is not part of the wedding repertoire (so not really "light" or "party" repertoire), it is part of the estrada world. The patriotic lyrics translate:

> I look at the blue lake
> I pick chamomiles in the fields
> I call you Russia
> The only one.
> Ask me several times
> There's no land that is dearer
> I was given a Russian name
> Here some time ago.
> I don't know greater happiness
> Than to live one life with you
> To be sad with you, my land
> And to celebrate with you.
> Your beauty was tainted by
> Neither the years, nor tragedy
> Ivans and Marias have always made us proud.
> Not all eagles have returned—
> Some are alive, and others are killed—
> But their glory belongs to you.[9]

By maintaining her diverse repertoire throughout these times of upheaval and into the American context, Shamayeva is making a strong statement about cosmopolitanism and Russian elements as defining characteristics of Bukharian music-making.

For the children of these first-generation immigrants, Central Asia is an important cornerstone of their identity, but one that is becoming an imagined place *constructed* through music rather than a locus of memory that is *conjured* through music. Younger Bukharians portray Central Asia as a vague "East," representing themselves through the party repertoire as "Middle Easterners." Alongside Central Asian dance costumes and moves, the doira frame drum, and the ever-present image of the Registan in Samarqand, Bukharian party music contains generic "Eastern" tropes actually quite foreign to maqom and Central Asian folk music such as "hijaz"-like scales (exploiting augmented seconds), instruments such as the 'ud and goblet drums, string accompaniment in the manner of the Egyptian firqa, and formulaic "belly dance" costumes and moves. Bukharian Jews are also starting to adopt the yodeling (*tahrir*) heard in Iranian classical music. The blending of these "Oriental" signifiers is also indebted to Bukharian Jewish life in Israel and the strong identification of Bukharian Jews there as "Eastern Jews" (Mizraḥim), a third Jewish category—not Ashkenazim or Sephardim—dominated by Jews originally from Arab countries and to a lesser degree Iran.

Orientalization is visually noticeable in the video clips uploaded by Bukharian Jews on YouTube, such as the scantily clad dancer flanked by an Egyptian anubis in Yuhan Benjamin's "Love Never Dies" (Figure 5.1), or the dancers accompanying Nargis Mallayeva as she performed a Russian version of her "1001 Nights" on the competition "Musical Debut" (Figure 5.2).[10] Artur Gulkarov has developed his own distinct repertoire by combining contortionist moves, Bollywood costumes and gestures, belly dance moves, and Russian glitz into a quasi-"Eastern" fusion.

Figure 5.1. Video still from Yuhan, "Love Never Dies" (2009).
Reproduced with permission.

Figure 5.2. Nargis Mallayeva performing "1001 Nights" on *Musical Debut*. Reproduced with permission.

Even with their "anything goes" aesthetic, party musicians are especially concerned with finding ways to keep distinctive Bukharian traditions in pop music. Ilyos Mallayev's poetry is well represented in the party repertoire, as is traditional Central Asian dance, and doira playing is essential. Party music has proven to be the ideal arena for Bukharian musicians to express the community's "traditional cosmopolitanism" by combining Central Asian folklore, Russian estrada entertainment, pan-"Mizrahi" and "Oriental" styles and signals, and American pop. Nargis's "Magic of 'I Love You'" (Audio Example 5.2◐) from *Desert Rain* is a seamless fusion, the English lyrics coordinated to the synthesized 6/8 rhythm in the standard way; a recurring verse in Persian sung by her mother, Muhabbat Shamayeva—the second time around, in an alternating shiru shakar style; and an Azerbaijani-style clarinet solo. In another example, Stas Kalontar's video for "Azizam" (video produced by D.J. Mike Alayev, words by Ilyos Mallayev) starts with an 'ud solo and an English introduction ("I wait upon the distant shore / To love you as love was never loved before") before launching into the Persian lyrics over a 6/8 dance groove played on electronic drum and doira (Figures 5.3–5.5).[11] The melody is in an "Eastern" scale, with characteristic augmented seconds, played mostly by unison violins with electric guitar interludes. The video features the dancing of Malika Kalontarova and her students, and doira playing by the Barayev brothers, as the background switches between the Registan, a stereotypical Eastern "palace" scene, and estrada-esque environments of lights, mirrors, and TV screens.

Figure 5.3. Stas Kalontar, "Azizam," opening shot of Registan with title in quasi-Eastern font. Reproduced with permission.

Figure 5.4. Stas Kalontar, "Azizam," Malika Kalontarova (center) surrounded by young dancers from her school. Reproduced with permission.

The party repertoire is extremely important to Bukharian Jewish Americans, especially the second generation, who want to see and hear themselves represented as cosmopolitan, modern, and at home in New York. However, young and old alike appreciate light music, and both heavy and light repertoires are essential pieces of Bukharian musical life. Almost all secular Bukharian cultural events require the presence of both maqom and party repertoire to satisfy the diverse needs of an audience representing many generations and regions. The seventieth birthday celebration of Ezro

Figure 5.5. Stas Kalontar, "Azizam," Kalontar (center) with Barayev brothers on doiras. Reproduced with permission.

Malakov and the "Golden Ilyos" concert to memorialize Mallayev's life both ran the stylistic gamut from maqom to pop. But the nature of light music is that it will always have a broader and more diverse audience than heavy music, and light music carries strong associations of the present while heavy music evokes the past. Thus, Bukharian musicians combine party aesthetics with the maqom and religious repertoires to reach as wide an audience as possible. A CD distributed at one Sefar Tŭĭ, for example, featured Ilyos Mallayev's religious poem "Pazmon Shudam" to the tune of "My Samarqand." Instead of the Russian chorus "Pesnyu vostochnuyu poĭ dushoĭ Samarqand / Kak tebya ya lyublyu gorod moĭ Samarqand" ("Eastern song, sing with your soul / My Samarqand, how I love you, my city Samarqand"), Khavasov sings in Persian "Erets Isroelam / Tuĭi jonu dilam / Makomu manzilam / Tu—Erets Isroel" ("My Erets Isroel / Marriage of my heart and soul / My place and home / You—Erets Isroel"). Such settings of religious texts to Central Asian pop melodies, as with the maqom settings of religious texts, allow poets and musicians to map the diasporic longings for both Central Asia and Israel onto each other.

Bukharian party music is quickly changing and expanding, as musicians continue to incorporate more and more styles and melodies. Whereas maqom and the religious repertoire have become increasingly defined musical corpuses in attempts to create cohesive ideas of Bukharian identity, the party repertoire has become a place for the cosmopolitan ideas of Bukharian identity to thrive, overlapping with multiculturalism's ideology of cultural pluralism. Bukharian musicians have responded to the many pressures they experience in New York's multicultural environment, especially the need to maintain cultural distinctiveness, by maintaining maqom, religious, and party repertoires simultaneously—striving for equal emphasis and combining them in innovative ways—rather than rejecting repertoires or styles altogether. Allowing party repertoire to exist alongside maqom and religious repertoire satisfies the musical interests and tastes of multiple generations of Bukharian Americans, without young Bukharians having to leave the fold. The balance of these three repertoires is seen as a form of adaptation and adjustment, rather than assimilation, which would require Bukharian Jews to choose between a Bukharian identity and a separate American identity.

6

Ziyorat

Bukharian Jews left Central Asia for many reasons. Some left to experience religious freedom and to pursue opportunities, and some because they had experienced difficulties and discrimination while living in the region. However, many Bukharians in New York retain personal and economic ties to Central Asia and speak fondly of their lives there. At times they romanticize Central Asia, especially as years of war and economic hardship in New York and Israel have diminished the luster of these new homes. Examples of every attitude toward Central Asia exist among Bukharian Jews, sometimes in the same person. Once a friend was describing the anti-Semitism he experienced in Uzbekistan before emigrating and his current distate for his former home, only to add that he was excited about an upcoming visit later that year with his family. Bukharian Jews regularly discuss visits to Central Asia for business reasons, musical collaborations, or public displays of solidarity, as in April 2008 when Lev Leviev traveled to Uzbekistan with numerous Bukharian dignitaries. The strong relationship goes both ways: when dignitaries from the Uzbek or Tajik government visit the United States, Bukharian Jews perform for them, and ambassadors from these countries often attend Bukharian events.

The close relationship that Bukharian Jews seemed to have with Central Asia struck me. In my own experience as the great-grandchild of European Jewish immigrants, my older relatives spoke in unequivocally negative terms about Europe, if they spoke about it all, and no one ever expressed any interest in visiting Poland, Ukraine, Germany, or the other places from which my ancestors came. "Good riddance" was the general sentiment. I knew what towns my ancestors came from and had heard some stories, but that was about it. From my perspective, it seemed unusual for these Jewish immigrants to retain such close contacts and affinities with the place that they had so recently evacuated en masse. Their situation also struck me as distinct from other American immigrant and minority

153

communities. Although they emigrated as an ethnic group in a short span of time and most came with refugee status, their regular back-and-forth with the geographic region of Central Asia seemed to distinguish them from other immigrants who left their homes quickly and under difficult conditions.

One important reason for Bukharian Jews to visit Central Asia is a *ziyorat,* a pilgrimage to the resting places of one's ancestors. Since beginning my research I had seen advertisements for these trips, such as a 2003 notice in the *Bukharian Times* (Figure 6.1). When Ezro Malakov invited me on a ziyorat he was organizing for the fall of 2010, I jumped at the opportunity to join him. This would finally be a chance to experience Jewish

Figure 6.1. Advertisement for a ziyorat (pilgrimage) in the *Bukharian Times* weekly, March 2003. The announcement reads: "Dear friends! You have a unique opportunity to visit relatives and memorial sites where your ancestors lived—fathers, grandfathers, great-grandfathers.... The World Congress of Bukharian Jews is organizing ten-day trips to Uzbekistan, with tours of three historic cities: Tashkent, Bukhara, and Samarqand.The tour is escorted by speakers of Russian, Bukharian, and English. You are provided with kosher food and comfortable hotels." Reproduced with permission.

Uzbekistan following mass migration, through the eyes of my closest Bukharian partner and one of the scene's most crucial figures.

The pilgrimage figures strongly in Central Asian culture. The term ziyorat also applies to a pilgrimage to the tomb (*mazor*) of a Muslim saint (T. Levin 1996:182–83). Ilyos Mallayev had already taken me on a poetic *ziyorati se hofizi buzurg* (pilgrimage to the graves of three great hofizes), as he communed with his musical inspirations: Levi Bobokhonov, Mikhoel Tolmasov, and Gavriel Mulloqandov (Mallayev 1999:352–55). In his "Shahrisabz" (Rubinov 2002:105), Roshel Rubinov uses the strongest Persian word for homeland—*vatan*—to describe his city and mentions a pilgrimage to the tomb of Bashir:

> Shahri Shahrisabz sitorazor ast,
> In shahri qadim chu sabzazor ast.
> Garchand, ki duram az vatanam man,
> Yodash bikunam kuhna diyor ast.
>
> . . .
>
> Gar khasta kunad Bashir ziyorat,
> Yobad ki shifo gar bemador ast.
>
> Translation:
> The city of Shahrisabz is abounding with stars,
> This ancient city is verdant,
> Although I am far from my homeland,
> I remember the old land.
>
> . . .
>
> If sick make a pilgrimage to Bashir,
> Find a cure for weariness.

Our ziyorat to Central Asia reinforced several key conclusions I had drawn after working so closely with the Bukharian community in New York. First, on the trip, music and poetry continually expressed the travelers' complex ideas about diaspora, combining multiple senses of homeland with an essential, singular sense of Bukharian identity contiguous with the past. Poems and musical genres came to life as we traveled from city to city, these Central Asian geographic sites just as important (albeit in different ways) to many in the community as the religious sites of the Land of Israel. Second, I saw even more strongly how Bukharian Jews had navigated a tremendous amount of upheaval during the twentieth century, and how in the United States, they were drawing on many of the same survival strategies that they employed as a minority population in Central Asia. Third, I continued to appreciate music's role as a nexus for managing senses of belonging and otherness, and the professional musician's special role in guiding the community and serving as an intercultural emissary. The strategy of using separate repertoires joined to different occasions and contexts, so successful in the American multicultural context, is based on well-established ways of managing repertoires in Central Asia and which proved equally adaptable upon return. During the trip, maqom was a continuous forum for

Muslim-Jewish interaction, in concerts and meetings that brought Bukharian Jews back together with their friends and neighbors. Music also at times united the Bukharian community at times, and at times brought to the fore the regional differences between them—a microcosm of the internal currents toward Jewish unity and diversity.

* * *

Constant Upheaval and the Impact of Globalization

Our ziyorat is to Tashkent, Samarqand, Shahrisabz, and Bukhara. Although organized by Malakov, none of the other travelers are professional musicians (and yet music is nearly constant; also, concerts are advertised as included in ziyorats organized by non-musicians).[1] In order to have enough participants, we are a diverse group, with members hailing from different places and many with relatives buried in more than one city. But for most of the thirty who are on the ziyorat, this is their first trip back to Uzbekistan since they had emigrated; for almost all of them that was in 1991 or 1992. Most are at least in their sixties, and several are well into their eighties, but they are committed to visiting the graves of their ancestors at least one more time while they are able to make the trip. The pilgrimage is also an opportunity to visit tourist attractions, to shop, and to eat the food and smell the scents they remember. To balance our various individual backgrounds with the overall collective endeavor, and to help us navigate the very different scene of Uzbekistan twenty years after most left, we will have a local tour guide. The excitement is palpable as the trip begins, everyone telling me about the beauty of Uzbekistan's cities.

Tashkent, the capital and long-standing seat of the Russian and Soviet authorities, embodies the multiple layers of Central Asia's governments and civilizations. Large dilapidated Soviet apartment buildings and offices give way to traditional houses with their outer walls facing the street to keep the inner courtyards cool. In Independence Square, the transformations from the Soviet Union to independent Uzbekistan are apparent. A World War II memorial has been rebuilt in Eastern-style architecture. An impressive monument of a mother holding a child, symbolic of the young country and the motherland, is topped by an enormous globe—with an enormous Uzbekistan on it. The globe used to be the biggest statue of Lenin in the world, more than one hundred feet tall. Our tour guide Furqat Pulatov explained, "The ninth of May [Victory Day, marking the surrender of Nazi Germany to the Soviet Union] is now just the 'Memorial Day.' No more military parades with *apparats*, like during the Soviet Union." Similarly, the Amir Timur monument began as a statue of General Konstantin Petrovich von Kaufman (1818–82), who became the first governor-general of the Russian Turkistan Protectorate in 1867. Then it became Lenin, Stalin, Marx, and now Timur (on the post-Soviet embrace of Timur in Uzbekistan, see Adams 2010:38–42).

The impact of language reform on Central Asia overwhelms. Downtown, Cyrillic and Roman compete for attention: governmental banners in Roman Uzbek announce "2200 Years of Tashkent" and the slogan "Uzbekistan: Great State of the Future!" ("O'zbekiston Kelajagi Buyuk Davlat!"). Signs, advertisements, and banners appear in both Cyrillic and Roman, and older signs in Cyrillic. Driving around the city, I hear an older friend of mine, a brilliant man, doing his best to sound out the Roman characters. His home city, where he lived for sixty years or so, now feels "foreign" to him, as he has tremendous difficulty reading the signs (compare also the language issues, regarding Bukhara, expressed to Cooper [2011:211–12]). Furqat begins speaking to the group in Persian, but a few people from Tashkent complain—they can't understand Persian very well, so Furqat settles on Russian. New immigrants often face communication difficulties as the mother tongues of parents differ from those of the children, but as usual, such issues are quite familiar to Bukharian Jews. In the Soviet Union, the mother tongue of Ezro's generation was Persian, and for many of their children, especially those from Tashkent, Russian (and now, for their children, English). All the passengers on the bus in this group of Bukharian Jews, a community so often portrayed as homogeneous by outsiders, speak different languages to one another and each hails from a different background.

The multiple layers of civilization illustrate Tashkent's status as an international city and the worldwide impact of globalization. The main bazaar, Chorsu, is a bustling market packed floor to ceiling with electronics, clothing, Disney character dolls, and knockoffs of all sorts, with stalls and kiosks run by Tajiks, Uyghurs, Koreans, and Uzbeks. In a food section, Germans are selling pork sausages. Back in our hotel I am shocked to run into one of my neighbors from my apartment building in Queens. She is writing an article on the contemporary art scene in Uzbekistan and is being shown around. I use her laptop to send an email to my wife. Below our hotel is the Ilkhom theater, which is currently showing an avant-garde updated version of Aeschylus' *Oresteia* to packed houses. The theater was established in 1976 by an Ashkenazic Jew (he was born in Tashkent to Ukrainian parents) named Mark Weil, and in his productions he tackled such controversial subjects as homosexuality in Muslim societies. Weil was murdered in 2007 in front of the theater, in a case still unsolved.

The Bukharian Jews are in their element navigating this mixture of culture and languages. Most of the general public in Tashkent speak Uzbek, and the young Uzbeks do not seem to know Russian very well; however, the Bukharians are completely comfortable speaking with cabbies and shop owners in Uzbek. I am surprised at the level of this fluency, since in New York I have not been exposed to this level of Uzbek-Bukharian interaction. Bukharian Jews in New York sing in Uzbek (mostly on recordings) and sometimes perform at Uzbek American events, but they never speak Uzbek among themselves. Their linguistic versatility contrasts with the Uzbeks we meet. For example, one fellow traveler (who speaks English, Russian, Uzbek, and Tajik) and I found ourselves out in a bazaar and some locals begin talking with us about the achievements of Uzbekistan. My friend tells them that I am a visiting professor from Iran, and to support the claim he speaks to me in Persian with an exaggerated Iranian accent. His switch allows us to communicate privately, as they do not speak Persian. We laugh about his linguistic strategy later. "What should I tell them, that you're an American Jew?"

Commemorating Loss, Performing Diaspora

Music is played on the bus, at meals, everywhere. Someone purchases a doira at one of the bazaars and on the bus one of the women plays a 6/8 beat, singing over it while others join in (Audio Example 6.1◉). Classic maqom recordings of Ezro and Neryo Aminov backed by large orchestras from the 1960s and 1970s provide the usual soundtrack, in the form of cassettes played on handheld portable machines. These dated sounds are clearly nostalgic for the pilgrims, who enjoy recalling days gone by with bittersweet emotion.

The first Tashkent cemetery is striking, packed with graves, most bearing the likenesses of the deceased, a regular practice among Soviet Jews. Jacob Malakov (Ezro's nephew) turns to me: "In America, some say we shouldn't do this, but I don't know why. It's so beautiful." I see "People's Artists" Berta Davidova, Maryam Yakubov, poets, musicians, and doctors. Most of the graves in this particular cemetery seem to date from the 1960s, and the years on the graves mostly stop with the 1990s. Ironically, the cemetery captures the vibrancy of Jewish life in Tashkent before emigration. It is a jarring contrast to the reality in 2010, when almost no Jews remain in the city.

Our first stop is the khonagoh, the small building at the cemetery for worship. Ezro sings Potaḥ from the Zohar and says healing blessings for the travelers. As a group, we first visit the grave of Ezro's older brother (and Jacob's father), Avrom, and his mother, Yeshuo. Jacob shakes his head, "I have to come all this way to visit my father." Ezro chants more from the Zohar (Audio Example 4.4◉), and prays along with Jacob, his brother Khaiko, his wife Bela, and Bela's sister, Yeshuo. The tour group gathers around, videotaping the proceedings. There is a public quality to Ezro and Khaiko's lamenting, as they weep and pray. Ezro's status as a ḥazzan and hofiz allows him to fulfill the familiar role of the gūyanda, or the public mourning role typically filled by women (including Ezro's own mother) in the past. They don't place stones on the graves, a custom I am used to, but Jacob washes the grave of his father and grandmother, they light candles, and they touch the graves and kiss their hands. After, we split up and people visit their relatives and friends, everyone taking pictures and documenting the trip. Before we leave, Ezro leads the group in more prayer. He also meets with the Muslim caretaker of the cemetery, pointing out several things that need repairing or upkeep. Bukharian Jews send money back to Central Asia to make sure their cemeteries and synagogues are cared for, and on ziyorats and other trips, they check up on the sites and make sure they are well kept.

Later that night, Ezro gives a concert at the hotel, inviting some local musicians to accompany him. Music and maqom in particular, as will be reinforced throughout the trip, is still one of the primary arenas through which Uzbeks and Bukharian Jews communicate and collaborate. The musicians play violin, doira, rubob, and soz to accompany Ezro. Matluba Dadaboyeva, a younger classical singer and a "People's Artist" (still an active title, *O'zbekiston xalq artisti*), sings songs made famous by the Bukharian legends Berta Davidova and Shoista Mullojonova. The members of the tour group sing along with her in an act of social and musical harmony.

The concert connects our group to their lives and friends in Uzbekistan, and it is quite heart-wrenching to compare this beautiful music-making session with the near dissolution of Central Asian Jewish life. Jacob is reunited with one of his closest childhood friends from the small town of Chirakchi, Tahir, who is now a government official. We also touch base with a Bukharian friend of Jacob's who lives in New York but who keeps an apartment in Tashkent. This same friend has many Uzbek friends that he grew up with and likes to visit three or four times a year.

The Bukharian singers are still very popular in Uzbekistan, and in a local record store (filled with bootleg mp3 CDs that contain the entire discographies of internationally famous bands) I see recordings by Avrom Tolmasov, Ezro, and others. The next day we visit the Yunus Rajabi museum, and I see Ezro's picture on the wall, along with pictures of other Bukharian Jews, such as Isak Katayev and Berta Davidova. Everywhere we go it seems people know Ezro as they meet him with hugs and huge smiles. As a prominent hofiz, he is a representative and community emissary. "Qurbon Olam!" They shout when they see him, naming his biggest hit. On an evening stroll to the Hamza Theater, Khaiko Malakov sings a stirring rendition of "O Tashkent," and he reminds me, the melody was written by Suleĭmon Yudakov, a Bukharian Jew. I think back to a Tajik man I met on the plane over to Tashkent—an immigrant who is living in Brooklyn and sending money home to his family, and who hadn't visited in over two years—who was eager to impress upon me his tolerant feelings for Jews. "We're brothers," he says. "I've read the Bible, the Torah, and the Quʿrān. They all say the same thing: One God."

Still, there are pangs of prejudice and discomfort as we travel. In one cafe, a trio of ours goes ignored and unserved. One of our number, in his early seventies, seems generally confused or amused by his interactions with those in the city. "Everyone is acting so polite now," he marvels. "Aka, aka,[2] salom aleykum, salom aleykum." "Well," another responds, "they're scared shitless." They tell me about the difficulties in the country after independence, such as racketeering and corruption. "This is why we had to leave the country." But perhaps tellingly, the most difficult moment of the trip comes near the end as we celebrate Shabbat with songs in the restaurant of the Tashkent hotel, and German tourists are eating at a table across the room. One of the men storms over to Ezro and furiously interrupts. "I'm not being racist, but you really shouldn't be singing like this all night!" He says this in English, and most of our group does not understand. An argument ensues between several members of each group, as Ezro tries to smooth things over. "Let's sing a little quieter," implores one of our group, but many are upset and angry, and they do not want to adjust their singing. This moment of deep tension and miscommunication is jarring, as despite some occasional tension, the Bukharian Jews are naturally comfortable and clearly at home with their former neighbors and surroundings.

Intracommunity Connections and Tensions

The interconnectedness of the global Bukharian diaspora hits home on our second day in Tashkent, when another tour bus pulls up with a ziyorat group in from Israel. Some in our group know some in theirs. People wave to each other, hug, reminisce, and tell stories. We end up spending a lot of time together over the trip, as our tours overlap a great deal. I have an Israeli counterpart, an Ashkenazic Jewish anthropology student named Yochai Primak interested in Bukharian culture, but unlike me, he is one of their tour guides.[3] The other tour guide is a gregarious Bukharian Hasidic man. Another of the travelers is a young Bukharian ḥazzan named Roshel, from Ramla, a Tel Aviv suburb with a significant Bukharian population. He sings some of Roshel Rubinov's tunes. He's eager to learn from Ezro and he spends as much time with him as possible on the trip. He knows the Bukharian way well, and he sings and prays beautifully.

Even as Bukharian Jews from New York and Israel reunite, tensions are beginning to emerge among our own group, which has clear divisions along city affiliations. Back in Uzbekistan, the forced unity of Bukharian Jews in New York formerly spread hundreds of miles apart has quickly evaporated. The Samarqandi Jews are especially eager to get to Samarqand, and the trip allows for more time in Tashkent than in Samarqand. They each want to eat the food of their cities, smell it, touch the earth. One Samarqandi Jew tells me that Tashkent is the *poitakht*, the capital, the big city, but Samarqand is where the real history and culture is. "I don't have much feeling for Tashkent." I ask him what life was like for him in Samarqand. "It was good, very good. It was good in Tashkent too. But—," he reminds me, "religion was hard."

As a solution, one bus leaves early the next morning to go to Samarqand. Naturally, I stay behind with the Malakovs and some others, and with the Israeli tour group we go to one of the two synagogues in Tashkent (the other synagogue historically served the Ashkenazic Jews in Tashkent, who mostly arrived after World War II [Z. Levin 2008b]). The building has been recently renovated with money from the Bukharian diaspora, reinforcing

Figure 6.2. Ezro Malakov singing at a Tashkent synagogue, 2010. Photo by the author.

the economic ties linking the community across the globe. "In memory of Eduard Nektalov" is embossed on the front in huge letters, commemorating a diamond dealer who was gunned down in broad daylight on Sixth Avenue in Manhattan in 2004. We meet two or three local residents who continue to attend the synagogue. Everywhere we go, I hear the same thing: there were twenty thousand Jews here, now about forty. We enter, Ezro sings, and we briefly read from the Torah before leaving (Figure 6.2). In the old Jewish neighborhood, new ostentatious houses are going up, one new house where there once were two. That afternoon we leave for Samarqand.

On the bus we pass cotton field after cotton field, with workers harvesting the crop. Uzbekistan was the major cotton producer for the Soviet Union, and all of the Bukharians on the trip had picked cotton at one time or another. Before entering Samarqand, we take a detour to an open-air restaurant in Sangzor, outside of the city of Jizzak. Our arrival is treated as an important event, as we are greeted with karnais and drums and filmed for Uzbek television. We eat *shashlik* (kebabs) and plov, drink vodka, and dance to music. Ezro gives another concert with local musicians, and Ezro continues his job as a community representative, giving speeches honoring the country and praising our hosts (Figure 6.3).

Samarqand looks much different from Tashkent: new buildings, clean, wide streets, and lots of restoration on the historical monuments. Many of the new structures are aesthetically similar to the

Figure 6.3. Ezro Malakov concert in Jizzak, Uzbekistan. Photo by the author.

catering halls and ballrooms in Queens. Samarqand was Timur's capital and it is also the birthplace of Uzbekistan's president, Islom Karimov. Clearly, the government has put a lot of money into this city. Everyone on the bus is impressed with and surprised by the city's makeover. Our hotel is bedecked with numerous images of Marilyn Monroe, and the TV in the lobby is continually playing music videos, mostly featuring American rap. But even more than in Tashkent, the old coexists with the new and the rich with the poor. We drive by Afrosiab, the ancient ruins of Samarqand, and people selling live chickens out of tiny coops in front of crumbling old houses. The highway is new, but most of the cars on it are thirty-year-old Ladas.

The cemetery in Samarqand has graves going back several hundred years. History speaks through the gravestones, as Cyrillic gives way to graves with mostly Hebrew characters and even some Persian script. The cemetery is on a hill, adjoining the Muslim cemetery; the two are separated by only a short wall (Figure 6.4). I make my own ziyorat to Levi Bobokhonov's grave. We have to leave quickly, and we walk through the Muslim cemetery. The Bukharians pick out friends and famous people, recalling their non-Jewish neighbors who featured so prominently in their former lives. As we walk down the path, I am surprised to realize that we are walking right into the historic Shahi Zinda complex, with its many stunning mausoleums. During our sightseeing I feel a huge relief to be able to communicate with the locals in Persian, still the main language of

Figure 6.4. At the outskirts of the Jewish cemetery in Samarqand, with wall separating Jewish from Muslim cemetery. The Shahi Zinda complex is in the background. Photo by the author.

Samarqand and Bukhara. But the day in Samarqand is rushed as there is a lot to see and the group needs to be back in the hotel before Shabbat.

That afternoon we visit the Mahalla (simply, "neighborhood"), the old Jewish quarter. We make our way to the Gumbaz (Blue Dome) Synagogue (Figure 6.5), built in the late nineteenth century under Russian rule, after the Russians lifted the ban on building new synagogues in place under the emir. The Samarqandi Jews hurriedly and happily read from the Torah, undeniably delighted by the opportunity to do something religious in this meaningful physical location. We then walk through to the Bibi Khanum Mosque and the large bazaar, the Guri Emir mausoleum (where Timur is buried), and the Registan—the complex of the Ulugbek Madrasa, Tillya Kori Madrasa, and the Sher Dor Madrasa that graces so many Bukharian Jewish CD covers. The economics of globalization quickly resurface in the square. A banner at the Registan welcomes the "Fifth International Meeting on the Silk Road," a joint conference held by the government of Uzbekistan and the World Tourism Organization, and I hear tourists speaking English and German. Women are praying in the Tillya Kori Madrasa, but mostly the Registan is filled with shops.

Samarqand, one of the oldest and most powerful sites of Bukharian Jewish heritage, seems emotionally important to the Samarqandis in a way that Tashkent was not to those from there. Borukh, the *mashgiaḥ* (supervisor of kosher food) on our trip, is a Bukharian Hasidic Israeli man

Figure 6.5. Gumbaz Synagogue in Samarqand. Photo by the author.

originally from Samarqand. He is beaming as he turns to me and says, "Samarqand is like Yerusholayim [Jerusalem]. The second city." The Samarqandis' attachment to their sites, especially Gumbaz, comes to the fore in a discussion with Ezro over where the group should hold Shabbat services. The Samarqandis want to walk over to Gumbaz, almost three miles away, but Ezro thinks we should worship at the hotel since so many people are elderly and it is hard for them to get around. I ask Ilya Yakubov, a former math teacher and a very knowledgeable elderly man that everyone simply calls "Domullo" (teacher), about this debate. "Well, for them, prayer has a very specific form (*shakl*), with the synagogue, the *tsitsit* [fringed prayer shawl]. When I was a little boy [i.e., under Stalin], we didn't have tsitsit or tfillin. It was forbidden in the Soviet Union. But my father explained that to God, these things, tsitsit and tefillin, aren't necessary. He would take me and my sister out to a field—there was no water, nothing—and we would pray the minḥo service."

Shabbat in Samarqand ends up, sure enough, at the hotel, and for morning services we are out in the cool air of the hotel's courtyard. We are together with the Israeli tour, and the young ḥazzan Roshel leads most of the service. The musaf service is led by an Israeli with an Ashkenazic nusaḥ. The lunch banquet is festive. We are joined by the minister of Uzbek Tourism and an ambassador from Ukraine, who is interested in adapting the ziyorat tour model for his country.

After the meal, the large group commences vigorous singing of shiro. We sing "Ruz ba ruz" ("Yom le Yom" in Persian) to the maqom melody "Tulkun," "Madh Guyand" ("Yehalel Niv" in Persian) to "Navruzi Sabo," "Ki Eshmero Shabbot," "Deror Yiqro," and "Yo Ribun Olam." The lay people sing the maqom melodies accurately, and in the absence of instruments they tap out zarbs on the table and vocalize instrumental breaks. Some of the singing reaches an almost competitive spirit, as some of the Samarqandi Jews are "enjoying" (*kaif kardan*) being home with a significant amount of vodka, and taking the opportunity to sing as loudly and extravagantly as possible; here the tension almost overboils due to the drunkenness bordering on disrespectful. Before things fall apart Ezro sings "Zulfi Pareshon" to ease the pressure, accompanying himself with a dinner plate. A number of speeches are made honoring Uzbekistan, our visitors, and Ezro for organizing the trip. Ezro stands and makes a speech of his own. He says many flattering things about Uzbekistan and the legendary figures in its history: Ulugbek, Amir Timur, Ibn Sina,

Figure 6.6. Ziyorat pilgrims dancing to local Uzbek musicians, Hotel Constantin, Samarqand. Photo by the author.

and Beruni. He also makes a point I have often heard him make in New York about the limiting and superficial aspects of nationalism: "Uzbekistan, Tajikistan, Turkmenistan, they are the same to us, there is no difference." His comments are clearly directed at the Uzbek dignitaries, revealing a confidence in his status as a community representative and the Bukharian Jews' transnational stance.

After the concluding services of Shabbat and a light meal, we are treated to yet another concert by local musicians and Ezro. This concert features a greater variety of styles than the others, maqom with lightly amplified instruments, heavily reverbed and amplified pop music, and singing over recorded orchestral accompaniment backing tracks from decades ago. A dancer in traditional costume dances to the upbeat numbers, and our group happily joins in (Figure 6.6).

At the Periphery of the Periphery

The next day we are to travel to Bukhara, stopping in Shahrisabz on the way. We drive through the stunning Urgut mountains, and arrive at the very small Jewish cemetery in the quiet city of Shahrisabz. Jacob turns to me in awe and says, "I can't believe I'm here. It's like a dream." Right in the middle of the cemetery is a small farm. We visit the grave of Ezro's mother's father, Ari ben Obo Borukhov, as well as Ezro's sister, who died at the age of eighteen. We also see the graves of Bella's and Yeshuo's mother and father. Ari's grave belies the humble and old quality of the Shahrisabz synagogue: no likeness, only Hebrew characters, and laid flat in the ground (Figure 6.7). Jacob tells me he's going to visit some of his friends in the village of Chirakchi, about forty miles away, where he grew up, and he invites me along. "You won't believe where we came from," he says. On the way, we pass one of the many cotton fields in Uzbekistan and Jacob sits up on the edge of his seat as his memory is jogged. "I picked cotton in this exact place!" he announces.

Ezro had worked in Chirakchi as a dentist for several years, and his brother Avrom Malakov was also a dentist. Growing up in Chirakchi, Jacob was part of a very small Jewish population, only a few families, much different from the substantial mahalla of Samarqand. They would drive to Shahrisabz for synagogue, since Chirakchi did not have one. Although driving is prohibited on Shabbat, they were out in the country, and of course, it was hard to follow rules strictly under Communism. We reunite with his old schoolmaster, an energetic elderly Russian woman, and his friends. Tahir has driven to meet us as well. We go out to a restaurant and garden for lunch. We overhear the music of a wedding being held inside, and we sit out at a large picnic bench and eat and drink vodka. Jacob discreetly gives gifts of American money to his friends. Unfortunately, we have to cut our visit short to return to the bus and get moving on to Bukhara.

Figure 6.7. Grave of Ari Ben Obo Borukhov, Ezro Malakov's grandfather. The stone was just washed by Malakov. Photo by the author.

Bukhara feels remote and provincial compared to Tashkent and Samarqand. The impact of the Russians establishing their seat of power in Tashkent and Karimov's investment in Samarqand is palpable. At the Ark, the emir's former palace, there is an empty wood frame where the throne used to sit—a physical manifestation of the shift in power, as the Russians removed it long ago for its valuable materials (Figure 6.8). I am also reminded of Bukhara's humbling age when visiting a Samanid mausoleum that predates Timur's buildings in Samarqand by several centuries, immediately apparent by its geometric stonework patterns instead of the Arabic script and familiar Islamic ornamentation. After some more sightseeing we take an uneventful plane ride back to Tashkent.

Figure 6.8. Former spot of the emir's throne, Bukhara. Photo by the author.

Further Cosmopolitanism

The trip from Bukhara to Tashkent feels almost like time traveling. Back in Tashkent I accompany the Malakovs to visit their old houses and neighbors. We are welcomed by the residents now living in Ezro and Bela's first home, but they do not know each other. Jacob's former house is another story: it it is now a Doctors without Borders office. We finally meet one of their old neighbors, an elderly woman who is overjoyed to see them. She asks Ezro for a blessing, and he obliges with a Muslim blessing and all of the appropriate gestures. His versatility is phenomenal: I see him perform in genres that I had not witnessed in almost ten years of working closely with him in New York.

After dinner we head out to see some musicians with Rafael Nektalov, the Bukharian musicologist, cultural advocate, and editor of the *Bukharian Times* in New York, who is in Tashkent on a different trip. In an oddly fitting end to the ziyorat, we end up in downtown Tashkent at a show for the "Guli" jewelry collection designed by President Karimov's daughter and frequent center of controversy Gulnara Karimova, attended by international journalists, models, and local businessmen and officials.[4] Nektalov is on this trip with a group including a young African American woman from New York and a man from Mexico City wearing a De La Soul T-shirt and tie-dyed pants shooting a video documentary. Their travel expenses have been paid, disclosing the public relations aspects of the event, which

Figure 6.9. Ezro Malakov performing with Abdulahad Abdurashidov and ensemble, Shodlik Palace hotel, Tashkent. Photo by the author.

is a glitzy display of and for Uzbekistan's elite. It is unsettling to be in this situation immediately after the humble Jewish cemetery in Shahrisabz and the quiet environs of Bukhara. Techno music is pulsing. Ezro reunites with an old friend, the ghijak master Abduhoshem Ismoilov, who has been hired to provide music and an element of local color. Ismoilov's job is circumscribed due to the fact that he has to fiddle along with the techno music piping through the speakers, but his professionalism carries him through.

The unifying power of maqom comes to the fore at the last concert for our ziyorat group, as we all reunite at the hotel in Tashkent. The nai player Abdulahad Abdurashidov joins Ezro with an instrumental ensemble, and the group trades exciting improvisations on an extended performance of "Zulfi Pareshon" (Figure 6.9 and Audio Example 6.2◉). Normally lyric songs and maqom melodies are not used as springboards for improvisation, but Abdurashidov begins extemporaneous passages between couplets, and Malakov quickly adjusts. Spontaneous duets, dramatic dynamic changes, trading of the spotlight, and liberal interpretations of the traditional lyric setting all contribute to a stirring musical conversation and an electric atmosphere. The Bukharian audience shows its appreciation with yells of encouragement, spontaneous applause, and showering of performers with wads of so'm (the local currency) and dollar bills. The rest of the evening is equally enjoyable. Alisher Alimatov, one of Turgun's sons, performs a piece of his father's repertoire after being announced with

Figure 6.10. Ezro Malakov and Roshel, a ḥazzan from Ramla, during our last concert of the trip. Photo by the author.

effusive praise by Rafael Nektalov. I'm asked to play tanbūr, and I perform a rudimentary rendition of "Navruzi Sabo." Bobomurod Hamdamov, a famous Uzbek singer of Ezro's generation, sings one of his hit songs over a backing track, and the members of our trip are overjoyed by this surprise. The travelers dance at the end of the concert (Figure 6.10), expressing their happiness at being back in Central Asia one last time before returning to their lives in the United States or Israel.

Before leaving Uzbekistan, I spend a day with Alisher. We go to the conservatory and observe a class taught by Mahmud Tojiboyev, one of Turgun's students. Portraits of great masters hang on the walls of the classroom: Turgun, Hoji Abdulaziz Rasulov, Domullo Halim Ibadov, Ota Jalol, and Ota Ghiyos. The students are learning songs in only the Uzbek language. The absence of Jewish masters from the wall and the Uzbek-only songs reinforce the Jewish role as minority musicians in Uzbekistan and the difference between the public and private spheres. An apparent lack of Jewish recognition in the public sphere contrasts with the previous night's festivities, the unwavering respect and admiration shown throughout the country for Ezro, and the conversations I have with Alisher. At his house, Alisher is an exemplary host, plays some solo pieces of his father's repertoire, and then makes a special point to tell me the appreciation his father had for the Jewish masters, and how Turgun used to undermine the nationalist sentiments surrounding the maqom. "My father was a messenger of music, only music," he says. "He liked freedom, not rules." Alisher is happy to see his Jewish friends, but he admits to not completely understanding why the entire Jewish population left. I ask him if Uzbekistan is much different without Jews. In an echo of Ezro telling me back in New York about how he missed the great instrumentalists of Uzbekistan, Alisher responds, "It's not really that different because they were less than one percent of the population. The only real difference is in music. There really aren't any good maqom singers around anymore. They're all in the United States and Israel."

On the plane back to New York I listen to Bukharian Jewish recordings and reflect on the trip. Throughout the Bukharian diaspora, remembrance is an essential component, and Central Asia exerts a strong pull. The cities of Bukhara, Samarqand, Shahrisabz, and Tashkent are their specific Bukharian Jewish homelands, coexisting with the general Jewish homeland of Israel and Jerusalem. They maintain these homelands simultaneously, aided by the very forces of globalization that helped shape their current dispersal. The United States is yet another homeland, the land of unprecedented religious freedom and economic opportunity.

Bukharian Jews' attachment to physical places, essentialist ideas, and classic diasporic conceptions suggests a reevaluation of the importance of these ideas to other minorities and immigrants, even as layers of diaspora and places that can be called "home" multiply. Various ideas of diaspora are put to multiple uses, for example, sustaining groups through upheaval and circumstances beyond their control. Peripheral groups can strategically employ deep-seated senses of otherness and imagined links to antiquity and lost homelands as economic resources in the cultural sphere.

As a group with a persistent minority status in their many homelands, Bukharian Jews have consistently transferred preexisting adaptation strategies from one environment to another. The mode of adaptation itself is viewed as a continuous tradition for Bukharian Jews, a necessary counterpart to the tenacity of the singular idea of identity that imagines an unchanging Bukharian Jewish culture with a direct line to antiquity. These two ideas may seem mutually exclusive or a paradoxical combination, but actually the process of balancing them is a key strategy for Bukharian Jews and, it would seem, for other groups that have an ongoing status at the margins. Furthermore, multiple approaches to adaptation and conflicts over the nature of change remind us of the internal diversity and unsettled conversations at the core of any ostensibly bounded "ethnic group."

As Bukharian Jewish professional musicians perform various repertoires, styles, and techniques they create general models for the lives of community members, offering "competing answers" to questions of "race and culture, people and nation" as they put the "product" of Bukharian Jewish ethnicity to use (referring once again to Musil's ideas noted in the Introduction [Musil 1978:1366, tr. 1990:162]). As nation-states and their constituent populations redefine who they are in an age of globalization, widespread cosmopolitanism, and mushrooming diasporas, the example of Bukharian Jews encourages us to focus on the myriad ways in which musicians representing communities in flux—especially professional musicians—put music to work in constructing senses of identity such as ethnicities.

Musicians construct senses of belonging and otherness, and accordingly, musical performance provides a crucial forum for dialogue and exchange between members of a group and their "others." From pre-Soviet Central Asia through the present globalized diaspora, music has been a primary medium of communication for Bukharian Jews and their neighbors, especially the Muslims whose culture defined much of Bukharian life and other Jewish communities. New geographic circumstances increase the senses of belonging and otherness that groups have to negotiate. Social relationships multiply, layer, and shift in emphasis; they are rarely replaced or resolved. The prevalence of multiculturalism in New York at the turn of the twenty-first century, which has parallels throughout the world, presented Jewish immigrants from Central Asia with a particular set of new questions, challenges, and opportunities. Bukharian Jewish musicians actively answered with products that defined their community's distinct ethnicity, and they put forward multiple ways for the community to use and reconsider traditional modes and repertoires. The products, "best interpreted, in turn, as new questions" (Blum 1994:277), are already encouraging further transformations, adaptations, and adjustments as people critique and reconsider multiculturalism's limitations.

As I fly from Tashkent to New York I imagine what it was like for my Bukharian friends making a trip like this twenty years ago, wondering what might lie ahead, and I reflect on my good fortune to know these people. Through my headphones I play "Yalalum" (Audio Example 6.3🔊); Mallayev 1999:360–62), Ilyos Mallayev's diasporic anthem, which ended every set by Ensemble Maqom, and which I also heard at a party in Israel eight years earlier.[5] "Yalalum" is quintessential Bukharian repertoire, existing in light-classical and party versions, and even a religious version with lyrics about Israel as the eternal Homeland over wedding-band instrumentation. Mallayev and the other Bukharian musicians I know have continually adapted and adjusted their repertoires and styles to address lives of constant change, always keeping their eyes on the past and present needs of the greater Bukharian community. Maqom, religious music, and party repertoire ebb and flow, reflecting the many different aspects of Bukharian Jewish American life. I sit back and listen.

> Dar dasti rafiqon guli navrastai noz,
> Mo ro begiriftand bo tabassum peshvoz,
> Az Osiyo dar Amriko kardem parvoz,
> Shoista, Malika u Muhabbat, Ilyos,
> Aknun zi shumo manam judoi nakunam,
> Yak lahza khayoli bevafoi nakunam,
> Mo ham ba shumo, shumo ba mo dust boshem,
> Be bazmi shumo kaif u safoe nakunam,
> Parvozi baland kaifi paru bol meshavad,

Dar mavji havo sohibi iqbol meshavad,
Dar Amriko har kas, ki biyoyad shabu ruz,
Mehmoni manu Rahmini Nektol meshavad,
Rahmin Nektol u Mulo Ishoqi Rabbai,
Peshboz begirem shumo ro bo tanbūru nai,
Boloi jamoat chu misoli posbon,
Dar har sukhani shumo biguyem: Labbai!

In the hands of friends, young beautiful flowers,
They greet us with smiles,
We flew from Asia to America,
Shoista, Malika, Muhabbat, Ilyos,
Now I should not be separated from you,
Let me not think unfaithful thoughts for even one moment,
Let us become your friends and you become ours,
I would not be happy without your celebration,
The long flight becomes the joy of wing and feather,
In the billows of air one becomes a prosperous master,
In America everyone that comes night and day,
Becomes my guest and that of Rahmin Nektol,[6]
Rahmin Nektol and Mullo Isḥoq our rabbi
Let us greet you with tanbūr and nai,
Head of the community like a watchman,
To your every word let us say: At your service!

Notes

Introduction
1. To avoid conflict with Jewish religious law (*halakhah*), Bukharian Jews usually hold Simḥat Torah parties after the sundown concluding the holiday. In 2007, Simḥat Torah ended on Friday, October 5, so the party was postponed until Sunday evening, following the Sabbath.
2. The words "music" and "musician" appear throughout this book in a general English-language sense, with singing and singers in the same category as instrumental music and instrumentalists. However, Bukharian Jews generally use the words *muzyka*, *mūsīqī*, and the English *music* only to describe music played on instruments, following the common usage in Central Asia. A cappella singing is called *be muzyka*, "without music." "To play [music]" is *navokhtan* (or *zadan*, "to strike" or "to hit"), whereas the verb "to sing" is *khondan*, which also means "to read."
3. For most of the Soviet Union's existence, emigration was extremely difficult. Only a very small number of Bukharian Jews had immigrated to New York beginning in the 1940s, via Israel and Europe. In 1963 there were enough Bukharian Jews to form the first Bukharian Jewish center and synagogue in New York (Ochildiev 2005:177). Even through the 1980s, almost all Bukharian emigration was to Israel, and only about 1,000 Jews from the entire USSR immigrated per year to the United States. In response to international sanctions, and with Gorbachev's reforms, emigration became easier. In 1987 the United States experienced a large spike in immigration, at which point the Immigration and Naturalization Service (INS) began denying refugee status to Soviet immigrants. During fiscal year (FY) 1987 the number of Soviet immigrants to the United States jumped over tenfold, reaching 30,000 in FY 1988, and "unmanageable" in 1989 (Beyer 1991:32). By 1989 the number of Bukharian Jews had reached an estimated 4,700 (Kaganovitch 2008:113–15). The status of Soviet refugees in the United States was contentiously debated until 1989 with the passage of the Lautenberg Amendment, which granted presumptive refugee status to Soviet Jews (Rosenberg 2003). Through 1999, the vast

majority of immigrants from Central Asia to New York fell into this refugee category (e.g., 93.5 percent of immigrants from Uzbekistan; New York City 2004b:37, 41).

4. Although "2,000 years" of exile is a cliché of Jewish history, a Jewish presence in Central Asia for that duration, or close to it, is plausible. At its height the Persian Achaemenid empire (ca. 770 BCE to 330 BCE) extended beyond the Iranian plateau into modern Central Asia territory, and most Jews remained in the empire even after Cyrus defeated the Babylonians in 539 BCE and allowed the Jews to return to Judea (see Sarshar 2002:5 for a useful map). Jews had been traders along the Silk Road since at least the first century CE, their dispersal making them "ideally situated to participate in trade" between the Roman and Parthian empires (Foltz 1999:31–32), and there is strong evidence of Jews in Merv (today Mary, Turkmenistan) and Khorezm before the Arab conquests that introduced Islam to the region in the seventh century CE (Zand 2000). A twelfth-century visitor to Samarqand, Benjamin of Tudela, estimated a Jewish population of 50,000 (certainly an exaggeration but a clear indication of a sizable community, see M. Adler 1907:59 and Zand 2000). Bukhara itself probably did not become a center of Jewish life until the late sixteenth/early seventeenth centuries.

5. For the year 2006, Kaganovitch (2008) estimated 28,000 in the entire United States, compared to 65,000 in Israel, 2,500 in Austria, 2,000 in Central Asia, and 4,500 elsewhere for a total of 102,000. Non-scholarly sources tend to give higher numbers for the New York population. In the *New York Times*, Moskin (2006) estimated "about 40,000" and the bukharianjews.com website (Pinkhasov n.d.) claims "about 60,000" in the United States and Canada.

6. The phrase "Land of Israel" refers to the diasporic concept (*Erets Isroel*), which overlaps with, but is not equivalent to, the contemporary Israeli nation-state.

7. Shi'a Muslims and Armenians, like Jews, constitute ethnoreligious minorities with important roles in the musical life of Central Asia. Some Shi'a Muslims may be descendants of slaves brought from Khorasan via Merv (T. Levin 1996:122; Fātemi 2005:223), others may have come as soldiers as a result of Nader Shah's conquests in Central Asia (Fātemi 2005:221–23). In Bukhara, the Shi'a male *mavrigikhon* (singer of "*mavrigi*-s," from Merv) is a popular wedding entertainer and a counterpart of the Jewish female sozanda, although this binary is sometimes overstated (Fātemi 2005:228).

8. On Soviet language reform in Central Asia, see Roy (2000:168–73) and Adams (2010:33–35), and on the specific impact of language policy on Bukhori, see Rzehak (2008).

9. Although I hesitated to use the term "current" to describe these regimes for fear of dating the book, the two leaders have been in power for decades and it seems that both will remain in power for the foreseeable future.

10. For example, the Bukharian Jewish writer Muhib (Mordekhai Bachayev, 1911–2007) was arrested in 1938 and spent the next fifteen years in jail, labor camps, and exile (Loy 2008a:137). He documented these events in his two-volume memoir, *Dar Juvoli Sangin* (In a Stone Sack) (Bachayev 2007).

11. Samarqand had been directly annexed into Russian Turkestan in 1868, while Bukhara remained nominally under the emir's jurisdiction—in

1873 the emirate became a Russian protectorate—until the emirate's dissolution in 1920. The Russians wanted to take advantage of the Jews' extensive textile connections and networks (Cooper 2012:72–73), so they extended to the Jews in Russian Turkestan much greater freedoms and opportunities, including the right to buy real estate, and the right to live and trade freely in Russia provided they join the Russian trade guilds (Zand et al. 2007:259). Increased economic opportunity and the removal of the threat of forced conversion resulted in major migrations from Bukhara to Russian Turkestan, in particular Tashkent and Samarqand. But in response, foreshadowing Soviet policies, the Russians forged a bizarre solution to what they viewed as a Jewish immigration problem. Beginning in 1887, the Russians made a stricter division between two categories: "native" (*tuzemnye*) Jews who could prove they were originally from the Russian Turkestan region and hence accorded the same rights as the local Muslims, and "foreign" (*inostrannye*) Jews that lived under Bukharan jurisdiction and as such were prohibited from buying land or participating in trade (Ivanov 2004; Shevyakov 2004). Although all Bukharian Jews (comprising both artificial categories) had lived in the same Central Asian cities for centuries, any newly "foreign" Jews were ordered to return to the Bukharan emirate by 1905. In reality, this decree was difficult to implement (Y. Yakubov 2008:16), and many Jews were able to stay active in business through bribes. Finally, after the overthrow of the tsar, Bukharian Jewish representatives negotiated with the new chairman of the province, achieving "native" status for the entire Jewish population.

12. Arkadi Il'yasov's life story (Loy 2008b) provides a typical example. His great-grandparents migrated from Mashhad to Herat in 1855. Il'yasov's family members moved to Mary in 1905 and Kerki in 1912 (both cities now in Turkmenistan), before half of the family moved on to Samarqand in 1937. Subsequently, some family members moved to Tashkent, Dushanbe, and Israel.

13. During the first decade of the 2000s, Leviev was one of the world's richest people: #227 on the Forbes list of billionaires in 2008 at a net worth of $4.5 billion. Although he now lives in London, and previously in Israel, he has built and supported several institutions in New York, mostly through his Ohr Avner Foundation and his work with the World Bukharian Jewish Congress, which serves as an international governmental body for the Bukharian diaspora. In addition to supporting the Queens Gymnasia (which also houses the Bukharian Jewish Museum) and the Bukharian Jewish Community Center in Forest Hills, he helped produce Ezro Malakov's *Musical Treasures of the Bukharian Jewish Community*, discussed in Chapter 4. The Ohr Avner Foundation funds a tremendous number of Jewish programs worldwide, including over ninety day schools, and it is the largest sponsor of Jewish institutions in the former Soviet Union. See http://www.fjc.ru (accessed 15 July 2014).

14. World Jewry is often divided into Sephardim and Ashkenazim, both categories arising from subsequent diasporas and dispersions following the exile from the Land of Israel in 70 CE. The Sephardim, officially exiled from the Iberian Peninsula (Sepharad) in 1492 and 1497, settled mainly in the Ottoman Empire, North Africa, and Italy (Corré et al. 2007; Zohar 2007:14). The Ashkenazim had settled in Germany (Ashkenaz) and northern France in the sixth century and spread to

Poland-Lithuania, Russia, and Eastern Europe ("Ashkenaz" 2007). These two categories roughly map onto another dichotomy, Jews who lived either "under the crescent" or "under the cross" (M. Cohen 1994, 2007). According to these strict definitions, Bukharian Jews are neither Ashkenazic nor Sephardic Jews. The Ashkenazic/Sephardic binary is strong in the United States; in Israel, a third category of "Mizraḥi" (Eastern) Jews serves as an umbrella category for those such as Bukharian Jews who do not fit either category.

15. Brooklyn, the borough with the second-highest number of immigrants, had 931,769 foreign-born residents, constituting 38 percent of the borough's population. According to census data, 53.6 percent of the Queens population age five and over speak a language other than English at home (www.census.gov; New York City 2004a:12–13; New York City 2004b:90–95).

16. For a comparison of 2000 and 2010 demographics, visit http://www.urbanresearchmaps.org/comparinator/pluralitymap.htm (accessed 12 December 2013).

17. "Dar dasti rafiqon guli navrastai noz / Mo ro begiriftand bo tabassum peshvoz."

18. The journalist Janet Malcolm's vexatious *Iphigenia in Forest Hills*, for example, contains misrepresentations and exoticizing statements such as, "No one really knows how or why or when these mysterious Jews came to Central Asia" (2011:10).

19. Bukharian Jews work in various professions and live within a wide range of economic situations. For example, although there are some very wealthy Bukharian Jews in the community, many older immigrants live on Social Security SSI (Supplemental Security Income). The jewelry business in and around 47th Street in Manhattan (the "diamond district") is an important industry for Bukharian Jews, including several musicians, but this industry yields a variety of monetary rewards. Shumiel Kuyenov works in the district, as does the young singer Yosef Munarov. Ochil Ibragimov is a jewelry designer with an independent business. Bukharian Jews are well represented in medicine and dentistry. Barbering is another major profession for Bukharian Jews; Roshel Rubinov worked as a barber for many years in addition to his many musical activities.

20. In a broad sense *hofiz* (*hāfiz, hāfez*) means "keeper," "protector," "guardian," or "retainer." In Central Asia and the greater Muslim world, hofiz can denote any "memorizer" of any area of knowledge and is specifically applied to one who has memorized the entire Qurʿān (al-Faruqi 1981:90; Blum 2001:365; Sultanova 2005:136). By committing the Qurʿān to memory, the hofiz becomes a "protector" of the words. The Qurʿānic hofiz not only knows the words but can also perform them with the proper technique and skill. Similarly, a Bukharian hofiz has committed many compositions to memory and can perform them in the proper manner.

21. During the preparation of this manuscript the entire collection of new Psalm settings had moved into production, to be released in 2014.

22. For example, scholars of "Jewish music" are still wrestling with Curt Sachs' often-quoted 1957 definition of Jewish music as "music by Jews, for Jews, as Jews," as well as the nationalist ideas of A. Z. Idelsohn (1882–1938) that sought to "demonstrate, through recordings, transcription, and analysis, that an essential continuity [in

Jewish music] was present" (Shelemay 1995:25; cf. Bohlman 2001:293) nearly one hundred years after his pioneering efforts (Móricz and Seter at al. 2012).

23. Theodore Levin, the author of the only major English-language work on Bukharian Jewish music prior to this book (two chapters in *The Hundred Thousand Fools of God* [1996]) conducted research in Russian. Edith Gerson-Kiwi (1950) and Johanna Spector (1967) probably used Hebrew when they communicated with Bukharian Jews in Israel; Spector's survey of Central Asian music mentions one encounter with a Bukharian Jew in Israel (1967:440) but otherwise is based on the work of Soviet ethnographers. Elena Reikher (2005–2006) used Russian for her interviews with the sozanda Nina Bakayeva in Israel (pers. comm.); her survey of Bukharian Jewish artists (2009–2010) is based on secondary sources. Djumaev's (2008) interview with Tūhfakhon, conducted with Angelika Jung in Bukhara, may have been in Russian and/or Persian. Walter Zev Feldman communicated with Bukharian Jews in Uzbek when he carried out research among Bukharian Jews in Central Asia and New York. Alexander Knapp's discussion of Bukharian cantillation (2010) relies only on Idelsohn's description from 1922 and Levin's liner notes (T. Levin 1991). The anthropologist Alanna E. Cooper used Russian and Hebrew; her book does not discuss music, but she is included here as the author of the only other scholarly monograph on Bukharian Jews (2012). With respect to non-English language publications, Otanazar Matyakubov, who worked with Levin (documented throughout T. Levin 1996), published several pieces discussing Bukharian Jews including interviews with Ilyas Mallayev (Matyakubov 2009) probably conducted in Russian. Angelika Jung works closely with Ari Bobokhonov (see Jung 2010), and interestingly the two communicate primarily in Russian despite Persian fluency (personal communication). Most of this information is based on personal communications and observations, as these scholars rarely indicated their linguisitic competencies or choices in their publications.

Chapter 1

1. *Levicha Hofiz* is also titled *Pevets ego prevoskhoditelstva* in Russian ("His majesty's singer") and *Hofizi Saroñ Janobi Olī* in Tajik Persian ("His majesty's palace singer").

2. I did not attend the play, which was performed before I began my ethnographic research. I based my information on a videotape of the final performance and Mallayev's script. The footnotes in this paragraph explain some of the play's deviations from historical facts.

3. The emir at the time would have actually been Olim Khon's father, Emir Abdulahad Khon (r. 1885–1910). In fact, Levi Bobokhonov began singing at the court of Abdulahad Khon and most of the events in the play would have occurred during his reign.

4. This policy seems more appropriately associated with Abdulahad Khon's predecessor, Muzaffar Khon (r. 1860–1886).

5. Olim Khon went to St. Petersburg to study at the age of thirteen (ca. 1893–96). Abdulahad Khon also traveled widely, to St. Petersburg, Kiev, Odessa, Yekaterinoslav, Baku, Tiflis, Batumi, Sevastopol, and Bakhchisarai (Naumkin 1993:29, 32).

6. Shishakhon (Buluri Oshma) was a real sozanda, but her actions in the play are fictional; Takhalov (2005) actually says Shishakhon was Levi's sister. In actuality, some Bukharian Jews did practice polygamy before Soviet times (Z. Levin 2008a:99).

7. The company that recorded Levi Bobokhonov and other Central Asian masters was the London-based Gramophone Company, which had a Russian division with a pressing plant in Riga. The Russian imprint was the *Pishushchiĭ Amur* or Amour Gramophone label. According to Will Prentice (unpublished liner notes), the man who negotiated the contract with Levi was an Englishman named Fred Tyler (he is "Mr. Anderson" in *Levicha Hofiz*), who documented his experiences in a still unpublished memoir. Levi recorded for Gramophone in April 1911 and 1913, although only the 1911 recordings were released (the 1913 recordings were apparently destroyed by the company between 1933 and 1935). Thus, Levi's contract was negotiated while Levi was serving Olim Khon. The 1911 date resolves the contradiction in the conventional notions that (1) the recordings were made in 1909 and (2) Olim Khon was the emir at the time. Furthermore, although Tyler did secure permission from Olim Khon to record Levi, the negotiation only required that Gramophone also record the emir's band, which was a "native cavalry band under the leadership of a Russian conductor" (Tyler, unpublished memoir, quoted in Will Prentice, unpublished liner notes). Boris Bobokhonov, Levi's grandson, corroborates this in the conversations reported by Theodore Levin, saying, "The emir was a diplomat. He said, 'Let them record'" (T. Levin 1996:101). Thank you very much to Will Prentice for generously sharing the results of his research and his notes with me.

8. As noted in the introduction, at the time Bukhara and Samarqand were under different jurisdictions, Samarqand being under Russian rule since 1868 and Bukhara remaining nominally under the emir until 1920. One common story has Levi fleeing to Samarqand after falling out of favor with the emir in 1909 and returning to Bukhara when Olim Khon ascended the throne in 1910, and then going back to Samarqand in 1920 or 1923 after the Russians deposed the emir (T. Levin 1996:102; Prentice unpublished liner notes). The 1911 and 1913 recording dates confuse this chronology, unless Levi moved to Samarqand in 1909 and returned to Bukhara in 1910 of his own volition, or unless Abdulahad Khon compelled Levi to leave Bukhara in 1909 for some reason other than the recordings. Furthermore, as already noted, Tyler's documents make it seem highly unlikely that Levi was punished for making these recordings (and Boris Bobokhonov told Levin, "the emir never asked my grandfather to leave" [T. Levin 1996:101], although this statement can be interpreted various ways). Upon review, it seems most likely to me that Levi served both emirs continuously in Bukhara and simply moved to Samarqand with the fall of the emirate. As noted in footnote 12, I hypothesize that the story of Levi's initial flight to Samarqand is a conflation of his story with the earlier Jewish court singer Borukh (Kalkhok) Babayev's moving from Bukhara to Samarqand almost immediately after the city's annexation in order to return to Judaism after a forced conversion.

9. Boris Bobokhonov believes Russian secret police poisoned Levi because of his connection to the emir (T. Levin 1996:102). In Boris's telling, Levi was "perfectly healthy" only a few days prior to his death

(and not prematurely aged from the emir's treatment, as represented in *Levicha Hofiz*).

10. Most Bukharian Jews consider Ota Jalol to be a forced convert (Babakhonov [1951] 1958:11; T. Levin 1996:92; Ochildiev et al. 2007:311; Matyakubov 2009:26). "He was 100% Jewish!" announced one of my interviewees. The celebrated tanburist Yakub Davidov, David Davidov's father, is known to be Ota Jalol's nephew (Matyakubov 2009:150). Djumaev (2004) writes that Ota Jalol's reputation as a chala is probably mistaken, and he does not include Ota Jalol among those with the added chala distinction in his list of Manghit court musicians (Djumaev 2006:51). In a brief exchange in *Levicha Hofiz* between Shishakhon and the emir's mother, Ota Jalol is explained to be a chala, but otherwise, he is represented as a Muslim in the play. Ari Bobokhonov's foreword to his Shashmaqom edition suggests that Ota Jalol was Muslim: "Ota Jalol was like a father to my grandfather, his support, his advocate at the court. He had no anti-Semitic attitude. At the court were indeed all Muslims; Levi was the only Jew. ...[Ota Jalol] did everything to encourage and support Levi." ("Ota Jalol war für meinen Großvater wie ein Vater, sein Halt, sein Fürsprecher am Hofe. Er hatte keine antisemitische Haltung. Am Hofe waren ja alle Muslime, Levi war der einzige Jude. ...Er tat alles, um Levi zu fördern und zu unterstützen" [Jung 2010:7].)

11. The chalas saw the Russians as saviors of a sort, able to end their difficult liminal double lives (Kaganovitch 2005). Many chalas fled to Russian Turkistan and returned to Judaism. In 1905, when the Russians required all the immigrants ("foreign Jews") to return to Bukhara, the chalas' situation once again became desperate. Now "apostates," they could be put to death in the emirate.

12. Muzaffar was responsible for bringing music and dance to the Bukharan court, as his predecessors had severe religious views and were against having musicians in the palace (Fātemi 2005:228). Muzaffar's changes are probably responsible for the introduction of Jewish singers at the court and the appearance of Borukh Kalkhok in Bukharian Jews' collective memory. The information on Kalkhok here comes from Imonuel Rybakov, who conducted research in the Uzbekistan Central Archives and found Kalkhok's story included on a document written by David Kalontarov in 1893 describing the migration of Jews to Samarqand after Russian occupation. The document states that Kalkhok had converted to Islam under pressure as the emir's singer, but moved to Samarqand quickly in 1868 after learning that "anyone wishing to relocate from the neighboring khanates can completely rely on protection from Russia," and he remained in Samarqand until his death in 1891 (Rybakov 2013). Previous writing on Kalkhok disagrees somewhat on this story: he was described as either having simply converted (Sukhareva 1966:175) or having fled to Samarqand to avoid conversion (Takhalov 2005:195). Kalkhok's flight to Samarqand might have served as the narrative template for the very similar, but less historically likely, story of Levi Bobokhonov's escape from Abdulahad Khon. Oral tradition also held that Kalkhok had been thrown in prison by Muzaffar (Djumaev 2004), which similarly seems to have been adapted to Levi's biography and used in the plot of *Levicha Hofiz*.

13. According to Tūhfakhon, most of the dancers entertaining the emir's mother (Eshon Oïim) were Jews (T. Levin 1996:199), but according to Olmas Rasulov, only Mikhali Karkigi (also known as Khalilkhon) was permitted at the court (Fātemi 2005:227). Tovoi Karkigi, Mikhali Karkigi's mother (Tovoi Namatiyeva, 1857–1959, also known as Tovoi Urus because she could speak Russian at a time when very few Central Asians did), is also said to have entertained Eshon Oïim. As examples of Muslim sozandas, Olmas Rasulov mentions Anbari Ashk (Fātemi 2005:227), and another of Fātemi's informants, Aka Gadoy, mentions an Ironi sozanda at the court, Bakhmali Ironi (Fātemi 2005:228).

14. In Ibragimov's telling of the story, the emir essentially "fired" Levi over his Gramophone recordings but didn't imprison him. Rather, he threw gold in his face and called him a "prostitute," criticizing him for his willing to share his exceptional talents with anyone for a nominal price. Ibragimov then situated Levi's move to Samarqand outside the emirate as a professional one. See also Boris Bobokhonov's discussions with Levin (T. Levin 1996:98–106).

15. "Nye sleduet zabyvat', chto Alimkhan byl vysokoobrazovannym chelovekom, vladel russkim i frantsuzskim yazykami. Odna iz yego zhen byla frantsuzhenjoĭ.... v kontse p'esy on vse zhe osvobozhdaet Levicha iz zatocheniya."

16. Jewish women demonstrated a notable willingness to leave behind the social mores of old Central Asia, performing unveiled on public stages early on. (The first woman to perform unveiled in Uzbekistan was Tamara Khanum, a member of the Armenian [Christian] ethno-religious minority.) Bukharian Jewish women on the whole participated to a disproportionate degree in the *khujum* ("assault") campaigns of the 1920s aimed at changing women's roles, including the "*paranja* (veil) and *kalym* (bride price),... polygamy, child marriage, women's illiteracy, and the prevention of outdoor work" (Z. Levin 2008a:96).

17. Mikhali Karkigi continued to perform during the Soviet era and also became Tūhfakhon's teacher (T. Levin 1996:119). Other prominent sozandas of the Soviet era include Noshputi (1908–1961, Hevsi Bakayeva, mother of the sozanda Nina Bakayeva), Gubur (Hevsi Aronova, 1907–1971), and Chervonkhon (Adina Benyaminova). Note that due to the lack of research and documentation on sozandas, information such as dates are difficult to verify. In some cases I was able to find these years on gravestones, increasingly available on websites such as bjews.info.

18. Rashidov was made chief of state of the Uzbek Republic in 1950 and First Secretary of the Uzbek Party in 1959. He became a member of the Politburo in 1961, making him one of the most powerful governmental officials in Central Asia. Although Mallayev and Shamayeva speak admiringly of him, his name became synonymous with Soviet corruption for his role in the "Cotton Affair" scandal, in which he received funds from Moscow for Uzbekistan through falsified records of cotton production and bribery. In reaction to the crackdowns following the exposure of Rashidov's corrupt relationships with Moscow, Uzbek nationalism grew under his successor, Inomjon Usmonkhūjaev.

Chapter 2

1. Gilman (2006:45 et passim) takes the unusual step of describing both hybridization (melting pot) and cultural pluralism (mosaic) as "multi-culturalism" models, but I use the term specifically to refer to the latter, in accordance with the understanding of multiculturalism that dominated the discourse of educational and cultural institutions during the period of Bukharian Jewish immigration.

2. As Slobin has pointed out, the "mythic Old World" representation tells us very little "about the scope and diversity of the musical life of Eastern European Jews" (Slobin 1982a:30).

3. The Jewish race was a central topic in theories and pseudo scientific writings about race that dominated American and European sociology and anthropology. However, as generally light-skinned "others" in a United States dominated by a black-white racial binary, Jews had an unprecedented opportunity to present Jewish racial identity as something fluid, and as a kind of whiteness (historically almost all Jewish immigration to the United States has been from Europe, unlike the globally diverse immigration to Israel), although this was hardly an undisputed or tension-free transformation (Goldstein 2006; Painter 2010). It need not be stated that whiteness in the United States holds enormous privileges, and that black immigrants, black ethnics, and African Americans have not had the liberty to wrestle with questions of "assimilation" in the same way as European Americans. The language of the melting pot was particularly Eurocentric (King 2000:15–19).

4. Several Jewish race records were reissued on *Jewface* (2006), including early Irving Berlin compositions. Of Monroe Silver, heard on the compilation, a Victor Records publicist wrote in 1918: "[Silver's] tones are the tones of the Bowery, and as he speaks one can see his dark eyes gleaming and imagine the expressive gestures so typical of this canny, humorous race of Orientals." For more on the ethnic and racial strategies of Jewish composers see Most (2001) and my article on George Gershwin and Bill Finegan (Rapport 2008).

5. For example, Gdal Saleski's *Famous Musicians of a Wandering Race* [1927] was renamed *Famous Musicians of Jewish Origin* in 1949 (Móricz 2008:3). Jewish identity and its racial history remain a sensitive topic, and the impulse to define Jewishness in racial terms is persistent. See, for example, Harry Ostrer's *Legacy: A Genetic History of the Jewish People* (2012).

6. Race ostensibly contrasts with ethnicity in that historically race has been a category of biological inquiry, physical appearances, and innate characteristics (and heavily implicated in pseudoscience and social discrimination), whereas ethnicity is ostensibly a cultural distinction, "all those traditions, customs, activities, and practices that pertain to a particular group of people who see themselves and are seen by others as having distinct cultural features, a separate history, and a specific sociocultural identity" (Smedley 2007:31). See also Gilman (2006:182–83) and Horowitz (2011:81).

7. http://www.youtube.com/watch?v=OdOvAP5QITU.

8. According to Elazar (1986, see also Dufoix 2003:8), *edah* refers to the "Jewish polity," the "Jewish people as a whole." To avoid confusion, and because my interviewees did not seem to use the term *edah* in our

conversations, I use the terms "ethnic group" and *millat* to refer to the different Jewish groups.

9. Soviet ideology made distinctions between *"natsiya* [nation], *national'nost'* [nationality in the sense of ethnic group], *narod* [a people, in the sense of ethnic community], and *narodnost'* [small ethnic group, not fully constituted as a nationality]" (Katz 1975:380, translations in original). Turkic and Persian words for ethnic group and nationality remained only loosely related to this hierarchy (Roy 2000:14–15; Baldauf 1991:91–92). In Central Asia, the Russian terms became attached to the terms *khalq* and *millat*, both words originally from Arabic, meaning "folk," "people," "nation," *khalq* having the more general sense of "population" and *millat* typically used for religious communities or denominations.

10. Prior to the 1930s, Bukharian Jews were considered a distinct nationality from "Jews" per se, but still separate from Uzbek, Tajik, and other Central Asian national designations.

11. "In ihren Gesichtszügen, ihrem Körperbau und auch in ihrer geistigen Veranlagung finden sich Züge des altaischen und tatarischen Charakters, so dass sich der Verdacht aufdrängt, dass in ihren Adern viel nichtjüdisches, ja sogar nichtsemitisches Blut fliesst."

12. http://www.youtube.com/watch?v=YfhrtOUv4Wo.

13. Bukharian Jews may be distinct from many immigrant communities due to the historical consistency of their marginal status. Unlike for Bukharian Jews, for many immigrants the transformations in America seem to involve a difficult reorientation from majority to minority status: Mexicans and Han Chinese who never had to consider their "Mexicanness" or "Chineseness" in Mexico or China are suddenly faced with a racialized minority identity in which they are forced to self-consciously consider their history, music, language, appearance, and beliefs in relation to a non-Mexican or non-Chinese American majority (e.g., Zheng 2010:248–49). However, legitimate comparisons require more research on how other immigrants understand their experiences and the impact of preexisting ethnic categories on immigrant musical life.

14. Immigrant communities gaining critical mass or increased visibility in recent decades, including Colombians, Mande-speakers from West Africa, and Indo-Caribbeans, have each developed similar ensembles. Hear, for example, the array of ethnic groups represented on *New York City: Global Beat of the Boroughs* (2001).

15. Compare the career of Xiao Xiannien, a *yangqin* performer and teacher who plays in New York's EastRiver ensemble. He learned a wide variety of styles growing up, including Chinese folk music and operas, and playing as a professional with a ballet company and an orchestra that performs Chinese orchestral works. In New York, he has focused on traditional music and adapting the yangqin to new contexts (Rushefsky 2009). Martin Vejarano of the Colombian group La Cumbiamba eNeYé also moved from jazz to more ethnic and folk repertoires after immigrating to New York (Hamilton 2008).

Chapter 3

1. *Maqām, maqom,* or *makam* (meaning "place" in Arabic and Hebrew, also used in Persian and Turkish) is a term found throughout the

world for a variety of music concepts, and the Central Asian maqom shares some features with other maqām traditions, including some common nomenclature. However, the meaning of *maqom* in Central Asia and among Bukharian Jews generally is quite different, and at times antithetical, to the meaning of *maqām* in the Arab world or *makam* in the Turkish world. In the Arab and Turkish contexts, *maqāmāt* or *makamlar* (pl.) are modes often used as springboards for improvisations, implying particular kinds of intervallic combinations and melodic contours. The Central Asian maqoms, on the other hand, consist entirely of precomposed melodies. Performers memorize and execute these melodies with some variations, but these ornaments, flourishes, and modifications of melodic contour are understood as being exact performances of the composed, canonical tunes, and not as improvisations within a mode. For an overview of maqām traditions, see Powers et al. (2001).

2. During the final preparation of this manuscript, Angelika Jung was also preparing a new monograph on the Shashmaqom (Jung, forthcoming), which promises to reveal many new insights into the repertoire.

3. Although the correct ordering of melodies has definitely been a consistent concern for performers and theorists, we do not actually know how, or to what extent, musicians performed maqom in suites at the court or elsewhere before the Soviet era. The relevant theoretical treatises do discuss the organization and proper orders of the names of the modes (Jung 1988; Jung 1989; Djumaev 1992), but it remains unknown how musicians themselves approached the system in performance (Jung's forthcoming monograph may be instructive here). Djumaev does not offer any information on the subject in his survey of court aesthetics (Djumaev 2006). Even if long suite performances did take place at the court or elsewhere, there is no reason to assume that other approaches did not exist or were not prevalent. Musicians approached the Shashmaqom and other repertoires in multiple ways during the Soviet era, they continue to do so, and it is likely that they did in the more distant past as well.

   It is conceivable that the focus on fully intact suites or cycles is primarily a twentieth-century development linked to the Soviet nationalist projects, despite the rhetoric applying suite performance to pre-Soviet aesthetics and a specifically Sufi mystical path (e.g., in the liner notes to Academy of Maqom 2006). Bukharian Jews, in contrast, are not as attached to the equation of old pre-Soviet maqom performance with complete suites. Bukharian Jews may have a different stance than Uzbeks and Tajiks because they are not invested in the Sufi connection, which is loaded with political and religious connotations as the post-Soviet states seek to create distance from their Soviet pasts. Furthermore, although they were heavily represented as master maqom performers, Bukharian Jews did not largely populate the ranks of professional musicologists and academics studying the repertoire.

4. Ari Babakhanov included several pieces from the Chormaqom repertoire in his edition of the Shashmaqom, including Chargoh III, Bayot III, and Chapandozi Gulyor, "so they are not forgotten" (Jung 2010:17).

5. Djumaev writes that yakkakhoni began in the breaks of a Sufi zikr (Djumaev 2001:944). He makes no mention of it being a women's

genre. Here the term may more generically refer to solo or individual singing.

6. In the context of a Persian-language conversation, Aminov used the Hebrew word for "soul" (*neshomo*, instead of the Persian *jon*).

7. http://www.youtube.com/watch?v=9QK3tVi2eVQ.

8. See also Sultanova (2009) on the ustoz-shogird tradition in the Ferghana valley.

9. The "variety of ways people engage [recordings] in human contexts—through imagining the people behind the recording, but also simply through listening and then drawing on the recordings in their own performing" (Solis 2004:339)—is a rich and little-explored area of ethnomusicological inquiry. Rubinov's experiences with recordings is reminiscent of the pianist Fred Hersch on Thelonious Monk: "Since there was nobody around to teach me, and I figured things out for myself, what I would do is, I would sit at the piano and try to imagine that I was Monk...or whoever I was listening to. I would listen to a side and then go to the piano and try to just channel them in some way" (quoted in Solis 2004:341).

10. The tanbūr and sato are slightly different instruments, and both can be played by plucking or bowing.

11. For example, the Bukharian Israeli composer Benjamin Yusupov used recordings of a tanbūr in his *Haqqoni (Crossroads No. 4)* (2007), and the Uzbek pop star Yulduz Usmanova started her album *Yulduz* (1999) with the sound of the tanbūr.

12. Yu'ov is unattributed on the recordings; his participation was noted by my interviewees (see also Matyakubov 2009:115). On the recordings Levi's tanbūr has a tinnier timbre than today's instruments, since it has only three strings instead of four (the tinniness is not attributable to recording quality), and Yu'ov's doira has a much deeper, resonant low stroke than is generally heard today.

13. The Central Asian conception of composition is part of a far-reaching tradition of music theory that includes writings in Greek, Arabic, Persian, Hebrew, Indian, and European languages. For Plato, *harmonia* was "fitting together," "adapting," or "adjusting" one thing to another (Barker 1984:163–64). "[Greek] Melic composition (melopoïïa) together with rhythmic composition (rhythmopoïïa) was the process of selecting and applying the various components of melos and rhythm to create a complete composition" (Mathiesen 2001:329).

14. Saïdo's name is in the *takhallus* (signature) of the poem, but I was unable to find this poem in his divan.

15. For a detailed discussion of the ways in which Bukharian Jewish musicians set poems to melodies, see my dissertation (Rapport 2006:110–36).

16. Persian ghazals usually have a repeating word or group of syllables following the rhyme. This ending element is called the *radif* (row) of the poem.

17. This mukhammas is different from the four-line mukhammas blessings extemporized by the sozanda (T. Levin 1996:121).

18. Sūhbat implies not just discourse or conversation, but the overall social atmosphere, the "company," part of the world of "social gatherings held in private homes (variously called *mehmanī, ziyāfat, shau nishini, gap, saz söxbet,* etc.)" held throughout Central Asia (Blum 2001:365).

19. Hebrew poets, beginning with Dunash ben Labrat in tenth-century Spain, explicitly borrowed the Arabic meters (Cole 2007:23). Persian poets adopted the ʿarūz *terms* soon after al-Khalil, although they seemed to have already developed the Persian quantitative meters and they applied the ʿarūz system differently than Arab poets (Elwell-Sutton 1976:vii, 57).

20. "...sheʿru mūsīqī bo hamdigar paivast hast, donistani vazni ʿarūz baroi har yak mutribu saroyanda shart va zarūr ast."

21. *Zarb*, from the Arabic root ḍrb (appearing in words related to stroking, beating, or hitting), is the name of a goblet drum in contemporary Iranian Persian (and "rhythmic accompaniment" in general). *Usul* is from the Arabic word for "principles," "roots," "causes" (Tsuge 1974:4; al Faruqi 1981:21; Farmer [1943] 1997:596).

22. Talqin is usually represented as a continually alternating 3/4 + 3/8 rather than 9/8.

23. At odds with this nationalist ideology, the terminology in the Shashmaqom and the suite form itself reflect multiplicity, not singularity, with its array of melodies and sections evoking different regions and styles, including places along the Silk Road such as Iraq (ʿIroq), India (Mūghulcha), and Kashgar (Qashqarcha).

24. Similar linguistic issues emerged in the nationalization of the Uyghur muqams (Light 2008:32–35, 217–25). Reminiscent of Fitrat's suppression of Ota Jalol's Persian repertoire, Light writes, "Several people suggested that some of the traditional texts that Turdi Akhun sang may have been entirely in Persian, and this was one reason the muqam editors were uncomfortable about letting them be recorded or seen" (2008:217). Ömär Imin, one of the editors of the muqam texts for the standard version of the muqams, told him, "I am not an ethnic nationalist [millätči], but the Uyghur people must have pure Uyghur poetry" (2008:222; see also Harris 2008:77).

25. According to the foreword by Boboqul Faizulloyev, Shohnazar Sohibov, and Fazliddin Shahobov, the informants for the Belyayev edition, Uspenskiĭ's informants were Bobokhonov, Ota Jalol, Domullo Halim, Ota Ghios, Usto Shodī, and Mirzo Nasrulloi Tanbūrī (Belyayev 1950:13).

26. During informal conversations with Bukharian Jewish connoisseurs of maqom, I twice heard Yunus Rajabi described as a chala or from a chala family. This is a less common attribution than the description of Ota Jalol as a chala, but one that stems from the same questions of nationalism and ownership. I have even heard some Bukharian Jews say that Ibn Sina was Jewish (explaining that Sina equals Sinai), so such claims need to be treated with skepticism.

27. The questions of nationality and ownership that surround the Shashmaqom are part of a wider context involving the widespread Soviet policies that sought to sever links between religion and nationality. Belyayev and Uspenskiĭ's study of music in the Ferghana valley went unpublished because it contained too many dervish songs (Djumaev 1993:45), and Belyayev ([1962] 1975) not only fails to mention Bukharian Jews but also almost completely skirts any mention of Islam or Muslims in his study of Central Asian music. Uzbeks and Tajiks wrestled with their own position as ethnoreligious minorities on the periphery of the Soviet Union, their common Muslim culture split into Uzbek and Tajik nationalities and their religion suppressed as well.

28. In the special issue of *Ethnomusicology Forum* (Vol. 14, Issue 2) dedicated to "Music and Identity in Central Asia," Jews are mentioned only twice. There are notable exceptions to this pattern, including articles that discuss Jewish contributions to maqom history and Central Asian musical life by Matyakubov (2004, 2009) and Djumaev (2004, 2008), and of course Jung's edition of Ari Bobokhonov's Shashmaqom transcriptions (2010).

29. Here Mallayev is equating the maqom of Bukhara and Samarqand, both of which refer to the Bukharan Shashmaqom.

30. Most Bukharian Jews seem to share this opinion, evidenced by the fact that I only saw Belyayev's edition in collections and only heard his version mentioned by musicians. The Belyayev edition, with its Persian texts, is useful for Bukharian Jews in New York, who sing only Persian or Hebrew texts for the Shashmaqom melodies; classical Turkic poems are typically reserved for lyric songs and Chormaqom tunes.

31. Reminiscent of Aminov's description of the Bukharan style, Darvish Ali (16th/17th c.) wrote, "The *tanbūr* is one of the earliest musical instruments. According to Greek scholars the word consists of two parts: *tan* (heart) and *bura* (to pluck). And this name conveys the meaning of the words 'plucking the heart'" (quoted in, and translated by, Żerańska-Kominek 2009:36).

32. Of all the musicians I interviewed and worked with, only Ilyos Mallayev was comfortable voicing serious skepticism about the definitiveness of the Shashmaqom. He engaged the repertoire creatively in that he did not take the order or presentation of the modes for granted. For example, he theorized that there is a "seventh maqom," based on his observation that Maqom Dugoh has two sarakhbors—"Sarakhbori Dugoh" and "Sarakhbori Oromijon"—whereas all the other maqoms have only one. This line of reasoning is strongly based in practice, as the function of each sarakhbor is to introduce the pertinent and distinctive melodic elements and relationships of the entire maqom suite. He expressed interest in recreating this "seventh maqom," but unfortunately he died before he could find a sponsor for the project. Mallayev's reasoning about the snapshot quality of the Shashmaqom editions would make sense, especially given the inclusion of pieces such as "Bebokcha" and "Sinakhurush" found at the end of Maqom Buzruk in the Belyayev edition (1950). Probably, performer-composers would create pieces in the maqom style and they might become part of the repertoire over time, acquiring a relatively fixed location. If this is the case, it would be consistent with processes during and after the Soviet era, as composers create works that become adopted into the maqom repertoire.

33. Alternate spellings for maqom found in these group names include maqam, maqâm, maqām, and makam. The groups tend to substitute spellings indiscriminately. For the purposes of the book, I have standardized everything according to my transliteration and translation conventions.

34. As noted in the Introduction, through 1999 the majority of immigrants to New York City from Central Asia were Jews who had been granted refugee status following the passage of the Lautenberg Amendment. This number includes the prominent musicians featured in this book. While the Bukharian population joined the massive emigration of Jews during the 1990s, prominent Uzbek and Tajik

professional musicians would not have been under the same pressure to leave. Through 2011 the number of (Muslim) Uzbek and Tajik immigrants to New York has increased, although Jews still seem to account for most of the population and even continue to account for most of the recent immigrants (New York City 2013:55). These numbers are difficult to parse, especially since US census numbers account for country of origin (not Soviet nationality categories) and the Central Asian republics are often grouped together. Furthermore, ethnicity, nationality, and country of origin are not necessarily linked for the Jewish or non-Jewish populations: for example, ethnic Uzbeks might be immigrating from other countries of origin than Uzbekistan, such as Turkey, Afghanistan, or Tajikistan. Also these numbers do not reflect undocumented immigration.

35. "To Bodi Sabo" and "Ushshoqi Samarqand" are both setting of poems by the Mughal princess Zebunniso (Zīb un-Nisā, 17th c., writing under her pen-name "Makhfi," or "Hidden"), a favorite poet among Central Asians. In the liner notes to *Central Asia in Forest Hills, New York,* Zebunniso is incorrectly placed in the nineteenth century. "Makhfi" is also identified as the poet for "To Bodi Sabo" but Makhfi and Zebunniso are left unconnected, and Makhfi is incorrectly referred to as "he."

36. Aminov's recording of Maqom Navo is a complete rendition of the first vocal subsuite, without any instrumental selections or any melodies culled from the second vocal subsuite. Aminov is extremely faithful to the Belyayev version, his performances of the same poems coinciding almost note-by-note with the edition. Unlike *At the Bazaar of Love,* Aminov recorded the entire album in a home studio. He accompanies himself on the tanbūr (with the exception of the first tarona of "Orazi Navo," for which he overdubbed some rubob) with doira played by his son Yakov. No other voices or instrumentalists are featured, the end of the suite is in a much slower tempo than Mallayev's recording, and reverb is added. All of these factors make Aminov's reminiscent of the more "official" Shashmaqom recordings of the Soviet era, rather than the contemporary world music aesthetic described as "pre-Soviet" that Mallayev's recording is meant to evoke.

Ari Bobokhonov's edition of the Shashmaqom (Jung 2010), produced in Germany, includes recordings of Maqom Navo: one CD of the entire instrumental (mushkilot) suite performed by Bobokhonov solo on Afghan rubob, consisting of eight compositions and lasting forty-one minutes, and a second CD of the first subsuite of the vocal section, lasting about one hour.

37. Ari Bobokhonov situates the "Iroqi Bukhoro" suite not in Maqom Buzruk but in the sixth maqom, Maqom Iroq.

38. The Center for Traditional Music and Dance sponsors numerous Community Cultural Initiatives (CCIs) developed together with immigrant and ethnic communities. Although concerts are a feature of CCIs, the goal is establishing self-sustaining institutions for the transmission and continuation of cultural traditions. See http://www.ctmd.org/CCI.htm.

39. Jon Pareles's review (Pareles 2002) of the concert in the *New York Times* incorrectly identified Abukhai Aminov as Ezro Malakov (Malakov was originally scheduled to perform) and incorrectly stated that Krakauer performed with Ensemble Shashmaqom instead of Ensemble Tereza.

40. Fatima Kuinova, Honored (*Zasluzhinnaya*) Artist of Tajikistan and the only Bukharian Jewish recipient of the National Endowment for the Arts (NEA) National Heritage Award, also sang for Stalin, mentioned on her biography on the NEA website: http://www.nea.gov/honors/heritage/fellows/fellow.php?id=1992_08type=bio (accessed 9 August 2011).

41. The Persian couplet comes from Rubinov's poem, "Panj Panja Barobar Nest," which we had been translating together. Thus, the quotation is not just about learning and ignorance, but a reference to the practices of memorizing poetry and studying with a teacher in developing a mature, professional personality.

42. During the final stages of preparing this manuscript, Avrom Tolmasov moved back to Israel.

43. "Uzbek song, Tajik song, Bukharian song" all refer to the classical maqom repertoire.

44. With this list, Rubinov intended to highlight historic cities with reputations for traditional culture.

Chapter 4

1. In synagogues, cemeteries, and at mixed celebrations, women attend but do not sing, and because I am a Jewish man, my experience with religious repertoire has been limited to mixed and male-only contexts. A study of women's Jewish religious repertoires awaits research conducted by a woman with access to private women's contexts.

2. Originally eighteen, now there are nineteen benedictions. However, the "eighteen" has been retained (Elbogen [1913] 1993:24–25, 31–37).

3. Malakov's approach agrees with Ibragimov's demonstration of the Shahrisabz way. Ibragimov knows both styles well, since he is from Bukhara but also learned the repertoire of his maternal grandfather, who was from Shahrisabz.

4. The distortion in this recording is due to the extremely loud volume at which the musicians play.

5. On the emergence of ultra-Orthodoxy in nineteenth-century Hungary, see Silber (1992).

6. Ezro Malakov pronounced the name of the genre *shaydu ovoz* or *shayd ovoz*.

7. *Tarannum kardan* refers to praise singing, more specific than the verb *khondan*, which means to sing or to read.

8. On the development and spread of the Jerusalem-Sephardi style and the introduction of Arab/Turkic maqām/makam practices in the Eastern Sephardic liturgy, see Seroussi (2012).

9. An alternative to the Ashkenazic and Sephardic categories, Mizraḥi ("Eastern" or "Oriental," in relation to Israel), has been applied to the "other" Jewish communities with increasing frequency during the twentieth and twenty-first centuries. Bukharian Jews would seem to fall into this category, as they are neither Ashkenazic nor Sephardic, and they come from the "East." Especially in Israel, where Mizraḥi Jews are more numerous and have constructed a more cohesive identity, many Bukharian Jews identify with this larger group, and recordings by Bukharian Jews in Israel such as Yosi Niyazov (n.d.) contain guitar melodies harmonized in thirds, Arab rhythms, and other elements of Mizraḥi musical style. However, Mizraḥi Jews in general

share experiences that do not include Bukharian Jews; Mizraḥi Jews by and large lived in Arab countries and immigrated soon after the founding of Israel in 1948 or after the 1967 war. Bukharian Jews, on the other hand, lived in Persianate and Turkic societies, spent most of the twentieth century living under Soviet rule, and did not emigrate en masse until the 1980s. In New York, no strong Mizraḥi category exists, and Bukharian Jews are much more likely to self-identify as "Sephardic" than "Mizraḥi" if pressed, demonstrating the continuing weight of the Ashkenazic/Sephardic binary in American Jewish life.

10. The society was officially named in 1891 "Society of Lovers of Zion to Build Houses for the People of Bukhara, Samarkand, Tashkent, and Their Outskirts" (Cooper 2012:133). The name was shortened to "The Society of Bukharia and Its Outskirts" in 1904.

11. Some Bukharian Jewish histories offer alternatives to the Mamon narrative. According to Nisim Tājer (1970; see also Cooper 2004: 96–102), the local leaders in Bukhara, Nasi Mullah Yosef Hasid and Hakham Yitshak Cohen, argued with Mamon and another emissary (Hakham Zaḥaria Matsliakh from Yemen) about issues of ritual and practice. Yosef ben Zaḥaria ben Matsliakh and his father are mentioned by Wolff (1835:195) as "rivals of the great Joseph Mooghrebee." Nosonovskiĭ (2005) and Mavashev (2005) are more recent moments in the continuing debate over the Mamon narrative.

12. Compare similar issues with respect to the Mizo in India and Myanmar and the Abayudaya in Uganda (Charmé 2012:387–410).

13. In bjews.com forum "Ask a Rabbi," thread "Tanakh/Torah scrolls compared to other communities?" (accessed 27 November 2007).

14. http://www.bethgavrielcenter.com/content/History-Of-Bukharian-Jews.html (accessed 20 January 2009).

15. In the same interview, Aron Aronov—who speaks ten languages, including English—made a special point that the correct English translation of the word *millat*, which Malakov had used to describe the different Jewish groups such as Syrian Jews and Turkish Jews, was "ethnic group" and not "nation" or "community," thus underscoring the value placed on ethnicity for Bukharian Jewish Americans.

16. Shimon Ḥakham was instrumental in conserving the work of the most celebrated Judeo-Persian poet, Shāhin (fl. fourteenth century), publishing editions of his *Shāhin Torāh* and *Ardeshir-nāma* (Fischel 1971:1146; Paper 1986). His other contributions to Judeo-Persian literature include a translation of the entire Torah, translations of other biblical books, and his own compositions: *Musā-nāma* (all of the rabbinic stories relating to Moses), *Purim-nāma*, and *Sefer liqqute dinim* (a compendium of Jewish law and ritual similar to the *Shulḥan Arukh*).

17. Although the general Jewish populace has tended to embrace the use of local melodies and poetic forms, religious authorities have typically had mixed reactions to innovative uses of neighbors' styles. When Dunash ben Labrat began using Arabic meters for his Hebrew poetry, "he was accused, among other things, of 'destroying the holy tongue...by casting it into foreign meters,' and 'bringing calamity upon his people'" (Cole 2007:23).

18. *Hazaj* meters are the most common in Hebrew, due to the ease with which constructions beginning with a *sheva* can be made. In Hebrew, the meter is called *marnin*, and the foot consists of one *yated* and two *tenu'āh*-s ($\cup - + - + -$).

19. Despite the all-encompassing nature of this statement, there is some variety to the conventional associations of poetic meters with maqom rhythmic types. For just one immediate example with respect to the *nasr* type, the most common poem used for "Nasri Bayot" is a ghazal by Hiloli, which is not in a hazaj meter, but *mujtass musamman makhbun makhzuf* ($\cup - \cup - \cup \cup - - \cup - \cup - \cup \cup -$): Bi-o bi-o ki dil-ū jon-i man fi-do-i tu bod / Sa-rī ki bar tan-i man hast khok-i po-i tu bod.

20. Even the Bukharan jadid (reformist) Abdulrauf Fitrat wrote in Persian (Roy 2000:4). Inhabitants of Samarqand and Bukhara, although in Uzbekistan, are Persian-speaking.

21. There are of course local preferences and differences in addition to the many shared poets and poems. Several Persian-language poets who are popular in Central Asia, such as Mashrab and Hiloli, are virtually unknown in Iran. Multilingual Central Asians are also immensely fond of Turkic-language poets, such as Fuzuli, regardless of their mother tongue. Many poets wrote in Turkic and Persian languages, such as Navoi; most famous for his Turkic poetry, he also wrote in Persian under the pen name Foni (Bečka 1968:486).

22. A similar attitude toward language can be found in the Lubavitcher community. Hebrew has the highest spiritual value, but Yiddish, associated with Eastern European culture and the revered Rebbes of the past, also has potential for prayer and devotion (Koskoff 2001:80–81). Judeo-Spanish is also used for devotional texts, but it does not rival Hebrew in spiritual status.

23. Roshel Aminov published *Sitorarezhoi adab: Pandu hikmat* (2013), a collection of classical Persian poetry in Roman characters, in part to support his efforts teaching Persian poetry at his Shashmaqom Academy (see Chapter 3). Imonuel Rybakov's *Easy Bukharian* (2011), an introductory language textbook aimed at young Bukharian Jewish Americans, contains several Persian poems and songs, some traditional and some recent works by Ilyos Mallayev, Roshel Rubinov, and others.

24. Mikhoel Zavul's "Nigahdorat Khudo Boshad" (Zavul 1999:95) is another new poem set to a maqom melody typically heard in religious settings. Ezro Malakov called the melody khalqī, and Roshel Rubinov said that the melody is by Gavriel Mulloqandov, originally used for a poem called "Az Qadar Gardam."

25. Russian terms, such as *pauza, pripev*, and *forshlag* (grace note, from German *Vorschlag*), are often preferred among Bukharian Jews for music theory and performance.

26. The expansive history of Persian rule would seem to explain some of the linguistic and cultural affinities of Iranian and Central Asian Jewish communities with Jews in Azerbaijan and Dagestan (Eliyahu 1999).

27. Biblical translations are from the Jewish Publication Society edition of 1985 (Philadelphia).

28. *Qurbon* (sacrifice) is a word common to Hebrew, Arabic, and Persian that, in an Iranian and Central Asian context, has noteworthy Sufi overtones of willing submission. In Rumi's poems, for example, both Ishmael and Isaac are described as qurbons willing to submit themselves out of love to Abraham's knife (Renard 1986:633–40).

Chapter 5

1. This same 6/8 pattern is a cornerstone of many dance and popular musics in Iran and Central Asia. Among Iranians, the rhythm is called *shesh-o-hasht* (6/8) or onomatopoeically *damboli dimbo*, and it has become particularly associated with the culture and local popular music industry among the diasporic community in Los Angeles (Hemmasi 2010).

2. Tūhfakhon introduced some changes in response to the Soviet times, including male performers in her ensemble and augmenting it with string instruments (rubob, tor, ghijak) and accordion, synthesizer, and clarinet (T. Levin 1996:119, 122).

3. During most of the 2000s, Tūhfakhon had relocated to Denver to be with her family.

4. Narkolayev's classical playing can be heard on *At the Bazaar of Love* and *Asie centrale: Traditions classiques,* Ocora 560035–36.

5. My wife's grandfather, Al Drootin (b. 1916), is a representative example. His father was a klezmer in and around the town of Zaslav in the Volhynia province, once part of the Pale of Settlement of the Russian Empire (now Izyaslav, Ukraine). His father was a clarinetist and his father's father a flutist. All of the musicians were "Yiddish" (Jewish) musicians, although his father's group had a non-Jewish trombone player. Their group would play Jewish weddings and bar mitzvahs as well as Russian (non-Jewish) "high society jobs" for the "hoi polloi" [*sic*], as the Jewish musicians had a "tremendous reputation" for great dance music. Al, a clarinetist and saxophonist, immigrated to the United States in 1925. (He was born in Zaslav, not in the United States, as is given in various sources such as Leonard Feather's *Encyclopedia of Jazz in the '70s* and the online *All Music Guide*. A family member who was interviewed for the biography gave Boston as Al's birthplace, to seem more "American" and avoid association with the Soviet Union.) Although Al learned his father's repertoire, he and his brother (Benjamin "Buzzy" Drootin, 1920–2000) were career jazz musicians in Boston and New York. Al also played for Lester Lanin's orchestra and other society bands. He played very little klezmer music over the course of his career, until in the 1990s, scholar and performer Hankus Netsky (the Klezmer Conservatory Band) became interested in his repertoire and showcased him with a Klezmer Conservatory Band concert.

6. The Russian word Djumaev used to describe both the "Jewish people" and "other peoples" is *narod*, which as mentioned can also be translated as "nation."

7. See also the comparison between Angel Lee and Tang Liangxing's American careers: "In contrast to the experience of Angel Lee and other pop singers, instrumental Chinese music and its players are more favorably received in America" (Zheng 2010:252).

8. Translated by Michael and Wendy Grinberg.

9. Translated by Valerie Tregubenko.

10. http://www.youtube.com/watch?v=eCR6yc5NrDg and http://www.youtube.com/watch?v=qs-7xcKWLUM.

11. http://www.youtube.com/watch?v=d0H0ZssG9v0NR.

Chapter 6

1. Other members of the Malakov family on the trip included Ezro's wife Bella Khayimova and her sister, Ezro's brother Khaiko, and Jacob, the son of Ezro's brother Avrom who died in 1984. Khaiko's son Daniel was murdered in 2007, creating a tragic aura around the Malakov family during the trip. Daniel's murder and the trial of his former wife and her cousin were covered in most of the New York media outlets and even led to a book (Malcolm 2011, based on her article for the *New Yorker*). For an assessment of Malcolm's book, I highly recommend Joyce Carol Oates's review (2011).

2. *Aka* ("older brother") is a term of respect. Ezro Malakov, for example, is called *Ezro-aka* by nearly everyone in the Bukharian Jewish community.

3. Primak published some of his research of oral history interviews, conducted in Tajik, among older Bukharian Jews in Israel (Primak 2008). Most recently he is the coordinator of Bukharian Jewish Studies at the Ben-Zvi Institute in Jerusalem.

4. The following year, IMG cancelled Karimova's "Guli" show at Lincoln Center for New York Fashion Week, citing human rights abuses in Uzbekistan (Human Rights Watch 2011).

5. The translation here is from the version published in Mallayev's collection, which differs somewhat from the lyrics of the audio example.

6. Raḥmin Nektalov is one of the leaders of the Bukharian community.

Glossary

All words are from Persian or Hebrew, except where indicated.

Amida	a central prayer of Jewish worship
anusim	"forced ones," forced converts from Judaism, who continued to practice Judaism in secret
'Aravit	the evening prayer in Jewish worship
'arūz	classical system of Persian and Arabic prosody
ashula	song
ashulai kalon	"great song," a style in which singers alternate in rising tessituras and culminate in group singing (called katta ashula in Uzbek)
Ashkenazim	Historically Yiddish-speaking Jews who spread out from German-speaking lands; in contemporary usage "Western" Jews or Jews who trace their ancestry to Eastern Europe
avj	culmination, climax
bahr	poetic foot
bazm	banquet
be muzyka	a cappella (lit. "without music")
beit	couplet or line, consisting of two misra'
chang	hammered zither (not the historical vertical harp)
chala	a Jew who outwardly converted to Islam under duress
doira	frame drum, with jingles along the inside rim
dutor	a long-necked lute with two strings
Erets Isroel	the Land of Israel (both the diasporic concept and the nation-state)
estrada	stage, variety, pop music
ghazal	a classical poetic form commonly used in maqom
ghijak	spike fiddle
golut	exile, diaspora
goy	nation, gentile
Ḥakham	a title meaning "wise man" or "religious leader"
halakhah	Jewish law and interpretation
ḥazzan	cantor

195

ḥazzanut	cantorial singing
hofiz	singer, professional singer
jomma	Bukharian Jewish ceremonial embroidered coat
katta ashula	see ashulai kalon
kehillo	community
khalq	folk (noun)
khalqī	folk (adjective)
khonagoh	worship house in a cemetery
Khudo	God
maqom	mode, classical music
marsiya	elegy
meḥitsah	screen separating men and women in the synagogue (see parda)
millat	ethnic group, nation
minhag	custom (of a particular Jewish community)
Minḥo	the afternoon prayer in Jewish worship
minyan	quorum of ten Jewish men over the age of bar mitzvah
misraʿ	line or half-line of a poem (see beit)
Mizraḥim	"Eastern" Jews
motamī	mourning (surudi motamī: mourning songs)
musaf	an additional service in Jewish worship
mukhammas	a five-line poetic form, sometimes based on a preexisting ghazal
Mullo	a title meaning "religious leader" (the same as Mullah)
muzyka	instrumental music, melody
nai	flute
narod	folk (Russian)
nigun	melody, a Jewish song
nota	Western music notation (Russian)
nusaḥ	"version," a particular way of performing Jewish liturgical repertoire, applicable to an individual or a community
ohang	melody
parda	fret (on a musical instrument), division; also screen separating men and women in the synagogue (see meḥitsah)
piyyut	Jewish liturgical poem
plov	pilaf
qadim	old, ancient
qism	section (can be applied to a section or piece of music)
qofiya	rhyme
rajaʿ	line or half-line of a poem
roh	way, also specifically referring to a way of performing melodies
sabuk	light
sato	a long-necked lute similar to the tanbūr, often bowed
Sephardim	historically Judeo-Spanish–speaking Jews who spread out from Spain and Portugal; in contemporary usage "Middle Eastern" or non-Ashkenazic Jews
Shaḥarit	the morning prayer in Jewish worship
shakl	poetic form

Shashmaqom	canonical Central Asian repertoire of six modes: Buzruk, Rost, Navo, Dugoh, Segoh, ʿIroq
Shemaʿ	a central prayer of Jewish worship
sheʿr	poem, poetry
shiro	singing (specifically applied to Jewish religious repertoire)
shiru shakar	lit. "milk and sugar," a poem with alternating Persian and Turkic verses
shogird	student
shuʿba	Shashmaqom subsection, lit. "branch"
soz	"instrument," also a specific kind of long-necked lute
sozanda	female wedding and party entertainer
sukhan	discourse, sermon, speech
tanbūr	a long-necked lute, typically with four strings and diatonically fretted; the central melodic instrument of the Shashmaqom
tavr	path (see roh)
tor	a double-chested short-necked lute with double courses
Transoxiana	Central Asia, "land beyond the river Oxus" (English)
tūĭ	wedding, party, celebration of a life-cycle event
ustoz, usto	master, teacher
ustogī	mastery
usul	rhythmic cycle, typically played on the doira. Also called zarb.
vatan	homeland
vazn	meter, rhythm
vaznin	serious, heavy
yakkakhonī	solo singing
Yahudi	Jew
zarb	rhythm, rhythmic cycle, typically played on the doira. Also called usul.
zardūzī	embroidered skullcap
ziyorat	pilgrimage

Bibliography

Adams, Laura L. 2010. *The Spectacular State: Culture and National Identity in Uzbekistan*. Durham, NC: Duke University Press.

Adler, E. N. 1898. "The Persian Jews: Their Books and Their Ritual." *Jewish Quarterly Review* 10(4):584–625.

Adler, Marcus Nathan. 1907. *The Itinerary of Benjamin of Tudela*. London: Oxford University Press.

Al'meyev, R.V. 2004. "K etnologii bukharskikh evreyev" [On the Ethnology of Bukharian Jews]. In *Evrei v srednei azii: Voprosy istorii i kul'tury*, edited by E.V. Rtveladze, 26–38. Tashkent: Izdatel'stvo "Fan" Akademii nauk Respubliki Uzbekistan.

Altschuler, Mordechai. 2007. "Russia." In *Encyclopaedia Judaica*, 2nd ed., edited by Michael Berenbaum and Fred Skolnik, 17:531–87. Detroit: Macmillan Reference USA.

Altschuler, Mordechai, and Aviva Müller-Lancet. 1971. "Bukhara." In *Encyclopaedia Judaica*, 4:1470–76. New York: Macmillan.

Amitin-Shapiro, Z. L. 1931. *Ocherk pravovogo byta Sr.-Aziatskikh evreev/Ŭrta-osiyo yahudilarining huquqlari tughrisida* [Essay on the Legal Life of Central Asian Jews]. Tashkent: Uzbekskoye gosudarctsvennoye izdatel'stvo.

Aminov, Roshel, and Yakov Amin. 2004. "Neriye Amin Fund, Inc." http://www.neriyeaminfund.com/.

Aminov, Roshel, and Yakov Amin. 2011. *Sitorarezhoi adab: Pandu hikmat*. Self-published.

Appiah, Kwame Anthony. 2006a. "The Case for Contamination." *New York Times Magazine*, January 1.

Appiah, Kwame Anthony. 2006b. *Cosmopolitanism: Ethics in a World of Strangers*. New York: W.W. Norton.

Arapov, Dmitriy Yu. 1993. "The Bukhara Khanate at the End of the 19th Century." In *Bukhara. Caught in Time: Great Photographic Archives*, 12–23. Reading: Garnet.

Asʿadi, Humān. 2000. " 'Shashmaqām' beh ʿonvān yek sistem musiqāʾi" [Shashmaqom as a Musical System]. *Faslnāme-ye musiqi-ye Mahur* 6:9–39.

"Ashkenaz." 2007. In *Encyclopaedia Judaica*, 2nd ed., edited by Michael Berenbaum and Fred Skolnik, 2:569–71. Detroit: Macmillan Reference USA.

Augé, Marc. [1994] 1998. *A Sense for the Other: The Timeliness and Relevance of Anthropology*. Translated by Amy Jacobs. Stanford: Stanford University Press.

Avenary, Hanoch. 1971. "Nusaḥ." In *Encyclopaedia Judaica*, 12:1283–84. New York: Macmillan.

Avenary, Hanoch. 1979. *Encounters of East and West in Music*. Tel Aviv: Tel Aviv University.

Aviv, Caryn, and David Shneer. 2005. *New Jews: The End of the Jewish Diaspora*. New York: New York University Press.

Babakhonov, I. M. [1951] 1958. "K voprosu o priskhozhdenii gruppy evreev-musul'man v Bukhare (On the origin of a Judeo-Muslim community in Bukhara)." *Sovetskaya etnografiya* 3:162–63, reprinted, edited, and translated by Rudolf Loewenthal, *The Judeo-Muslim Marranos of Bukhara: Two Russian Articles*, Central Asian Collectanea, No. 1. Washington, DC.

Bachayev, Mordekhai (Muhib). 2007. *Kulliyot* (Collected Works). Jerusalem: Self-published.

Baldauf, Ingeborg. 1991. "Some Thoughts on the Making of the Uzbek Nation." *Cahiers du Monde russe et soviétique* 32(1):79–95.

Barker, Andrew. 1984. *Greek Musical Writings. I, The Musician and His Art*. Cambridge: Cambridge University Press.

Bečka, Jiří. 1968. "Tajik Literature from the 16th Century to the Present." In *History of Iranian Literature*, edited by Jan Rypka, 483–605. Dordrecht: D. Reidel.

Belyayev, Viktor, ed. 1950. *Shashmaqom. I, Maqom Buzruk*. Moscow: Gosudarstvyennoye muzikal'noye izdatyel'stvo/Nashriyoti davlatii muzikavi.

Belyayev, Viktor, ed. 1954. *Shashmaqom. II, Maqom Rost*. Moscow: Gosudarstvyennoye muzikal'noye izdatyel'stvo/Nashriyoti davlatii muzikavi.

Belyayev, Viktor, ed. 1957. *Shashmaqom. III, Maqom Navo*. Moscow: Gosudarstvyennoye muzikal'noye izdatyel'stvo/Nashriyoti davlatii muzikavi.

Belyayev, Viktor, ed. 1959. *Shashmaqom. IV, Maqom Dugoh*. Moscow: Gosudarstvyennoye muzikal'noye izdatyel'stvo/Nashriyoti davlatii muzikavi.

Belyayev, Viktor, ed. 1967. *Shashmaqom. V, Maqom Segoh* and *Maqom 'Iroq*. Moscow: Gosudarstvyennoye muzikal'noye izdatyel'stvo/ Nashriyoti davlatii muzikavi.

Belyayev, Viktor. [1962] 1975. *Central Asian Music: Essays in the History of the Peoples of the U.S.S.R.* Edited and translated by Mark and Greta Slobin. Middletown, CT: Wesleyan University Press.

Bent, Ian D., and Stephen Blum. 2001. "Repertory [Repertoire]." In *The New Grove Dictionary of Music and Musicians*, 2nd ed., edited by Stanley Sadie, 16:196–98. London: Macmillan.

Benyaminov, Meyer. 1992. *Bukharian Jews*. English rev. ed. New York.

Beyer, Gregg A. 1991. "The Evolving United States Response to Soviet Jewish Emigration." *International Journal of Refugee Law* 3(1):30–59.

Blum, Stephen. 1994. Conclusion to *Music-Cultures in Contact: Convergences and Collisions*, edited by Stephen Blum and Margaret J. Kartomi, 250–77. Basel: Gordon and Breach.

Blum, Stephen. 2001. "Central Asia." In *The New Grove Dictionary of Music and Musicians*, 2nd ed., edited by Stanley Sadie, 5:363–72. London: Macmillan.

Bohlman, Philip V. 2001. "Diaspora." In *The New Grove Dictionary of Music and Musicians*, 2nd ed., edited by Stanley Sadie, 7:292–94. London: Macmillan.

Bohlman, Philip V. 2002a. "Inventing Jewish Music." In *Yuval VII: Studies in Honor of Israel Adler*, edited by Eliyahu Schliefer and Edwin Seroussi, 33–74. Jerusalem: Hebrew University Magnes Press.

Bohlman, Philip V. 2002b. *World Music: A Very Short Introduction*. New York: Oxford University Press.

Bregel, Yuri. 2003. *An Historical Atlas of Central Asia*. Leiden: Brill.

Calmard, J. 2003. "Cultural and Religious Cross-Fertilization between Central Asia and the Indo-Persian World." In *History of Civilizations of Central Asia. V: Development in Contrast: From the Sixteenth to the Mid-Nineteenth Century*, edited by Chahryar Adle and Irfan Habib, coedited by Karl M. Baipakov, 812–20. Paris: UNESCO.

Castelo-Branco, Salwa El-Shawan. 2001. "Performance of Arab Music in Twentieth-Century Egypt: Reconciling Authenticity and Contemporaneity." In *The Garland Encyclopedia of World Music. VI, The Middle East*, edited by Virginia Danielson, Scott Marcus, and Dwight Reynolds, 557–561. New York: Routledge.

Chafets, Zev. 2007. "The Missionary Mogul." *New York Times*, 16 September.

Charmé, Stuart Z. 2012. "Newly Found Jews and the Politics of Recognition." *Journal of the American Academy of Religion* 80(2):387–410.

Clifford, James. 1994. "Diasporas." *Cultural Anthropology* 9(3):302–38.

Cohen, Judah M. 2009. *The Making of a Reform Jewish Cantor: Musical Authority, Cultural Investment*. Bloomington: Indiana University Press.

Cohen, Judith R. 1990. "Musical Bridges: The Contrafact Tradition in Judeo-Spanish Songs." In *Cultural Marginality in the Western Mediterranean*, edited by Frederick Gerson and Anthony Percival, 121–27. Toronto: New Aurora Editions.

Cohen, Judith R., and Joel Bresler. 2009. "The Music of the Sephardim." *Early Music America* 15(4):61–62, 64.

Cohen, Mark R. 1994. *Under Crescent and Cross: The Jews of the Middle Ages*. Princeton, NJ: Princeton University Press.

Cohen, Mark R. 2007. "The Origins of Sephardic Jewry in the Medieval Arab World." In *Sephardic and Mizrahi Jewry: From the Golden Age of Spain to Modern Times*, edited by Zion Zohar, 23–39. New York: New York University Press.

Cohen, Robin. 1997. *Global Diasporas: An Introduction*. London: UCL Press.

Cole, Peter, trans. and ed. 2007. *The Dream of the Poem: Hebrew Poetry from Muslim and Christian Spain, 950–1492*. Princeton, NJ: Princeton University Press.

Cooper, Alanna E. 1998. "The Bukharan Jews in Post-Soviet Uzbekistan: A Case of Fractured Identity." *Anthropology of East Europe Review* 16(2):42–54.

Cooper, Alanna E. 2000. "Negotiating Identity in the Context of Diaspora, Dispersion and Reunion: The Bukharan Jews and Jewish Peoplehood." Ph.D. dissertation, Boston University.

Cooper, Alanna E. 2003. "Feasting, Memorializing, Praying, and Remaining Jewish in the Soviet Union: The Case of the Bukharan Jews." In *Jewish*

Life after the U.S.S.R., edited by Zvi Gitelman with Musya Glants and Marshall I. Goldman, 141–51. Bloomington: Indiana University Press.

Cooper, Alanna E. 2004. "Reconsidering the Tale of Rabbi Yosef Maman and the Bukharan Jewish Diaspora." *Jewish Social Studies* 10(2):80–115.

Cooper, Alanna E. 2008. "Rituals in Flux: Courtship and Marriage among Bukharan Jews." In *Bukharan Jews in the 20th Century: History, Experience, and Narration,* edited by Ingeborg Baldauf, Moshe Gammer, and Thomas Loy, 187–208. Wiesbaden: Reichert.

Cooper, Alanna E. 2011. "Where Have All the Jews Gone? Mass Migration from Independent Uzbekistan." In *The Divergence of Judaism and Islam: Interdependence, Modernity, and Political Turmoil,* edited by Michael M. Laskier and Yaacov Lev, 199–224. Gainesville: University Press of Florida.

Cooper, Alanna E. 2012. *Bukharan Jews and the Dynamics of Global Judaism.* Bloomington: Indiana University Press.

Corré, Alan D., Ezer Kahanov, Cecil Roth, Hyman Joseph Campeas, and Yitzhak Kerem. 2007. "Sephardim." In *Encyclopaedia Judaica,* 2nd ed., edited by Michael Berenbaum and Fred Skolnik, 18:292–305. Detroit: Macmillan Reference USA.

Crosland, Alan, dir. 1927. *The Jazz Singer.* Warner Bros.

Diner, Hasia. 2004. *The Jews of the United States, 1654 to 2000.* Berkeley: University of California Press.

Djumaev, Alexander. 1992. "From Parda to Maqām: A Problem of the Origin of the Regional System." In *Regionale maqam. Traditionen in Geschichte und Gegenwart: Materialien der 2. Arbeitstagung der Study Group "maqām" des International Council for Traditional Music vom 23. bis 28. März 1992 in Gosen bei Berlin,* edited by Jürgen Elsner and Gisa Jähnichen, 145–62. Berlin: Humboldt-Universität.

Djumaev, Alexander. 1993. "Power Structures, Culture Policy, and Traditional Music in Soviet Central Asia." *Yearbook for Traditional Music* 25:43–50.

Djumaev, Alexander. 1997. "Najm al-Dīn Kaukabī Bukhārī and the Maqām Theory in the 16th to 18th Centuries." In *The Structure and Idea of Maqām: Historical Approaches. Proceedings of the Third Meeting of the ICTM Maqām Study Group Tampere–Virrat, 2–5 October 1995,* edited by Jürgen Elsner and Risto Pekka Pennanen, 27–37. Tampere: Department of Folk Tradition, University of Tampere.

Djumaev, Alexander. 1999. Liner notes to *Ari Bobokhonov and Ensemble: Shashmaqam.* New Samarkand Records SAM CD 9002. Compact disc.

Djumaev, Alexander. 2001. "Sacred Music and Chant in Islamic Central Asia." In *The Garland Encyclopedia of World Music. VI, The Middle East,* edited by Virginia Danielson, Scott Marcus, and Dwight Reynolds, 935–47. New York: Routledge.

Djumaev, Alexander. 2004. "Bukharskie evrei i muzykal'naya kul'tura Sredneĭ Azii" [Bukharian Jews and the Musical Culture of Central Asia], in *Evrei v Sredneĭ Azii: Voprosy istorii i kul'tury,* edited by E.V. Rtveladze, 84–102. Tashkent: Izdatel'stvo "Fan" Akademii nauk Respubliki Uzbekistan.

Djumaev, Alexander. 2005. "Musical Heritage and National Identity in Uzbekistan." *Ethnomusicology Forum* 14(2):165–84.

Djumaev, Alexander. 2006. "The Old Aesthetics of the Bukharan Šašmaqām: Its Origin, Meaning and Destiny." In *Maqām Traditions of Turkic Peoples: Proceedings of the Fourth Meeting of the ICTM Study Group "Maqām," Istanbul 18–24 October 1998*, edited by Jürgen Elsner and Gisa Jähnichen, 47–56. Berlin: Trafo.

Djumaev, Alexander. 2008. "Musical Traditions and Ceremonies of Bukhara." *Anthropology of the Middle East* 3(1):52–66.

Dufoix, Stéphane. 2003. *Diasporas*. Translated by William Rodarmor. Berkeley: University of California Press.

Dugger, Celia W. 1997. "A Virtuoso Far from Home: Uzbeks' Classical Master Reclaims Role in Queens." *New York Times*, 20 February.

During, Jean. 1993. "Musique, Nation & Territore en Asie Interieure." *Yearbook for Traditional Music* 25:29–42.

During, Jean. 1994. *Quelque chose se passe: Le sens de la tradition dans l'Orient musical*. Paris: Éditions Verdier.

During, Jean. 1998. *Musique d'Asie centrale: l'esprit d'une tradition*. Arles: Cité de la Musique/Actes Sud.

During, Jean. 2005. "Power, Authority, and Music in the Cultures of Inner Asia." *Ethnomusicology Forum* 14(2):143–64.

Elazar, Daniel J. 1986. "The Jewish People as the Classic Diaspora: A Political Analysis." In *Modern Diasporas in International Politics*, edited by Gabriel Sheffer, 212–57. London: Croom Helm.

Elbogen, Ismar. [1913] 1993. *Jewish Liturgy: A Comprehensive History*. Philadelphia: Jewish Publication Society.

Eliyahu, Piris. 1999. *The Music of the Mountain Jews*. Yuval Music Series, 5. Jerusalem: Jewish Music Research Center.

Farmer, Henry George. [1943] 1997. "Saʿadyah Gaon on the Influence of Music." In *Studies in Oriental Music. I, History and Theory*, edited by Eckhard Neubauer, 573–695. Frankfurt am Main: Institute for the History of Arabic-Islamic Science at the Johann Wolfgang Goethe University.

al-Faruqi, Lois Ibsen. 1981. *An Annotated Glossary of Arabic Musical Terms*. Westport, CT: Greenwood Press.

Fātemi, Sāsān. 2005. "La musique legere urbaine dans la culture iraini-enne: Réflexions sur les notions de classique et populaire" [Light Urban Music in Iranian Culture: Reflections on the Notions of Classic and Popular]. Ph.D. dissertation, Universite Paris X—Nanterre.

Feldman, Walter Zev. 1994. "Bulgărească/Bulgarish/Bulgar: The Transfor-mation of a Klezmer Dance Genre." *Ethnomusicology* 38(1):1–35.

Feldman, Walter Zev. 2004. Program notes to *Music and Dance of the Jewish Wedding: Bukharan Wedding*, held at 92nd Street Y, 8 December.

Fischel, Walter J. 1971. "Ḥakham, Simon." In *Encyclopaedia Judaica*, 7:1146. New York: Macmillan.

Foltz, Richard C. 1999. *Religions of the Silk Road: Overland Trade and Cultural Exchange from Antiquity to the Fifteenth Century*. New York: St. Martin's Press.

Frank, Gelya. 1997. "Jews, Multiculturalism, and Boasian Anthropology." *American Anthropologist* 99(4):731–45.

Friedman, Sandy. 2005. "Eastern Influence: Bukharian Jewish Music and Culture Lives—in Howard Country." *Baltimore Jewish Times*, Howard County edition, 18 November, 21–22.

Frigyesi, Judit. 2002. "Orality as Religious Ideal: The Music of East-European Jewish Prayer." In *Yuval VII: Studies in Honor of Israel Adler*, edited by Eliyahu Schliefer and Edwin Seroussi, 113–53. Jerusalem: Hebrew University Magnes Press.

Frye, Richard N., C. Edmund Bosworth, Yuri Bregel, G. A. Pugachenkova, E. V. Rtveladze, Barbara Schmitz, Michael Zand, and Anke von Kügelgen. 1990. "Bukhara." In *Encyclopedaedia Iranica*, edited by Ehsan Yarshater, 4:511–45. New York: Bibliotheca Persica Press.

Galchinsky, Michael. 1994. "Glimpsing Golus in the Golden Land: Jews and Multiculturalism in America." *Judaism* 43(4):360–68.

Genshtke, V. L., and T. E. Vaganova. 2004. "Nekotorye svedeniya o sredneaziatskikh evreyakh (po putevym ocherkam G. Lansdella)" [Some Information about the Central Asian Jews (from the travel notes of H. Lansdell)]. In *Evrei v Srednei Azii: Voprosy istorii i kul'tury*, edited by E.V. Rtveladze, 39–50. Tashkent: Izdatel'stvo "Fan" Akademii nauk Respubliki Uzbekistan.

Gerson-Kiwi, Edith. 1950. "Wedding Dances and Songs of the Jews of Bokhara." *Journal of the International Folk Music Council* 2:17–18.

Gilman, Sander L. 2006. *Multiculturalism and the Jews*. New York: Routledge.

Gilman, Sander L. 2008. "Foreword: Are Jews Musical? Historical Notes on the Question of Jewish Musical Modernism." In *Jewish Musical Modernism, Old and New*, edited by Philip V. Bohlman, vii–xvi. Chicago: University of Chicago Press.

Gilroy, Paul. 1993. *The Black Atlantic: Modernity and Double Consciousness*. Cambridge, MA: Harvard University Press.

Goldstein, Eric L. 2006. *The Price of Whiteness: Jews, Race, and American Identity*. Princeton, NJ: Princeton University Press.

Goldschmidt, Ernst Daniel, and Ruth Langer. 2007. "Liturgy." In *Encyclopaedia Judaica*, 2nd. ed., edited by Michael Berenbaum and Fred Skolnik, 13:131–39. Detroit: Macmillan Reference USA.

Gutierrez, Ramon A. 1994. "Ethnic Studies: Its Evolution in American Colleges and Universities." In *Multiculturalism: A Critical Reader*, edited by David Theo Goldberg, 157–67. Cambridge: Blackwell.

Hall, Stuart. 1990. "Cultural Identity and Diaspora." In *Identity: Community, Culture, Difference*, edited by Jonathan Rutherford, 222–37. London: Lawrence and Wishart.

Hamilton, Gabrielle. 2008. "Martin Vejarano: Healing Wounds through Music." *CTMD The Global Beat of the Boroughs e-Newsletter*, March. http://www.ctmd.org/pages/enews0508martin.html (accessed 12 December 2012).

Harris, Rachel. 2008. *The Making of a Musical Canon in Chinese Central Asia: The Uyghur Twelve Muqam*. Hampshire, UK: Ashgate.

Ḥayimov, Yoqub. 1982. *Sadoqat: Qissa, Ocherk, Hikoyalar, Bir Pardali P'esalar*. Toshkent: G'afur G'ulom nomidagi Adabiyot ba san'at nashriyoti.

Hemmasi, Farzaneh. 2010. " 'Living in Every Persian Body': The Rhythmic Definition of Iranian Los Angeles." Paper presented at the annual meeting for the Society of Ethnomusicology, Los Angeles, November 10–14.

Hertzberg, Arthur. 2007. "Jewish Identity." In *Encyclopedia Judaica*, 2nd ed., edited by Michael Berenbaum and Fred Skolnik, 11:292–99. Detroit: Macmillan Reference USA.

Hirsch, Francine. 2005. *Empire of Nations: Ethnographic Knowledge and the Making of the Soviet Union*. Ithaca, NY: Cornell University Press.

Hirshberg, Jehoash. 1990. "The Encounter with Bracha Zephira." Chap. 9 of *Paul Ben-Haim: His Life and Works*. Translated by Nathan Friedgut and edited by Bathja Bayer. Jerusalem: Israeli Music Publications.

Horowitz, Bethamie. 2011. "Old Casks in New Times: The Reshaping of American Jewish Identity in the 21st Century." In *Ethnicity and Beyond: Theories and Dilemmas of Jewish Group Demarcation*, edited by Eli Lederhendler, 79–90. New York: Oxford University Press.

Hourani, Albert. 1991. *A History of the Arab Peoples*. Cambridge, MA: Belknap Press of Harvard University Press.

Hrushovski, Benjamin. 1981. "Note on the Systems of Hebrew Versification." In *The Penguin Book of Hebrew Verse*, edited by T. Carmi, 57–72. New York: Penguin Books.

Human Rights Watch. 1995. "Uzbekistan." In *Human Rights Watch World Report 2005*. http://www.humanrightswatch.org/wr2k5/wr2005.pdf (accessed 14 February 2006).

Human Rights Watch. 2011. "Fashion Week Cancels Show of Uzbek Dictator's Daughter." http://www.hrw.org/news/2011/09/15/fashion-week-cancels-show-uzbek-dictator-s-daughter (accessed 9 January 2014).

Idelsohn, Abraham Zvi. 1922. *Hebräisch-Orientalischer Melodienschatz. III, Gesänge der Persischen, Bucharischen und Daghestanischen Juden*. Jerusalem: Benjamin Harz Verlag.

Idelsohn, Abraham Zvi. [1929] 1967. *Jewish Music in Its Historical Development*. New York: Schocken Books.

Ivanov, V. A. 2004. "Epokha Turkestanskogo general-gubernatorstva v istorii sredneaziatskikh (bukharskikh) evreyev" [The Era of the Turkistan Governor-Generalship in the History of Central Asian (Bukharian) Jews]. In *Evrei v Sredneĭ Azii: Voprosy istorii i kul'tury*, edited by E.V. Rtveladze, 103–23. Tashkent: Izdatel'stvo "Fan" Akademii nauk Respubliki Uzbekistan.

Joselit, Jenna Weissman. 1992. " 'Merry Chanuka': The Changing Holiday Practices of American Jews, 1880–1950." In *The Uses of Tradition: Jewish Continuity in the Modern Era*, edited by Jack Wertheimer, 303–25. New York: Jewish Theological Seminary of America.

Jung, Angelika. 1988. "The Maqâm Principle and the Cyclic Principle in the Uzbek-Tajik Shashmaqam." In *Maqam, Raga, Zeilenmelodik: Konzeption und Prinzipien der Musikproduktion: Materialen der 1. Arbeitstagung der Study Group "Maqam" beim International Council for Traditional Music vom 28. Juni bis 2. Juli 1988 in Berlin*, edited by Jürgen Elsner, 200–15. Berlin: Nationalkomitee DDR des International Council for Traditional Music in Verbindung mit dem Sekretariat Internationale Nichtstaatliche Musikorganisationen.

Jung, Angelika. 1989. *Quellen der traditionellen Kunstmusik der Usbeken und Tadshiken Mittelasiens: Untersuchungen zur Entstehung und Entwicklung des Shashmaqam*. Hamburg: Verlag der Musikalienhandlung.

Jung, Angelika, ed. 2010. *Der Shashmaqam aus Buchara: überliefert von den alten Meistern* [The Shashmaqom of Bukhara: Handed Down by the Old Masters]. Notated by Ari Bobokhonov. Berlin: Verlag Hans Schiler.

Jung, Angelika. Forthcoming. *Der Shashmaqam aus Buchara: Beiträge zum Verständnis der klassischen Musik Mittelasiens* [The Shashmaqom of Bukhara: Contributions to the Understanding of Classical Central Asian Music]. Berlin: Verlag Hans Schiler.

Kadinsky, Sergey. 2010. "Bukharian History Comes to the Academy." *New York Jewish Week*, 15 January.

Kaganovitch, Albert. 2005. "The Muslim Jews in Central Asia." *Museo-on. com: Kulturen der Welt erleben*. http://www.museo-on.com/go/museoon/en/home/db/archaeology/_page_id_925.xml (accessed 7 December 2007).

Kaganovitch, Albert [Kaganovich]. 2007. *The Mashhadi Jews (Djedids) in Central Asia*. Berlin: Klaus Schwarz.

Kaganovitch, Albert. 2008. "The Bukharan Jewish Diaspora at the Beginning of the 21st Century." In *Bukharan Jews in the 20th Century: History, Experience, and Narration*, edited by Ingeborg Baldauf, Moshe Gammer, and Thomas Loy, 111–16. Wiesbaden: Reichert.

Kantor, Jodi. 2009. "First Family Reflects a Nation's Diversity." *New York Times*, 21 January.

Karamatov, Faizullah M., and Ishak Radjabov. 1981. "Introduction to the Shashmaqam." Translated by Theodore Levin. *Asian Music* 13(1):97–118.

Katz, Zev. 1975. "The Jews in the Soviet Union." In *Handbook of Major Soviet Nationalities*, edited by Zev Katz, 355–89. New York: Free Press.

Kaykāvūs ibn Iskandar ibn Qābūs, 'Unṣur al-Ma'ālī. 1994. *Qābūsnāma*. Edited by Ghulām Ḥusayn Yūsūfī. Intishārāt-i 'Ilmī va Farhangī.

Kennedy, Hugh. 2002. *An Historical Atlas of Islam*. Leiden: Brill.

Kenvin, Helene Schwartz. 2010. *Silk Road Adventures: Among the Jews of the Caucasus and Central Asia*. Los Gatos, CA: Robertson.

King, Desmond. 2000. *Making Americans: Immigration, Race, and the Origins of the Diverse Democracy*. Cambridge: Harvard University Press.

Kirshenblatt-Gimblett, Barbara. 2002. "Sounds of Sensibility." In *American Klezmer: Its Roots and Offshoots*, 129–73. Berkeley: University of California Press.

Kligman, Mark. 2009. *Maqām and Liturgy: Ritual, Music, and Aesthetics of Syrian Jews in Brooklyn*. Detroit: Wayne State University Press.

Knapp, Alexander. 2010. "Learning to Chant the Bible in the Bukharan-Jewish Tradition." In *Sacred Knowledge: Schools or Revelation? Master-Apprentice System of Oral Transmission in the Music of the Turkic Speaking World*, edited by Razia Sultanova, 17–25. Köln: Lambert Academic.

Koplik, Sara. 2008. "The Experiences of Bukharan Jews outside the Soviet Union in the 1930s and 1940s." In *Bukharan Jews in the 20th Century: History, Experience, and Narration*, edited by Ingeborg Baldauf, Moshe Gammer, and Thomas Loy, 91–109. Wiesbaden: Reichert.

Koskoff, Ellen. 2001. *Music in Lubavitcher Life*. Urbana: University of Illinois Press.

Kurin, Richard, and Diana Parker. 2002. "The Festival and the Transnational Production of Culture." In the program book for the 2002 Smithsonian Folklife Festival. http://www.silkroadproject.org/smithsonian/ (accessed 23 February 2006).

Lansdell, Henry. 1885. *Russian Central Asia, including Kuldja, Bokhara, Khiva, and Merv*. London: Sampson Low.

Levin, Theodore. 1984. "The Music and Tradition of the Bukharan Shashmaqam in Soviet Uzbekistan." Ph.D. dissertation, Princeton University.

Levin, Theodore. 1991. Liner notes to *Bukharan Jewish Ensemble Shashmaqam, Central Asia in Forest Hills, New York*. Smithsonian Folkways 40054. Compact disc.

Levin, Theodore. 1996. *The Hundred Thousand Fools of God: Musical Travels in Central Asia (and Queens, New York)*. Bloomington and Indianapolis: Indiana University Press.

Levin, Theodore, and Abduvali Abdurashidov. 2005. Liner notes to *Invisible Face of the Beloved: Classical Music of the Tajiks and Uzbeks. Music of Central Asia Vol. 2*. Smithsonian Folkways SFW CD 40521. Compact disc and DVD.

Levin, Theodore, and Otanazar Matyakubov. 1991. Liner notes to *Bukhara: Musical Crossroads of Asia*. Smithsonian Folkways SF 40050. Compact disc.

Levin, Theodore, and Razia Sultanova. 2001. "The Classical Music of Uzbeks and Tajiks." In *The Garland Encyclopedia of World Music. Volume 6, The Middle East*, edited by Virginia Danielson, Scott Marcus, and Dwight Reynolds, 909–20. New York: Routledge.

Levin, Theodore, Razia Sultanova, and F. M. Ashrafi. 2001. "Uzbekistan." In *The New Grove Dictionary of Music and Musicians*, 2nd ed., edited by Stanley Sadie, 26:180–89. London: Macmillan.

Levin, Ze'ev. 2008a. "The Khujum Campaign in Uzbekistan and the Bukharan Jewish Women." In *Gender Politics in Central Asia: Historical Perspectives and Current Living Conditions of Women*, edited by Christa Hämmerle, Nikola Langreiter, Margareth Lanzinger, and Edith Saurer, 95–112. Köln: Böhlau.

Levin, Ze'ev. 2008b. "When It All Began: Bukharan Jews and the Soviets in Central Asia, 1917–1932." In *Bukharan Jews in the 20th Century: History, Experience, and Narration*, edited by Ingeborg Baldauf, Moshe Gammer, and Thomas Loy, 23–36. Wiesbaden: Reichert.

Lewis, Geoffrey L. 1999. *The Turkish Language Reform: A Catastrophic Success*. Oxford: Oxford University Press.

Light, Nathan. 2008. *Intimate Heritage: Creating Uyghur Muqam Song in Xinjiang*. Berlin: Lit.

Loeb, Laurence D. 2000. "Jewish Music and the Iranian-Jewish Music Professional." *Teru ʿā: Yahudīān-e Īrānī dar tārikh-e mo ʿāser* 4:25–38.

Loeffler, James. 2010. *The Most Musical Nation: Jews and Culture in the Late Russian Empire*. New Haven, CT: Yale University Press.

Loy, Thomas. 2008a. "About a Friend: Reflections on the Memoirs of Mordekhay Bachayev." In *Bukharan Jews in the 20th Century: History, Experience, and Narration*, edited by Ingeborg Baldauf, Moshe Gammer, and Thomas Loy, 127–44. Wiesbaden: Reichert.

Loy, Thomas. 2008b. "Close Relatives: The Life Narration of Abrasha (Arkadi) Levayevich Il'yasov." In *Bukharan Jews in the 20th Century: History, Experience, and Narration*, edited by Ingeborg Baldauf, Moshe Gammer, and Thomas Loy, 145–75. Wiesbaden: Reichert.

Malakov, Ezro, ed. 2007. *Musical Treasures of the Bukharian Jewish Community/Muzykal'naya sokrovishchnitsa bukharskikh evreyev*. Tel Aviv: World Bukharian Jewish Congress.

Malcolm, Janet. 2011. *Iphigenia in Forest Hills: Anatomy of a Murder Trial*. New Haven, CT: Yale University Press.

Mallayev, Ilyos. 1999. *Devon (Sadoi dil + Qalb sadosi)*. New York: Self-published.

Mallayev, Ilyos. 2003. *Shir u-shvāḥāh* [Song and Praise]. Photocopied manuscript of religious poems in Persian language, using both Cyrillic and Hebrew alphabets. Israel.

Mathiesen, Thomas J. 2001. "Greece, §I, 1: Ancient." In *The New Grove Dictionary of Music and Musicians*, 2nd ed., edited by Stanley Sadie, 10:327–48. London: Macmillan.

Matyakubov, Otanazar. 2004. *Maqomot*. Tashkent: Musiqa.

Matyakubov, Otanazar. 2009. *Besedy s Il'yasom: o muzykal'nykh traditsiyakh staroĭ Bukhary* [Interview with Ilyas: The Musical Traditions of Old Bukhara]. New York: Congress of Bukharian Jews of the USA and Canada.

Mavashev, David. 2005. "Nasledie Khakhama Ĭosefa Mamana Maaravi" [The Heritage of Khakham Yosef Maman Maaravi]. *Zametki po evreĭskoĭ istorii* 5(54). http://berkovich-zametki.com/2005/Zametki/Nomer5/Mavashev1.htm (accessed 28 November 2007).

Meiendorf, Egor Kazimirovich, ed. 1870. *A Journey from Orenburg to Bokhara in the Year 1820*. Translated by E. F. Chapman after original French compiled by Carl Hermann Scheidler. Revised by Pierre-Amadée Jaubert. Calcutta: Foreign Department Press.

Mehta, Suketa. 2003. "The Meltingest Pot." *New York Times Magazine*, 5 October.

Moreen, Vera B. 1987. *Iranian Jewry's Hour of Peril and Heroism: A Study of Bābāī ibn Luṭf's Chronicle, 1617–1662*. New York: American Academy for Jewish Research.

Moreen, Vera B. 1990. *Iranian Jewry during the Afghan Invasion: The Kitāb-i Sar Guzasht-i Kāshān of Bābāī b. Farhād*. Stuttgart: Franz Steiner.

Moreen, Vera B. 2010. "Iranian Jewish History Reflected in Judaeo-Persian Literature." In *Contacts and Controversies between Muslims, Jews and Christians in the Ottoman Empire and Pre-Modern Iran*, edited by Camilla Adang and Sabine Schnidtke, 397–411. Würzburg: Ergon.

Móricz, Klára. 2008. *Jewish Identities: Nationalism, Racism, and Utopianism in Twentieth-Century Music*. Berkeley: University of California Press.

Móricz, Klára, Ronit Seter, Judah M. Cohen, Alexander Knapp, Steven J. Cahn, Rebecca Cypess, and Edwin Seroussi. 2012. "Colloquy: Jewish Studies and Music." *Journal of the American Musicological Society* 65(2):557–92.

Moskin, Julia. 2006. "The Silk Road Leads to Queens." *New York Times*, 18 January, F1, F6.

Most, Andrea. 2001. "'We Know We Belong to the Land': Jews and the American Musical Theater." Ph.D. dissertation, Brandeis University.

"Mudzhiza—znachit 'chudo'" ("Mūjiza Means 'Miracle'"). n.d. Review of *LevichaHofiz*. http://www.bukharianjewishcongress.org/theater/616-mudzhiza-means-miracle (accessed 21 July 2010).

Mukhtarov, A. 2003. "The Manghīts." In *History of Civilizations of Central Asia. V: Development in Contrast: From the Sixteenth to the Mid-Nineteenth Century*, edited by Chahryar Adle and Irfan Habib, coedited by Karl M. Baipakov, 53–62. Paris: UNESCO.

Murphy, Michael. 2012. *Multiculturalism: A Critical Introduction*. New York: Routledge.

Musil, Robert. [1978] 1990. *Precision and Soul: Essays and Addresses*. Edited and translated by Burton Pike and David S. Luft.

Chicago: University of Chicago Press. Originally published in volumes 8 and 9 of Musil's *Gesammelte Werke*, edited by Adolf Frisé. Reinbek bei Hamburg: Rowohlt Verlag.

Naumkin, Vitaly. 1993. *Bukhara. Caught in Time: Great Photographic Archives*. Reading: Garnet.

Nektalov, Rafael. 1999. "Pevets Ego Prevoskhoditelstva." *Vestnik*, 13 April.

Nektalov, Rafael. 2005. *Itskhak Mavashev: Vospominaniya sovremennikov* [Itsḥoq Mavashev: Memories of His Contemporaries]. New York: Liberty/ Yitzhak Mavashev Foundation: Research Institute of Bukharian Jewry in Diaspora.

Nektalov, Rafael. 2013. Interview with Roshel Rubinov. *Bukharian Times*, 2–8 August, 8, 35.

Netsky, Hankus. 2002a. "American Klezmer: A Brief History." In *American Klezmer: Its Roots and Offshoots*, edited by Mark Slobin, 13–23. Berkeley: University of California Press.

Netsky, Hankus. 2002b. "The Klezmer in Jewish Philadelphia, 1915–70." In *American Klezmer: Its Roots and Offshoots*, edited by Mark Slobin, 52–72. Berkeley: University of California Press.

Netzer, Amnon. 2007. "Meshed." In *Encyclopaedia Judaica*, 2nd ed., edited by Michael Berenbaum and Fred Skolnik, 14:76–77. Detroit: Macmillan Reference USA.

New York City Department of City Planning Population Division. 2004a. *The Newest New Yorkers 2000 Briefing Booklet*. http://www.nyc.gov/ html/dcp/html/census/nny.shtml (accessed 10 April 2005).

New York City Department of City Planning Population Division. 2004b. *The Newest New Yorkers 2000: Immigration in the New Millennium*. http://www.nyc.gov/planning (accessed 10 April 2005).

New York City Department of City Planning Population Division New York City Department of City Planning Population Division. 2013. *The Newest New Yorkers: Characteristics of the City's Foreign-born Population, 2013 Edition*. http://www.nyc.gov/population (accessed 2 January 2014).

Nosonovskiĭ, Mikhail. 2005. "Byl Rav Ĭosef Mamon Magribi spasitelem evreev Bukhary?" [Was Rav Yosef Mamon Magribi the Savior of the Bukharian Jews?] *Al'manakh "Evreĭskaya Starina"* 4(28). http:// berkovich-zametki.com/2005/Starina/Nomer4/MN72.htm (accessed 28 November 2007).

Nurjanov, Nizam. 1980. "Traditsii sozanda v muzykal'no-tantseval'noĭ kul'ture tadzhikov na rubezhe XIX–XX vekov" [Sozanda tradition in Tajik music and dance culture at the turn of the 19th–20th centuries]. In *Muzyka narodov Azii i Afriki*, edited by V. S. Vinogradova, III:111–57. Moscow: Sovyetskiĭ Kompozitor.

Oates, Joyce Carol. 2011. "Reporter for the Defence." *Times Literary Supplement*, 6 May, 8–9.

Ochildiev, David. 2005. *A History of the Bukharan Jews*. New York: Mir Collection.

Ochildiev, David, Robert Pinkhasov, and Iosif Kalantarov. 2007. *A History and Culture of the Bukharian Jews*. New York: Club "Roshnoyi— Light."

Olufsen, Ole. 1911. *The Emir of Bokhara and His Country: Journeys and Studies in Bokhara (with a Chapter on My Voyage on the Amu Darya to Khiva)*. London: William Heinemann.

Ostrer, Harry. 2012. *Legacy: A Genetic History of the Jewish People*. New York: Oxford University Press.

Painter, Nell Irvin. 2010. *The History of White People*. New York: W.W. Norton.

Paper, Herbert H. 1986. Introduction to *The Musā-nāma of R. Shim'on Ḥakham*, edited by Herbert H. Paper. Judeo-Iranian Text Series, No. 1. Cincinatti: Hebrew Union College Press.

Pareles, Jon. 2002. "World Music Review: Music of Soviet Jews Finds a New Homeland." *New York Times*, 22 May.

Peterson, Richard A., and Roger M. Kern. 1996. "Changing Highbrow Taste: From Snob to Omnivore." *American Sociological Review* 61(5):900–907.

Pinkhasov, Peter. n.d. "The History of Bukharian Jews." http://www.bukharianjews.com/modules.php?op=modloadname=Sectionsfile=ind exreq=viewarticleartid=2page=1 (accessed 21 February 2006).

Pinkus, Benjamin. 2007. "Cosmopolitans." In *Encyclopaedia Judaica*, 2nd. ed., edited by Michael Berenbaum and Fred Skolnick, V:232. Detroit: Macmillan Reference USA.

Pollack, Howard. 2006. *George Gershwin: His Life and Work*. Berkeley: University of California Press.

Powers, Harold, et al. 2001. "Mode." In *The New Grove Dictionary of Music and Musicians*, 2nd ed., edited by Stanley Sadie, 16:775–860. London: Macmillan.

Prell, Riv-Ellen. 2011. "The Utility of the Concept of 'Ethnicity' for the Study of Jews." In *Ethnicity and Beyond: Theories and Dilemmas of Jewish Group Demarcation*, edited by Eli Lederhendler, 102–7. New York: Oxford University Press.

Prentice, Will. n.d. Unpublished liner notes to CD of Levi Bobokhonov's archival Gramophone Company recordings.

Primak, Yochai. 2008. "Protecting the Integrity of the Community: Interpreting Jewish Life in Pre-Soviet Central Asia. Notes from Rabbanith Miriam's Life History." In *Bukharan Jews in the 20th Century: History, Experience, and Narration*, edited by Ingeborg Baldauf, Moshe Gammer, and Thomas Loy, 177–85. Wiesbaden: Reichert.

Puzhol', K. 2004. "Svyazi mezhdu Tsentral'noy Aziyeǐ i Palestinoǐ, ili puti affektivnogo sionizma, 1793–1917" [Connections between Central Asia and Palestine, or Paths of Affective Zionism, 1793–1917]. In *Evrei v sredneǐ azii: Voprosy istorii i kul'tury*, edited by E.V. Rtveladze, 132–50. Tashkent: Izdatel'stvo "Fan" Akademii nauk Respubliki Uzbekistan.

Rajabi, Yunus. 1959. *Bukhoro maqomlari/Bukharskiye makom'i*. Edited by Il'yas Akbarov. Uzbek khalq muzikasi/Uzbekskaia narodnaia muzyka, 5. Tashkent: Uzbekiston SSR Davlat Nashriyeti.

Rapport, Evan. 2006. "The Musical Repertoire of Bukharian Jews in Queens, New York." Ph.D. dissertation, Graduate Center of the City University of New York.

Rapport, Evan. 2008. "Bill Finegan's Gershwin Arrangements and the American Concept of Hybridity." *Journal of the Society for American Music* 2(4): 507–30.

Reikher, Elena. 2005–2006. "The Female Sozanda Art from the Viewpoint of Professionalism in the Musical Tradition: A Preliminary Survey." *Musica Judaica* 18:70–86.

Reikher, Elena. 2009–2010. "Bukharan Jews in the Art Music of Central Asia." *Musica Judaica* 19:137–70.

Renard, John. 1986. "Images of Abraham in the Writings of Jalāl ad-Dīn Rūmī." *Journal of the American Oriental Society* 106(4):633–40.

Rice, Timothy. 2003. "Time, Place, and Metaphor in Musical Experience and Ethnography." *Ethnomusicology* 47(2):151–79.

Roberts, Sam. 2010. "Listening to (and Saving) the World's Languages." *New York Times*, 28 April.

Ro'i, Yaacov. 2008. "The Religious Life of the Bukharan Jewish Community in Soviet Central Asia after World War II." In *Bukharan Jews in the 20th Century: History, Experience, and Narration*, edited by Ingeborg Baldauf, Moshe Gammer, and Thomas Loy, 57–75. Wiesbaden: Reichert.

Rosehope, Cara, prod. 2011. "Shalom from the Silk Road: The Story of the Bukharians." *Encounter* on ABC Radio National, 13 February. Transcript and audio at http://www.abc.net.au/rn/encounter/stories/2011/3132959.htm (accessed 7 August 2011).

Rosenberg, Victor. 2003. "Refugee Status for Soviet Jewish Immigrants to the United States." *Touro Law Review* 19 (Winter/Spring):419–50.

Rosman, Moshe. 2007. *How Jewish Is Jewish History?* Oxford: Littman Library of Jewish Civilization.

Rotar, Igor. 2005. "Islam and Karimov." *Transitions Online*, http://www.tol.cz/look/TOL/article.tpl?IdLanguage=1IdPublication=4NrIssue=106NrSection=3NrArticle=13682 (posted 10 March 2005). Also http://www.eurasianet.org/departments/insight/articles/pp031105a.shtml.

Rowland, Richard H., et al. 1992. "Central Asia." In *Encyclopaedia Iranica*, edited by Ehsan Yarshater, 5:159–242. Costa Mesa, CA: Mazda.

Roy, Olivier. 2000. *The New Central Asia: The Creation of Nations*. Originally published as *La Nouvelle Asie centrale ou la fabrication des nations* (Editions du Seuil, 1997). New York: New York University Press.

Rubinov, Roshel. 2002. *Ilhomi dil: Ash'or* [Heart's Inspiration: Poems]. New York: Self-published.

Rushefsky, Pete. 2009. "Xiao Xiannian: New Sounds for Chinese Strings." *Journal of New York Folklore* 35. http://www.nyfolklore.org/pubs/voic35-3-4/xiao.html.

Rybakov, Imonuel. 2011. *Easy Bukharian*. Rego Park, NY: Association of the Bukharian Jewish Youth of the USA "Achdut-Unity."

Rybakov, Imonuel. 2013. "O evreĭskikh korifeyakh shashmakoma 19-20 vekov" [About Jewish Shashmaqom Luminaries of the 19–20 Centuries]. *Bukharian Times*, 2–8 August, 16.

Rzehak, Lutz. 2008. "The Linguistic Challenge: Bukharan Jews and Soviet Language Policy." In *Bukharan Jews in the 20th Century: History, Experience, and Narration*, edited by Ingeborg Baldauf, Moshe Gammer, and Thomas Loy, 37–55. Wiesbaden: Reichert.

Sahim, Haideh. 2003. "Iran and Afghanistan." In *The Jews of the Middle East and North Africa in Modern Times*, edited by Reeva Spector Simon, Michael Menachem Laskier, and Sara Reguer, 367–88. New York: Columbia University Press.

Sarshar, Houman, ed. 2002. *Esther's Children: A Portrait of Iranian Jews*. Beverly Hills: Center for Iranian Jewish Oral History.

Satlow, Michael L. 2006. *Creating Judaism: History, Tradition, Practice*. New York: Columbia University Press.

Saulny, Susan. 2011. "Race Remixed: Black? White? Asian? More Young Americans Choose All of the Above." *New York Times*, 29 January.

Schuyler, Eugene. 1877. *Turkistan: Notes of a Journey in Russian Turkistan, Khokand, Bukhara, and Kuldja*. New York: Scribner, Armstrong.

Seroussi, Edwin. 1989. *Mizimrat Qedem: The Life and Music of R. Isaac Algazi from Turkey*. Jerusalem: Renanot Institute for Jewish Music.

Seroussi, Edwin. 1990. "The Turkish Makam in the Musical Culture of the Ottoman Jews: Sources and Examples." *Israel Studies in Musicology* 5:43–68.

Seroussi, Edwin. 2012. "Judeo-Islamic Sacred Soundscapes: The 'Maqamization' of the Eastern Sephardic Jewish Liturgy." In *Jews and Muslims in the Islamic World*, edited by Tsevi Zohar, 1–24. Bethesda, MD: University Press of Maryland.

Seroussi, Edwin, et al. 2001. "Jewish Music." In *The New Grove Dictionary of Music and Musicians*, 2nd ed., edited by Stanley Sadie, 13:24–112. London: Macmillan.

Shay, Anthony. 2009. "Choreographing Masculinity: Hypermasculine Dance Styles as Invented Tradition in Egypt, Iran, and Uzbekistan." In *When Men Dance: Choreographing Masculinities across Borders*, edited by Jennifer Fisher and Anthony Shay, 287–308. New York: Oxford University Press.

Shelemay, Kay Kaufman. 1995. "Mythologies and Realities in the Study of Jewish Music." *the world of music* 37(1):24–38.

Shelemay, Kay Kaufman. 1998. *Let Jasmine Rain Down: Song and Remembrance among Syrian Jews*. Chicago: University of Chicago Press.

Shevyakov, A. I. 2004. "Evrei Tashkentsoĭ oblasti v kontse XIX–nachale XX veka" [Jews of the Tashkent Region in the Late 19th–early 20th Century]. In *Evrei v Sredneĭ Azii: Voprosy istorii i kul'tury*, edited by E.V. Rtveladze, 175–84. Tashkent: Izdatel'stvo "Fan" Akademii nauk Respubliki Uzbekistan.

Shiloah, Amnon. 1992. *Jewish Musical Traditions*. Detroit: Wayne State University Press.

Silber, Michael K. 1992. "The Emergence of Ultra-Orthodoxy: The Invention of a Tradition." In *The Uses of Tradition: Jewish Continuity in the Modern Era*, edited by Jack Wertheimer, 23–84. New York: Jewish Theological Seminary of America.

Singer, David, ed. 1991. *American Jewish Year Book 1991*. New York: American Jewish Committee and the Jewish Publication Society.

Sklare, Marshall, and Joseph Greenblum. 1967. *Jewish Identity on the Suburban Frontier: A Study of Group Survival in the Open Society*. New York: Basic Books.

Slobin, Mark. 1982a. *Tenement Songs: The Popular Music of the Jewish Immigrants*. Urbana: University of Illinois Press.

Slobin, Mark. 1982b. "Bukharan Music in Israel." In *Yuval* IV, edited by Israel Adler and Bathja Bayer, 225–39. Jerusalem: Hebrew University Magnes Press.

Slobin, Mark. 1986a. "Multilingualism in Folk Music Cultures." In *Explorations in Ethnomusicology: Essays in Honor of David P. McAllester*, edited by Charlotte J. Frisbie, 3–10. Detroit Monographs in Musicology, 9. Detroit: Information Coordinators.

Slobin, Mark. 1986b. "A Fresh Look at Beregovski's Folk Music Research." *Ethnomusicology* 30(2):253–60.

Slobin, Mark. 1993. *Subcultural Sounds: Micromusics of the West*. Hanover, NH: University of New England Press.

Slobin, Mark. [1989] 2002. *Chosen Voices: The Story of the American Cantorate*. Urbana: University of Illinois Press.

Smedley, Audrey. 2007. *Race in North America: Origin and Evolution of a Worldview*. 3rd ed. Boulder: Westview Press.

Solis, Gabriel. 2004. "'A Unique Chunk of Jazz Reality': Authorship, Musical Work Concepts, and Thelonious Monk's Live Recordings from the Five Spot, 1958." *Ethnomusicology* 48(3):315–47.

Sollors, Werner. 1986. *Beyond Ethnicity: Consent and Descent in American Culture*. New York: Oxford University Press.

Spector, Johanna. 1967. "Musical Tradition and Innovation." In *Central Asia: A Century of Russian Rule*, edited by Edward Allworth, 434–84. New York: Columbia University Press.

Spinetti, Federico. 2005. "Open Borders. Tradition and Tajik Popular Music: Questions of Aesthetics, Identity and Political Economy." *Ethnomusicology Forum* 14(2):185–211.

Stonequist, Everett V. 1935. "The Problem of the Marginal Man." *American Journal of Sociology* 41(1):1–12.

Sukhareva, Ol'ga Aleksandrovna. 1966. *Bukhara: XIX–nachalo XX v. (Pozdnefeodal'nyĭ gorod i ego naseleniye)*. [Bukhara: 19th–Early 20th Century. (The Late Feudal City and Its People)]. Moscow: Nauka.

Sultanova, Razia. 2005. "Music and Identity in Central Asia: Introduction." *Ethnomusicology Forum* 14(2):131–42.

Sultanova, Razia. 2009. "Master–Apprentice (Usto–Shogird) Training System in the Ferghana Musical Tradition." In *Sacred Knowledge: Schools or Revelation? Master-Apprentice System of Oral Transmission in the Music of the Turkic Speaking World*, edited by Razia Sultanova, 36–52. Köln: Lambert Academic.

Summit, Jeffrey A. 2000. *The Lord's Song in a Strange Land: Music and Identity in Contemporary Jewish Worship*. New York: Oxford University Press.

Tājer, Nisim. 1970. *Tōldōt Yehūdē Būkhārāh: be-Būkhārāh u-ve-Yisrāēl mi-shenat 600 'ad 1970* [History of Bukharian Jews: In Bukhara and in Israel from 600 to 1970]. Tel Aviv.

Takaki, Ronald. [1993] 2008. *A Different Mirror: A History of Multicultural America*. Rev. ed. New York: Back Bay Books.

Takhalov, Suleĭman. 2005. "Traditsionnoye muzykal'noye tvorchestvo" [Traditional Music]. In *Istoriya Bukharskikh Evreyev: Novyĭ i Noveĭshiĭ Period (1865–2000)* [The History of the Bukharian Jews. The New and Newest Period (1865–2000)], edited by Robert Pinkhasov, 178–228. New York: World Congress of Bukharian Jews Club "Roshnoi-Light."

Taylor, Charles. 1992. *Multiculturalism: Examining the Politics of Recognition*. Introduction by Amy Gutmann and comments by Susan Wolf, Steven C. Rockefeller, Michael Walzer, Jurgen Habermas, and K. Anthony Appiah. Princeton, NJ: Princeton University Press.

Thomson, Virgil. [1935] 2002. "George Gershwin." In *Virgil Thomson, a Reader: Selected Writings, 1924–1984*, edited by Richard Kostelantz, 149–54. New York: Routledge.

Tietze, Andreas, and Joseph Yahalom. 1995. *Ottoman Melodies, Hebrew Hymns: A 16th Century Cross-Cultural Adventure*. Bibliotheca Orientalis Hungarica Vol. 43. Budapest: Akadémiai Kiadó.

Tsuge, Gen'ichi. 1974. "Âvâz: A Study of the Rhythmic Aspects in Classical Iranian Music." Ph.D. dissertation, Wesleyan University.

Tsui, Ying-fai. 2001. "Ensembles: The Modern Chinese Orchestra." In *The Garland Encyclopedia of World Music. VII, East Asia: China, Japan, and*

Korea, edited by Robert C. Provine, Yosihiko Tokumaru, and J. Lawrence Witzleben, 227–232. New York: Routledge.

Turino, Thomas. 2004. "Introduction: Identity and the Arts in Diaspora Communities." In *Identity and the Arts in Diaspora Communities*, edited by Thomas Turino and James Lea, 3–19. Warren, MI: Harmonie Park Press.

Wahrman, Dror. 1991. *Ha-Būkhārīm u-shekhūnātam bi-yerūshalayim* [The Bukharians and Their Neighborhood in Jerusalem]. Jerusalem: Hūtsāt yad yitsḥāq ben-tsvi.

Waters, Mary C., and Philip Kasinitz. 2010. "Discrimination, Race Relations, and the Second Generation." *Social Research* 77(1):101–32.

Whitlock, Monica. 2002. *Land beyond the River: The Untold Story of Central Asia*. New York: St. Martin's Press.

Williams, Ken. 2010. "Samir Breaks Taboo, Becoming First Gay Star in Bellydance Superstars' 'Bombay Bellywood.'" *San Diego Gay and Lesbian News*, 28 September. http://www.sdgln.com/news/2010/09/27/samir-breaks-taboo-becoming-first-gay-star-bellydance-superstars-bombay-bellywood (accessed 12 December 2012).

Wishna, Victor. 2003. "A Lost Tribe, Found in Queens." http://www.jewsweek.com/ and http://www.sdjewishjournal.com/stories/oct03_5.html (accessed 25 February 2006).

Wolff, Joseph. 1835. *Researches and Missionary Labours among the Jews, Mohammedans and other Sects*. 2nd ed. London: J. Nisbet.

Wong, Deborah. 2006. "Ethnomusicology and Difference." *Ethnomusicology* 50(2):259–79.

Wyatt, Robert, and John Andrew Johnson, eds. 2004. *The George Gershwin Reader*. New York: Oxford University Press.

Yakubov, Arkadiy, ed. 2005. *The Congress United Us/Kongress Ob'yedinil Nas*. New York: Congress of Bukharian Jews of the USA and Canada.

Yakubov, Yefim. 2008. "The 'Declaration of Rights of Native Jews'—The Final Legislative Act Induced by the 'Bukharan Jewish Question.'" In *Bukharan Jews in the 20th Century: History, Experience, and Narration*, edited by Ingeborg Baldauf, Moshe Gammer, and Thomas Loy, 11–21. Wiesbaden: Reichert.

Yuhan. 2006. "Yuhan!" http://www.yuhanny.com (accessed 25 February 2006).

Yusupov, Benjamin. 2007. *Haqqoni (Crossroads No. 4)*. Hamburg: Sikorski.

Zand, Michael. 2000. "Bukhara; vii. Bukharan Jews." In *Encyclopedia Iranica*, vol. 4, edited by Ehsan Yarshater, 530–45. New York: Bibliotheca Persica Press.

Zand, Michael, Aviva Muller-Lancet, and Elena Reikher. 2007. "Bukhara." In *Encyclopaedia Judaica*, 2nd ed., edited by Michael Berenbaum and Fred Skolnik, 4:257–67. Detroit: Macmillan Reference USA.

Zangwill, Israel. [1909] 1919. *The Melting-Pot, Drama in Four Acts*. New York: Macmillan.

Zavul, Mikhoel. 1999. *Munojot*. New York: Self-published.

Żerańska-Kominek, Sławomira. 2009. "Tales and Fables of the Chang (Harp) in Darvish Ali's Risalei Musiqi." *Asian Music* 40(2):33–51.

Zheng, Su. 2010. *Claiming Diaspora: Music, Transnationalism, and Cultural Politics in Asian/Chinese America*. New York: Oxford University Press.

Zohar, Zion, ed. 2007. *Sephardic and Mizrahi Jewry: From the Golden Age of Spain to Modern Times*. New York: New York University Press.

Discography

Academy of Maqom [Maqâm]. 2006. *Invisible Face of the Beloved: Classical Music of the Tajiks and Uzbeks. Music of Central Asia, 2.* Smithsonian Folkways SFW 40521.

Aminov [Amin], Roshel. 2002. *Sadoi dil bo ovozi tanbūr/My Soul Cries with the Voice of the "Tanbur."* Produced by Albert Narkolayev.

Aminov [Amin], Roshel. 2005. *Bukharian Classical Shashmakom* [Disc 1: R. Amin's recording of Maqom Navo; Disc 2: Reissued recordings of Neryo Aminov.] Self-produced.

Bobokhonov, Ari, and Ensemble. 1998. *Shashmaqam.* New Samarkand Records SAM CD 9002.

Beth Gavriel Bukharian Jewish Congregation. 2003. *Erets Isroel.* Sponsored by Bukharian Organization Ateret Menaḥem, B'nei Barak, Israel.

Bukharan Jewish Ensemble Shashmaqam. 1991. *Central Asia in Forest Hills N.Y.* Smithsonian Folkways 40054.

Coleman, Anthony, prod. and arr. 1999. *With Every Breath: The Music of Shabbat at BJ.* Knitting Factory Records.

Ensemble Maqam. 1998. *Bukharian Jewish Folk Music.* Self-produced.

Ibragimov, Ochil. n.d. *Ohangi dil: Surudhoi pandu nasihat/Melodiya dushi: Al'bom nastavleniĭ [Heart Song: Songs of Moral Advice].* Self-produced

Katayev, Isak. n.d. *Oromijon.* Produced by Slava Katayev.

Khavasov, Ilyusha. 2002. *My Samarqand.* Self-produced.

Kuyenov, Shumiel, and David Davidov. 2009. *Tar Navasi: Classic Uzbek Music.* Produced by Abe Mor.

Levin, Theodore, and Otanazar Matyakubov, recorders. 1991. *Bukhara: Musical Crossroads of Asia.* Smithsonian Folkways 40050.

Malakov, Ezro, prod. 1998. *Shiro, Shahariti Shabboti, Zohar.* Self-produced.

Malakov, Ezro, prod. 2000. *Eternal Music of Bukharian Jewish Hymns: Shirey Kodesh, Shaharit Shel Shabbat, Havdalah and Zohares.* Self-produced.

Malakov, Ezro, prod. 2003. *Eternal Music of Bukharian Jewish Hymns: Shirei Shabbat Kodesh, Brit Millah, Purim, Pesach, Shavuot, Chanukkah, Magelat Ester, Selikhot, Rosh Hashanah, Sukkot, Simkhat Torah.* Self-produced.

215

Malakov, Ezro, prod. 2007. *Musical Treasures of the Bukharian Jewish Community/Muzykal'naya sokrovishchnitsa bukharskikh evreev/Otser ha-muzykah shel kehillat yehudei bukharah*. Tel Aviv: World Bukharian Jewish Congress.

Mallayev, Ilyos. 1997. *At the Bazaar of Love: Timeless Central Asian Maqam Music*. Shanachie 64081.

Mazal Tov, et al. 2003. *Moshe Narkolayev: Vospominaniye* [Memories]. Self-produced.

Mullojonova, Shoista. 2004. *I'm Singing for You*. Self-produced.

Nabiev, Jurabeg. 1997. *Maqām Navā*. Ocora 560102.

Nargis. 2001. *Desert Rain*. Self-produced.

Narkolayev, Albert. 2003. *Shirin jon*. Self-produced.

Narkolayev, Albert. 2005. *Azizam*. Self-produced.

Niyazov, Nison. 2006. *Bulbul maro bedor kard*. Self-produced.

Niyazov, Yosi. n.d. *Yosi Niyazov*. Sponsored by Bukharian Organization Ateret Menaḥem, B'nei Baraq, Israel.

Ottens, Rita, and Joel Rubin, eds. 2002. *Cantor Isaac Algazi: Sweet Singer of Israel*. Wergo SM16222.

Prentice, Will, comp. 2002. *Beyond the Revolution: A 1909 Recording Expedition in the Caucasus and Central Asia by the Gramophone Company*. Topic TSDC921.

Rubinov, Roshel. 2002. *Tamanno*. Self-produced.

Rubinov, Roshel. 2007. *Pesni moeĭ dushi* [Songs of My Soul]. Self-produced.

Shamayeva, Muhabbat. 2003. *Yallalum*. Self-produced.

Tolmasov, Avrom. 1997. *Giriya*. Raphael Brothers Records RBR 1010.

Usmanova, Yulduz. 1999. *Yulduz*. Double T DTM912612.

Various Artists. 1993. *Asie centrale: Traditions classiques*. Ocora Radio France CD C 560035–36.

Various Artists. 1999. *Ouzbekistan: Les Grandes voix du passé (1940–1965)*. Ocora 560142.

Various Artists. 2001. *New York City: Global Beat of the Boroughs*. Smithsonian Folkways SFW 40493.

Various Artists. 2002. *The Silk Road: A Musical Caravan*. Smithsonian Folkways SFW 40438.

Various Artists. 2003. *Az qudrati Khudovand* [By the Strength of God]. World Bukharian Jewry Rabbi's Association/World Bukharian Jewish Congress.

Various Artists. 2005. *The Rough Guide to the Music of Central Asia. Uzbekistan to Kazakhstan: Sounds of the Silk Road*. World Music Network RGNET 1129.

Various Artists. 2006. *Jewface*. Reboot Stereophonic RSR006.

Index

Abdughani, Ota Ghiyos, 65, 170
Abdullayeva, Nasiba, 134, 141, 146
Abdurashidov, Abdulahad, 169–70
Abdurashidov, Abduvali, xvii, 81–82
Abramov, Yosef, 50, 55, 71, 73, 78
Afghanistan, 8, 9, 23, 27, 119
Aga Khan Music Initiative in Central
   Asia (AKMICA), 76, 81
Alayev, Mike, 141, 149
Alimatov, Alisher, 58, 169–70
Alimatov, Turgun, 58, 66, 94, 170
Alpert, Michael, 84
alphabets, 5, 26, 54, 157, 162, 166–67
   See also multilingualism; *and specific*
     languages
Aminov, Abukhai, 50, 71, 73, 79, 84
Aminov, Neryo, xv, 67, 82
   singing with maqom orchestras,
     58–59, 158
   as teacher, xvi, 29
   See also musical items cited
Aminov, Roshel, xv, 81–82
   as ḥazzan, 103–4
   performances of, 79
   as teacher, 18, 87–89
   See also schools: Traditional School
     of Bukharian and Shashmaqom
     Music; sound recordings
amplification, 1, 17, 48, 81, 145, 166
anti-Semitism, 7, 38, 65, 143, 153,
   159–60
Arab music, 131, 134, 142, 144, 148,
   149, 184–85n3, 190n9
Armenians, 4, 141, 176n7
Aronov, Aron, 12, 34, 45
Ashkenazic Jews, 131, 177n14

in Central Asia, 44–45, 160
influence on Bukharian Jewish
   religious practice, 112, 114
and Jewish American identity, 36–38
relation to Bukharian Jews, 9, 44–46,
   83–86
ashulai kalon, 25, 53, 61, 85, 105, 128
assimilation, 5
   Bukharian Jewish concerns about,
     21, 33, 42, 44, 129
   and Hanukkah, 125
   and Jewish customs and practices,
     13, 45–46
   and multiculturalism, 34–35, 38, 99
   in Soviet Central Asia, 30
   See also conversion
atheism, 5, 6, 27
auctions, 1, 101, 107

Babayev, Borukh (Kalkhok), 24, 82,
   181n12
Balkhi, Eli, 112
Barayev, Matat, 50, 55, 72, 117–19
Barayev, Osher, 32, 47, 50, 57, 72,
   75, 85
Barayev, Solomon, 129
Belyayev, Viktor. *See* Shashmaqom:
   editions of
Benjamin, Yuhan, 15, 42, 115, 141,
   144–45, 148
blessings, 16, 100–1, 108, 134, 158, 168
Bloomberg, Michael, 34, 127
Bobokhonov, Ari, 15, 29, 68–69, 75,
   129–30
   See also Musical Treasures;
     Shashmaqom: editions of

Jewish, 3, 17, 38, 41–43, 50, 99, 113–14, 116, 143
Land of Israel (concept), 4, 7, 115, 123–26, 151, 155
and multiple senses of homeland, 123, 126, 151, 155, 171
Uzbek, 80
Different Mirror, A (Takaki book), 38–39
discrimination
against Jewish people, 4, 6, 8, 30
against Muslim people, 30
doira (frame drum)
in maqom, 56, 58, 60–61, 75, 81, 91, 92–93, 159
in religious music, 1, 98, 125
in party music, 25, 133–34, 136, 148, 149–50, 158
Drootin, Al, 193n5
Dushanbe, xv, 67, 89

Elishayev, Simḥa, 105, 127–28
English language, 16, 26, 72, 101, 105, 134, 141, 146, 149, 160
ensembles
Ensemble Maqom, xv–xvii, 6, 47, 70–79, 172
Ensemble Shashmaqom, xvi, 47, 70–73, 79
folkloric and heritage, 46–47, 140
maqom orchestras of Soviet era, 29, 57–60, 65, 68, 75, 122, 140, 158
Mazal Tov, xvii, 133–35, 140, 141, 145
estrada, 15, 139–40, 146–48, 149
Ethnic Folk Arts Center. *See* Center for Traditional Music and Dance
ethnicity, 3, 17, 32, 36, 37–39, 41, 46–48, 66, 125, 171, 183n6
See also Bukharian Jews: as ethnic group
Europe, 3, 7, 8, 37–38, 98–99, 129, 142, 153

Faizulloyev, Boboqul, 82
Feldman, Walter Zev, 39, 54, 72
Ferghana valley, 25, 51, 53
Fitrat, Abdurauf, 65
folk music (khalqī), 53, 63, 78, 88, 148
food and drink, 5, 48, 81, 156, 160, 161
at celebrations, 1, 107, 134, 139
dietary laws, 37, 97, 106, 114
osh plov, 107
plov, 1, 42, 46, 147
sacred meals, 13, 98, 106, 107, 165
frame drum. *See* doira

ghazal, 61–62, 75, 83, 87, 92, 94, 120
globalization, 9, 33, 69, 84, 123, 157, 171

economics of, 44, 69–70, 163
and party music, 146
Gramophone Company. *See* sound recordings
Gulkarov, Artur, 139, 148
Gulkarov, Isḥoq, 139
Gurg, Yusefi, 22–23, 82
gūyanda (female mourner). *See under* women

Ḥakham, Shimon, 116, 191n16
halakhah. *See* religious law and practice, Jewish
Hamdamov, Bobomurad, 170
haqqoni, 108
Hasidic Jews, 46, 109, 160, 163
Ḥayimov, Hillel, 120
Ḥayimov, Yoqub, 27
ḥazzan, 14–15, 103–5, 111–12, 130, 140, 160
ḥazzanut, 96, 102, 105, 160, 165
Yerushalmi, 112, 130
Hebrew language, 13, 120, 166–67
poetry, 116–18, 191n18
songs, 28, 48, 134
unifying Jewish people, 43, 99
used in maqom, 54, 68
See also prayer; religious texts
Hiloli, 62, 192n19
historical narratives, 21, 32, 39, 191n11
hofiz (singer), 14, 31, 49, 61, 79, 83, 90, 95
knowledge of poetry, 63, 87
technique, 53, 86–87, 116
holidays
Jewish, 99, 104
Navruz, 14, 80
Uzbekistan Independence Day, 80
See also Sabbath; Simhat Torah
Holocaust. *See* World War II
hybridity, 126, 129, 131, 145, 148
and diaspora, 123–24
and multiculturalism, 35
hymns. *See under* religious repertoire

Ibadov, Domullo Halim, 23, 170
Ibragimov, Ochil, 50, 72, 78, 93, 178n19
as ḥazzan, 15, 103
Idelsohn, Abraham Zvi, 41, 44, 178n22
improvisation, 94, 102, 169
Indian music, 78, 135, 140
Inoyatov, David, 82
instrumental music, 52, 78, 119, 122

multilingualism, 19, 28, 33, 34
  Bobokhonov/Jung edition of
    Shashmaqom, 68–69
  in Central Asia, 27, 120, 192n21
  as part of Bukharian Jewish identity,
    68, 142, 145
  in party music, 140–41, 145–46, 149
Munarov, Yosef, 91–92, 178n19
musical items cited
  "Ajab Ajab" (Tolmasov), 107
  "Anenu," 106, 128
  "'Arūsi Zebo" (Rubinov), 134, 138–39
  "Azizam" (Kalontar/Mallayev),
    149–50
  "Ba Dilbar" (Sabzanov), 53, 78
  "Ba Gulistan" ("To Bodi Sabo")
    (Aminov), 71, 78, 83, 88, 189n35
  "Bukharian Jewish Wedding Song,"
    78
  "Castanets," 141
  "Chapandozi Bayot," 119
  "Chapandozi Gulyor," 119, 185n4
  "Chapandozi Ushshoq," 93
  "Chi Ajab Umri Javoni" (Niyazov),
    107
  "Chuli Iroq," 88
  "Chu Sanjid" ("Yehalel Niv"), 117, 119
  "Deror Yiqro," 116, 165
  "Georgian Miniatures" ("Eastern
    Melody") (Mallayev), 78
  "Halleluyo," 107
  "Hava Nagila," 134
  "Hayom Harat Olam," 41
  "Hotel California," 134
  "Idi Purim" (Mallayev), 120–21
  "Iroqi Bukhoro," 61, 74
  "I Turn to You," 134
  "Khanuko" (Mallayev), 125
  "Khudovando (Goali, Goali)," 102–3
  "Ki Eshmero Shabbot," 165
  "Lekha Dodi," 41
  "Let's Get Loud," 134
  "Love Never Dies" (Benjamin), 148
  "Madh Guyand" ("Yehalel Niv"), 117,
    119, 165
  "Mahvashi Nozuk," 78, 88
  "Magic of 'I Love You,'" 149
  "Mūghulchai Buzruk," 52–52
  "Mūghulchai Dugoh," 58, 117–18,
    119
  "Mūghulchai Segoh," 119
  "My Favorite Things," 140
  "My Russia" ("Glyazhu v ozera
    sinie"), 147
  "My Samarqand," 134, 146–47, 151
  "Nasri Bayot," 52, 71, 119, 192n19

"Nasri Chorgoh," 71, 82, 117
"Nasri Uzzol," 74
"Nasrulloi," 74–75, 83, 119
"Navruzi Ajam," 61, 93
"Navruzi Sabo," 119, 165, 169–170
"Nigahdorat Khudo Boshad," 192n24
"Ohista, Ohista" (Tolmasov/
  Mallayev), 93
"O Khonum," 78
"Ozod Kun Khudoyo" (Niyazov), 109
"Panj Panja Barobar Nest"
  (Tolmasov/Rubinov), 93–94, 107
"Pazmon Shudam" (Mallayev), 123,
  151
"Pedar" (Rubinov), 94
"Qashqarchai Mūghulchai Buzruk,"
  53
"Qashqarchai Rok," 120–21
"Qurbon ba Tu Man Yerusholayim"
  (Mallayev), 124–25
"Qurbon Olam" (Mulloqandov), 53,
  55, 61, 78, 107, 159,
"Ruz ba Ruz" ("Yom le Yom"), 165
"Sarakhbori Buzruk," 74
"Sarakhbori Dugoh," 188n32
"Sarakhbori Navo," 78, 88, 89
"Sarakhbori Oromijon," 188n32
"Savti Navo," 88
"Sayora," 91
"Shastu Shastu Chor," 53, 88
"She Bangs," 134
"Shirinjon," 78
"Simkhu No," 107
"Soqinomai Bayot," 93
"Soqinomai Savti Kalon," 125
"Talqinchai Mūgulchai Buzruk," 53
"Talqinchai Savti Kalon," 93
"Talqini Bayot," 71, 119
"Talqini Uzzol," 61, 74
"Tamanno" (Mallayev, Rubinov arr.),
  92
"Tulkun," 165
"Ufori Iroqi Bukhoro," 107
"Ufori Mūghulchai Segoh," 33,
  124–25
"Ufori Savti Kalon," 78
"Ufori Tulkun," 125
"Ufori Uzzol," 74, 78, 137, 139
"Ushshoqi Samarqand," 71, 107,
  189n35
"Vasfi Tūro" (Mallayev), 120
"Yalalum" (Mallayev), 11, 78, 172–73
"Yehalel Niv," 117, 119, 165
"Yerushalayim" (Mallayev), 120
"Yigdal," 25, 106
"Yom le Yom," 116–18, 165

"Yo Ribun Olam," 102–3, 116, 165
"Yor Yor," 53
"Zhonushka" (Davidyan), 141
"Zulfi Pareshon" (Aminov/
   Mulloqandov), 78, 89, 165, 169
Musical Treasures of the Bukharian
   Jewish Community (Malakov/
   Bobokhonov collection), xvi, 16,
   18, 127–31, 177n13
Muslim-Jewish relations, 5–7, 23, 25,
   30, 31, 70–83, 84, 159, 168–72
Muslims, 4, 6, 23, 43–44, 46, 66, 79,
   114, 140, 141, 162, 172
   religious life, 30, 31, 58, 135, 155, 168
   Shi'ites in Central Asia (Ironi), 4, 176n7
   Sufi practices, 53, 77, 81, 185n3
   See also Muslim-Jewish relations;
     Tajiks; Uzbeks
mutrib, 25

Najara, Israel, 102, 113, 116, 117
namud, 87
Narkolayev, Albert, 133–34, 141
Narkolayev, Roma, 75, 133, 140
Nasirov, Ota Jalol, 22, 24, 27, 28, 65,
   170, 181n10
nationalism, 35, 66, 145
   Bukharian Jews and Central Asian
     nations, 7, 30, 68–69, 122, 143,
     145, 166
   and Jewish musical life, 17, 97, 18,
     127
   and language, 28, 64–65, 68
   and maqom, 51, 52, 55, 64–69, 126,
     170, 185n3
   Soviet Central Asia, 5, 36, 42–43, 65,
     184n9
Nektalov, Eduard, 161
Nektalov, Rafael, 129–30, 168, 170
New York, demographics of, 10–11
New York Times, The, 11–12, 71, 73
Niyazov, Nison, 107, 109
Niyazov, Yosi, 129

Obo Deroz, Mullo, xvi, 112
organizations
   American Sephardi Federation, 113
   Ateret Menaḥem Organization, 120
   Center for Jewish History, 41
   Congress of the Bukharian Jews of
     the USA and Canada, 6, 35
   National Endowment for the Arts,
     39, 72
   Queens Council for the Arts, 79
   World Bukharian Jewish Congress,
     xv, 9, 113, 177n13

World Music Institute, 39, 48
   See also Center for Traditional Music
     and Dance
orientalism, 140, 148–49
otherness, 123, 171–72
   Bukharian Jews in relation to
     Ashkenazic Jews, 36
   Bukharian Jews in relation to
     Muslims 23, 35
   and concept of repertoire, 46
   and ethnicity, 38
   and Jewish identity, 37–38, 42–43, 65,
     125–26
Ottoman Empire, 113, 116

Palestine. *See* Israel/Palestine
Paliy, Galina, 133
party music, 1, 12–13
   absence in multiculturalist
     situations, 48, 146
   definition of, 135–42
   gender and sexuality, 139–40
   media, 135, 141, 148–50
   in religious repertoire, 107
   See also estrada; popular music;
     sozanda; weddings
Persian Jewry, 8, 119–20, 122–23
Persian language, 13, 18–19, 26, 27
   associations, 54, 120
   diminishing use among Bukharian
     Jews in US, 86, 89, 91–92
   everyday communication, 3, 4, 5, 30,
     157–58, 162–63
   Judeo-Persian, 5, 30, 113
   poetry, 16–17, 23, 93–94, 119–21,
     123–25, 128, 151, 155
   and Shashmaqom editions, 65, 67–68
   speeches, 82, 101, 165–66
   translations of Hebrew texts, 98, 113,
     116, 119
   use in maqom, 1, 54, 68, 75
   See also ghazal; poetry
pilgrimage, 6, 20, 59, 154–56
Pinḥasov, Daniel, 99, 103
Pinkhasova, Yafo. *See* Tūhfakhon
poetry, 53, 54, 78, 92–94, 146
   contests, 25
   form and genre, 16, 53, 61–62, 125
   and hofiz knowledge, 87
   meter, 62–63, 75, 117–20, 125,
     192n19
   new religious, 119–21, 123–25, 128, 151
   shiru shakar, 141, 149
   See also ghazal; *and specific*
     languages
polygamy, 22, 27, 180n6

popular music, 15, 48, 134
  and Bukharian Jewish youth, 141
  and cosmopolitanism, 144
  and traditional Central Asian
    elements, 149–51
  See also estrada; party music
prayer, 14, 98
  Bukharian compared to Syrian, 117
  Bukharian use of pan-Sephardic
    elements, 112
  in Central Asia on pilgrimage, 158,
    160, 163–65
  Muslim call to prayer, 31
  notations and recordings of, 128, 130
  pre-Soviet Central Asia, 6, 105
  Soviet Central Asia, 164
  synagogue performance styles,
    99–106
  unifying Jewish people, 43, 99
  See also ḥazzan; ḥazzanut; religious
    repertoire; synagogues
Primak, Yochai, 160
professional musicians
  as community leaders, 12, 14, 16–17,
    155, 171–72
  diverse repertoires of, 15–16, 24–25,
    47, 68, 74, 78, 120, 141–42, 146
  and innovation, 131
  Jewish professionals in majority
    contexts, 23–24, 142, 143
  and maqom, 51, 58–59, 68, 86–87
  and recording industry, 25
  and religious music, 105–7, 116,
    119–21
  roles, 14–15, 103, 136, 140

Queens, demographics of, 10–11

rabbis
  Ashkenazic, 46, 114
  commissioning of religious
    recordings, 120
  influence on women's singing,
    109–11
  Malakov lineage, xvi
  Sephardic, 113–114
  Simḥat Torah, 107
  and synagogue worship, 99–101, 105
race, 10, 17, 36, 37–39, 44, 171,
  183nn3–6
rap music, 141
Rahmon, Emomalī, 6, 82
Rajabi, Yunus
  Malakov admiration for, 127
  museum, 58–60, 159
  relation to Bukharian Jews, 65

Shashmaqom edition, 52, 65, 67
  Uzbek State maqom ensemble, 57, 68
Rashidov, Sharof, 29, 30, 182n18
Rasulov, Hoji Abdulaziz, 25, 32, 71, 170
recordings. See sound recordings
religious law and practice, Jewish
  Bukharian comparisons of Soviet
    and American contexts, 96–97;
    110–11
  impact on research, 18
  multiple interpretations of, 36, 37,
    42, 45–46, 97–99, 110–11
  Soviet Central Asia, 14, 28, 30, 96,
    118, 164, 166
  and women, 58, 97, 98, 99, 110–11
religious repertoire, Jewish, 1, 12, 47
  cantillation, 112, 117
  definition of, 98–108
  hymns, 25, 41–42, 102, 106, 116–19
  liturgy, 98, 113–14
  paraliturgy, 98, 102, 107–8, 110–11
  and party music, 151
  recordings of, 41–42, 108–9, 128
  represented in Levicha Hofiz, 25
  shiro, 106–7, 116–22, 165
  Soviet suppression of, 28, 30
  and women, 97, 98, 99, 109, 110–11, 140
  See also ḥazzan, ḥazzanut; Musical
    Treasures; prayer
religious texts, Jewish, 98
  Psalms, 16, 100, 119, 122, 124–25,
    131, 143
  Torah, 1–2, 96, 100–1, 107, 110–11,
    112, 114, 118, 120, 122, 128, 159,
    161, 163, 191n16
  Zohar, 108, 128, 158
repertoire, concept of, 17–18, 46, 64
reverb, 1, 77, 81, 94, 166
rhythm
  dance rhythms, 1, 134, 135, 138–39,
    144, 193n1
  maqom rhythms, 63, 93, 117–119,
    135, 136–38, 192n19
  See also poetry: meter
Roussos, Demis, 142
Rubinov, Roshel, xvi-xvii
  on assimilation in United States, 42
  compositions of, 53, 92–93, 119, 134,
    138–39, 160
  as ḥazzan, 103–4
  inspired by Levi Bobokhonov, 32–33
  in Levicha Hofiz, 21–22, 32, 90
  maqom performance, 52, 57, 68, 83,
    85, 90, 93
  on musical transmission, 55–56,
    89–90

Turkic languages
  everyday communication, 4, 80, 157
  and Shashmaqom editions, 65, 67–68
  songs, 28
  use in maqom, 54, 68, 93, 170
Turkish music, 41, 116, 134, 142–44,
  184–85n3

Union of Soviet Socialist Republics
  (USSR)
  emigration from, 7–8, 175n3
  language reform, 157
  national categories, 5, 30, 36, 42, 43,
    64–65, 184n9
  "People's Artist" honor, xvii, 15, 28,
    30
Usmanova, Yulduz, 25
Uspenskiĭ, Viktor, 64, 65
ustoz-shogird. See transmission,
  musical
Uzbek identity and Islam, 65–66
Uzbekistan, 3, 5–7, 16, 29-31, 43, 52,
  58, 59, 65, 68, 77, 79, 80, 82, 91,
  118, 122, 127, 129, 130, 140, 144,
  153, 156, 161, 165–66
Uzbek language. See Turkic languages
Uzbeks, 4, 7, 31, 43, 58, 66, 67, 68, 69,
  94, 142, 157–58
  New York immigrants, 7, 70, 79–80,
    141, 145, 188n34

venues, 15–16
  Carnegie Hall, 58, 70, 72, 74, 94
  Kaye Playhouse, 84, 85
  Lincoln Center, 79
  Miller Theater, 81
  92nd Street Y, 50, 54
  Queens Theater in the Park, 21, 32,
    58
  Symphony Space, 79

Wagner, Richard, 65, 143
weddings, 13, 15–16, 28, 48, 54, 98,
  133–39, 145
  relation to maqom, 50, 54–55, 90–91,
    134–35
  wedding songs, 53, 71, 78
  See also ceremonies; party music;
    sozanda
Weil, Mark, 157
Weiner, Anthony, 127
whiteness, 38, 183n3
women, 25, 135–36, 140, 182n16
  female mourners, 46, 108,
    110–11, 158
  and Jewish religious repertoire, 13,
    18, 46, 108, 109–11
  and maqom, 14, 28, 58, 94
  women-only gatherings, 98, 135
  See also sozanda
world music, 14, 15, 25–26, 69–79, 90,
  145–46
World War II, 37–38, 109, 123, 156,
  160

Yagudayeva, Firuza, 71, 73, 79, 85
Yahudi, Yusuf, 113
yakkakhoni, 53, 128
Yakubov, Maryam, 158
Yehoshua, Yitshak, 101, 109
Yiddish language, 16
"Yigdal," 25, 106
"Yo Ribun Olam," 102–103, 116, 165
Yudakov, Suleĭmon, 15, 159
Yūlchiyeva, Munojot, 25
Yusupov, Benjamin, 186n11

Zavolunova, Virginia, 89, 94
Zavul, Mikhoel, 27, 62, 78, 93
Zirkiyev, Borukh, 65
ziyorat. See pilgrimage